Critical Issues in Education

MW00325756

Joseph Murphy, Series Editor

The Effective Principal:
Instructional Leadership for High-Quality Learning
BARBARA SCOTT NELSON AND ANNETTE SASSI

Redesigning Accountability Systems for Education
SUSAN H. FUHRMAN AND RICHARD F. ELMORE, EDS.

Taking Account of Charter Schools:
What's Happened and What's Next?
KATRINA E. BULKLEY AND PRISCILLA WOHLSTETTER, EDS.

Learning Together, Leading Together:
Changing Schools through Professional Learning Communities
SHIRLEY M. HORD, ED.

Who Governs Our Schools? Changing Roles and Responsibilities
DAVID T. CONLEY

School Districts and Instructional Renewal
AMY M. HIGHTOWER, MICHAEL S. KNAPP,
JULIE A. MARSH, AND MILBREY W. MCLAUGHLIN, EDS.

Effort and Excellence in Urban Classrooms:
Expecting—and Getting—Success with All Students
DICK CORBETT, BRUCE WILSON, AND BELINDA WILLIAMS

Developing Educational Leaders: A Working Model:
The Learning Community in Action
CYNTHIA J. NORRIS, BRUCE G. BARNETT,
MARGARET R. BASOM, AND DIANE M. YERKES

Understanding and Assessing the Charter School Movement
JOSEPH MURPHY AND CATHERINE DUNN SHIFFMAN

School Choice in Urban America: Magnet Schools and the Pursuit of Equity
CLAIRE SMREKAR AND ELLEN GOLDRING

Lessons from High-Performing Hispanic Schools:
Creating Learning Communities
PEDRO REYES, JAY D. SCRIBNER, AND
ALICIA PAREDES SCRIBNER, EDS.

Schools for Sale: Why Free Market Policies
Won't Improve America's Schools, and What Will
ERNEST R. HOUSE

Reclaiming Educational Administration as a Caring Profession
LYNN G. BECK

THE EFFECTIVE PRINCIPAL

INSTRUCTIONAL LEADERSHIP FOR HIGH-QUALITY LEARNING

Barbara Scott Nelson and Annette Sassi

Teachers College, Columbia University
New York and London

Published by Teachers College Press, 1234 Amsterdam Avenue, New York, NY 10027

Copyright 2005 by Teachers College, Columbia University

All rights reserved. No part of this publication may be reproduced or transmitted in any form or by any means, electronic or mechanical, including photocopy, or any information storage or retrieval system, without permission from the publisher.

The vignette at the beginning of the introduction is reprinted by permission from *Young Mathematicians at Work: Constructing Fractions, Decimals, and Percents* by Catherine Twomey and Maarten Dolk. Copyright © 2002 by Catherine Twomey Fosnot and Maarten Dolk. Published by Heinemann, a division of Reed Elsevier, Inc., Portsmouth, NH. All rights reserved.

Excerpts from the article written by Margaret Riddle in Chapter 3 are reprinted by permission of the publisher from Schifter, D., ed., *What's Happening in Math Class?*, *Volume 1* (New York: Teachers College Press, © 1996 by Teachers College, Columbia University. All rights reserved.), pp 138–142.

The cases of Marianne Cowan and Joseph Garfield in Chapter 6 contain excerpts from "Leadership Content Knowledge," by M. K. Stein and B. S. Nelson, 2003, *Educational Evaluation and Policy Analysis*, 25(4), 423–448. Copyright 2003 by the American Educational Research Association. Reprinted by permission of the publisher.

The work described here was conducted at the Education Development Center, Inc., Newton, MA, and supported by funds from the Spencer Foundation under grant 20000084 and the National Science Foundation under grant ESI-92-54479. Any opinions expressed herein are those of the authors and do not necessarily represent the views of these organizations.

Library of Congress Cataloging-in-Publication Data

Nelson, Barbara Scott.
    The effective principal : instructional leadership for high-quality learning / Barbara Scott Nelson and Annette Sassi.
        p.   cm.—(Critical issues in educational leadership series)
    Includes bibliographical references and index.
    ISBN 0-8077-4607-X (cloth : alk. paper)—ISBN 0-8077-4606-1 (pbk. : alk. paper)
    1. Elementary school principals—United States.   2. Educational leadership
United States.   3. Mathematics—Study and teaching (Elementary)—United
States.   I. Sassi, Annette.   II. Title.   III. Series.

    LB2831.92.N45 2005
    372.12'012—dc22   2005043067

ISBN 0-8077-4606-1 (paper)
ISBN 0-8077-4607-X (cloth)

Printed on acid-free paper
Manufactured in the United States of America

12   11   10   09   08   07   06   05   8   7   6   5   4   3   2   1

CONTENTS

Preface   vii

Introduction   1

PART I
Principals' Knowledge of Mathematics and Mathematics Learning   7

1. Principals' Knowledge of Elementary Mathematics:
   Knowing Where You're Going   9

2. Principals' Ideas About Learning and Teaching Mathematics   32

PART II
Principals' Use of Knowledge in Their Work   55

3. Working with Teachers: Situating Ideas in Practice   57

4. Assessment: Situating Ideas in Formal Accountability Structures   77

5. "Education and Politics Meet at the Crossroads":
   Engaging Stakeholder Audiences as Learners   98

PART III
How Principals' Knowledge of Mathematics Learning and Teaching
Affects How They Build a Sense of Community in Their Schools   121

6. Learning Through Instructional Leadership   125

7. The Engaged Instructional Leader: "I'm in This, Too."   150

Conclusion   171

Appendix: Research Methodology   179
References   185
Index   193
About the Authors   206

W E BEGAN this work with school and district administrators in 1993 while we were conducting a program on elementary mathematics for teachers, based on the 1989 *Curriculum and Evaluation Standards for School Mathematics* of the National Council of Teachers of Mathematics (NCTM). As part of that program, we offered a series of seminars on elementary mathematics instruction for the principals of participating teachers' schools and the mathematics coordinators and assistant superintendents of their districts. This group of about 40 administrators could see how the ideas in the NCTM standards affected teachers' work in important ways; and they wondered whether or not these ideas might affect their own work too, particularly in such areas as classroom observation, the mentoring of teachers, and communicating with parents and other community stakeholders.

These administrators' curiosity set us and our colleagues on a series of teaching experiments (cf. Ball, 1993; Lampert, 1990; Steffe & Thompson, 2000). Specifically, we offered administrators workshops and courses on mathematics education, learned what worked pedagogically for them, and studied their ideas about mathematics, learning, and teaching as they emerged in—and often changed—our work together. We also conducted several more conventionally designed studies about how some of these administrators connected new ideas to their ongoing administrative practice. As part of this overall program of work, we and our colleagues also developed the *Lenses on Learning* curriculum (Grant et al., 2003a, 2003b, 2003c). We learned a great deal about administrator learning while developing the *Lenses* material, which also informed the perspective of this book.

The teaching experiments and research studies provided the data for this book. While the data collection was somewhat different in different projects, it generally included ethnographic observations of the workshops and seminars we offered, transcriptions of audiotapes of those seminars, extensive interviews with the administrators, ethnographic observations of them at work in their schools, and interviews with some of the teachers with whom they worked. We also examined a number of artifacts that grew out of principals' work such as their notes taken when observing classes, teacher evaluation forms, and meeting agendas and minutes. (See the appendix, "Research Methodology," for more detail.) While the original group of administrators numbered about forty and the number we explicitly studied in depth was under twenty, by the end of the decade we had worked with close to a hundred administrators.

Not only is our work solidly grounded in administrators' practice, it also has a strong theoretical core. We argue that ideas about mathematics, learning, and teaching influence both *what* administrators are able to perceive about instruction in their schools and *how* they choose to take action. We have studied the relationship between administrators' ideas and their administrative actions by focusing on the nature of their professional judgment. By that we mean the reasoning and judgment involved in taking practical actions in their day-to-day work.

School administrators regularly make judgments in complex situations. For instance, when observing in classrooms administrators make subtle decisions about what is important to attend to in order to judge the adequacy of the instruction. They interpret the significance of such features as the noise level of the classroom, the amount and kind of student activity, and any of a wide range of teacher behaviors. Decisions about which facts matter also help shape the related practical activities in which administrators engage: the notes they make about what they observe, what they say when they consult with the teacher, what recommendations for further action they make. All of these activities require the exercise of wise professional judgment.

Our view of professional judgment has been influenced by philosophical explorations of practical judgment (Nussbaum, 1990; Wiggins, 1978) and the application of such perspectives to teaching (Pendlebury, 1995; see also Sassi, 2002). In this work the mutability, indeterminacy, and particularity of the practical world come to the fore; and how one chooses to act rests as much on an interpretation of the particulars of the situation as on general rules of action. Therefore, how one pays attention and to what one pays attention are critical in the exercise of practical judgment.

Before launching into the body of this book we wish to acknowledge our debts to those who have helped in various ways. Our colleagues Catherine Miles Grant and Amy Shulman Weinberg, with the help of Sheila Gay Buzzee Holland, collected and analyzed the data on the work of several school principals. Their very fine work on these cases and the discussions with them about all of the cases are integral to the shape of this book. Over the years a number of other researchers and teacher educators worked with us, including Ellen Davidson, Jim Hammerman, Christine Kaplan, and Jessica Bleiman. We were ably assisted in logistical matters by Sheila Flood and Glenn Natali.

We also wish to acknowledge the help of a number of colleagues who have read and commented on chapters of this book while it was in development: Deborah Schifter, Amy Morse, Amy Shulman Weinberg, Greta Johnson, Kristen Reed, and the members of the Professional Development Study Group. A special debt is due to Mark Smylie and Suzanne Wilson who read an earlier draft of the book in its entirety and gave us extraordinarily helpful comments. While we are indebted to all these colleagues for challenging our thinking and helping us sharpen our analysis, the interpretations in this book, and any errors, are entirely ours.

We wish to acknowledge our special debt to the school and district administrators who invited us to think with them about how their ideas about mathematics, learning, and teaching affected their work, and agreed to share their stories to help others learn. These were all very busy professionals, dedicated first and foremost to the children who attended their schools, but they made time to come to our seminars, and allowed us to watch them at work in their schools and interview them an extraordinary number of times. Always, they were patient with us and very gracious. They told us that our talks together provided for them a rare, and valued, opportunity for reflection and intellectual growth. We appreciate that they gained something of value from our work together, but we suspect that we learned even more.

Finally, we wish to thank our families for their support. Thanks to Brian and Claire Wilson for always making space for Annette to write and for their constant support over the years of this project. And thanks to Ernestine, Joan, Alicia, and Julia for understanding that Barbara's working vacations could be a good thing.

INTRODUCTION

Each day at the start of math workshop [the investigative part of math class] Dawn Selnes, a fifth-grade teacher in New York City, does a short minilesson on computation strategies. She usually chooses five or six related problems and asks the children to solve them and share their strategies with one another. Crucial to her choice of problems is the relationship between them. She picks problems that are likely to lead to a discussion of a specific strategy. She allows her students to construct their own strategies by decomposing numbers in ways that make sense to them. . . .

On the chalkboard today is the string of problems the children are discussing. Although the string ends with fractions, it begins with a few whole number multiplication problems, and Alice is describing how she solved 9 × 30. "I just used all the factors," she explains. "I thought of it as nine times three times ten. I knew that nine times three was twenty-seven, so times ten is two hundred and seventy."

Dawn asks for other strategies, but most of the children have treated the problem similarly, so Dawn goes to the next problem in her string, 15 × 18. Several children use the distributive property here. Tom's strategy is representative of many, and several children nod in agreement as he explains how he did 10 × 18 and got 180, and then took half of that to figure out the answer to 5 × 18. He completes the calculation by adding 180 to 90, for an answer of 270. Lara's strategy is similar, if not as elegant, but it makes sense to her. She multiplies using tens, too, but she breaks up the eighteen instead of the fifteen and multiplies 10 × 15, and then 8 × 15. These two products together also result in 270.

Ned agrees with their answer, but with a smile he says, "Yeah, but you didn't even have to calculate. It's the same as nine times thirty, because the thirty is halved, and the nine is doubled."

Although all the children in the class are comfortable with this doubling and halving strategy and understand why it works (having explored it thoroughly with arrays earlier in the year), they have not all thought to use it, because Dawn has turned the number around. It might have been more obvious if she had written 18 × 15 directly underneath 9 × 30. But she wants to challenge them to think.

Now Dawn moves to fractions. She writes 4½ × 60 as the third problem. Several children immediately raise their hands, but Dawn waits for those still working to finish. Alice is one of them, so she asks her to share first, "What did you do, Alice?"

"I split it into four times sixty first," Alice begins, "and I did that by doing four times six equals twenty-four. Then times ten is two hundred and forty. Then I knew that a half of sixty was thirty. So thirty plus two hundred and forty is two hundred and seventy."

"My way is kind of like yours," another classmate, Daniel, responds, "but I subtracted."

"But then you would get the wrong answer," Alice tells him, looking puzzled.

"No, what I mean is I did five times six times ten. That was three hundred. Then I subtracted the thirty."

"And where did you get the five?" Several of his classmates are also now puzzled.

"That was easier for me than four and a half. But that's why I took thirty away at the end," Daniel explains, very proud of his strategy.

Dawn checks to see whether everyone understands by asking who can paraphrase Daniel's strategy. Several children do so, and Dawn seems satisfied that the group appears to understand.

"That's a really neat strategy, isn't it?" Daniel beams and Dawn turns to Ned, "And what did you do Ned? Your hand was up so quickly. Did you see a relationship to another problem again?"

Ned laughs, "Yep. Just doubling and halving again. It's the same as nine times thirty. The nine was halved and the thirty was doubled."

Several children make surprised exclamations. . . . Dawn smiles and goes to the next problem: $2\frac{1}{4} \times 120$. This time everyone's hand is up quickly, and Dawn calls on Tanya, who has not yet shared. Tanya, as well as the rest of the class, has made use of the doubling and halving relationships in this string of problems.

—Catherine Twomey Fosnot and Maarten Dolk,
Young Mathematicians at Work

THIS CLASSROOM VIGNETTE draws attention to the character of high-quality elementary mathematics classrooms. Students and teacher are exploring problem-solving strategies, in this case solving multiplication problems. The strategies build on the students' conceptual understanding of factoring and the distributive property of multiplication, which they had previously explored. The teacher is directing their attention to a particular strategy—halving and doubling—while at the same time acknowledging other valid approaches. Computational practice and problem solving are integrated.

School administrators, especially principals, are faced with having to make sense of such classrooms and provide instructional leadership that supports and promotes them. For many administrators, this may seem a daunting task because they are not accustomed to classrooms like this. What should they know and what should they be able to do?

Since the mid-1990s there has been renewed interest in viewing school and district administrators as instructional leaders. The thought is that administrators should be knowledgeable about the content and quality of the educational program in their schools and with processes that support it. These include the evaluation of instruction, professional development for teachers, the nature and quality of the curriculum, and the nature of testing and assessment. Knowledgeable administrators would work with their faculties to improve instruction. In this view, no longer would it be adequate for principals to be absorbed by such managerial tasks as school governance, personnel management, finance, or building management. Rather, an integration of instructional concerns and school management would be called for (Rowan, 1995; Knapp et al., 2002; Spillane & Halverson, 1998; Stein & D'Amico, 2000; Stein & Nelson, 2003). The No Child Left Behind (NCLB) legislation passed in 2002 gives increased impetus to this trend. School and district administrators are now being held accountable as rarely before for the nature and quality of instruction.

The development of more cognitive orientations toward learning and teaching in the last few decades will make these goals even more complex for many principals. These orientations toward instruction have resulted in new learning goals for students, the development of new instructional strategies to meet these goals, and the implementation of new forms of educational assessment to monitor student achievement and plan for instructional improvement. Further, in recent years there has been considerable interest in viewing schools as learning communities (A. L. Brown & Campione, 1994, 1996) in which teachers and administrators can engage together in a "community of practice" (J. S. Brown & Duguid, 1991). From the learning communities or "communities of practice" perspective, instructional leadership is conducted by a wide range of people, in schools and out, who are concerned with particular instructional issues (Prestine & Nelson, 2003; Spillane, Halverson, & Diamond, 2001).

All of these developments call into question whether the traditional forms of school organization and leadership are sufficient (Murphy, 1999; Nelson, 1998; Prestine & Nelson, 2003; Rowan, 1995) and raise the issue of just what kind of understanding of teaching and learning administrators need.

This book explores the relationship between what administrators know about academic subjects—including how they are learned and how they are taught—and their work as instructional leaders. Such knowledge has been called "leadership content knowledge," that is, the content knowledge that is necessary for leadership (Stein & Nelson, 2003). In particular, we explore what a group of elementary principals knows about elementary mathematics, what they know about how mathematics is learned and taught, and how that knowledge affects their work. (Because our work has included assistant superintendents and mathematics curriculum coordinators, we have occasionally drawn on data we have about their work as well.) For example, we look at what principals see when they observe mathematics lessons, how they work with teachers, the kind of cultures they foster in their buildings, how they themselves continue to learn through their work, and the kinds of relationships they build with parents and other stakeholders in their communities. While our analysis is restricted to the area of elementary mathematics, it can be taken as a case that illuminates issues to be considered in instructional leadership in other subject areas as well.

Of course, there are additional aspects of instructional leadership that leaders' knowledge might affect: recruitment of teachers, selection of professional development programs for teachers, acquisition of instructional materials, management of relations with the district's central office, and so on. By not discussing these we do not mean to suggest that they are not important, nor that principals' ideas about mathematics, learning, and teaching do not affect their actions in these areas. Rather, in this book we discuss those administrative areas that most absorbed the time and attention of the principals whose work we studied.

The interests of some readers are likely to be focused on organizational, political, and policy issues that may appear to receive little explicit attention in this book. For such readers, we have made references throughout the text to the ways in which our argument about the importance of principals' knowledge and beliefs can be seen to inform other debates. We invite such readers to delve for a short time into the world of elementary mathematics instruction, engaging with the mathematical and pedagogical ideas that interest the principals whose work we examine here. It may be that some organizational and policy issues look subtly different from this knowledge-based perspective.

ORGANIZATION OF THE BOOK

This book comprises three parts, which can be viewed as a nested set of explorations, starting "inside the heads" of principals, so to speak, in Part I and then moving outward in subsequent sections to consider increasingly larger aspects of school context. In each chapter we present several cases, each describing the thinking and the work of a particular elementary principal. Such grounded images have the advantage of presenting new ideas in contextualized fashion and providing a way for readers to imagine themselves in the shoes of the administrator in the case. Through these first-person accounts, we provide insights into what is both possible and challenging for elementary principals as they develop new ideas about mathematics, learning, and teaching and work to connect these ideas to their administrative practice.

Part I is about elementary principals' ideas about the nature of mathematics as an enterprise, the effects of the amount and kind of mathematics knowledge that they have, and the significance of their ideas about the nature of mathematics learning. Chapter 1 presents and analyzes three cases that illustrate the effects of principals' knowledge of elementary mathematics. Chapter 2 presents and analyzes the effects of three principals' beliefs about how children learn mathematics.

Part II examines several aspects of principals' administrative work. Chapter 3 analyzes how principals' mathematics knowledge and views on mathematics learning and teaching affect their ability to help teachers improve their instructional practice. Chapter 4 explores the relationship between principals' knowledge of mathematics instruction and how they work with formal accountability structures. Chapter 5 examines how administrators communicate about mathematics instruction to two important constituencies, school boards and parents.

Part III focuses on how principals can learn about mathematics, learning, and teaching in and through their own administrative practice, and how such learning leads them to build and participate in communities of practice of different sorts in their schools. Chapter 6 focuses on the conditions under which administrators gain important insights into the nature of learning and teaching in the context of their own practice. Chapter 7 discusses how principals' views of the nature of learning affect the way they build a culture for learning in their schools.

Finally, we follow these three major parts with a conclusion in which we argue that effective instructional leadership requires a thorough understanding of contemporary pedagogy and a deep appreciation of the complexity of subject matter knowledge. We draw out the implications of this argument for mathematics education, educational policy, and school improvement.

By agreement, all names of administrators, districts, and schools are pseudonyms.

Principals' Knowledge of Mathematics and Mathematics Learning

A CENTRAL PREMISE of this book is that the nature of administrators' understanding of mathematics, learning, and teaching substantially affects the nature of the instructional leadership that they exercise. Ideas about mathematics, learning, and teaching influence what administrators are able to perceive about instructional life in their schools, what they value, and how they choose to take action.

This is a particularly important issue in an era in which instructional methods and texts have been changing dramatically to reflect ideas about mathematics, teaching, and learning that are based on current research in cognitive psychology and mathematics education. Such research shows that children learn mathematics best when they explore mathematical ideas in the context of solving complex problems, thereby simultaneously building structures of mathematical ideas in their minds and connecting mathematical facts and problem-solving procedures to those ideas (Kilpatrick, Swafford, & Findell, 2001). That is, what counts as effective and high-quality elementary mathematics instruction is rigorous thinking intertwined with mastery of computational procedures.

These goals for student learning are now embodied in many new texts, curricula, and high-stakes tests. But many administrators were educated before these goals for mathematics instruction had been developed, and in-service opportunities for administrators generally have not provided opportunities to explore such new ideas deeply. Therefore, many administrators' ideas about what is important in mathematics instruction are out of alignment with the best teaching that may be going on in their schools and districts. This misalignment affects administrators' ability to recognize and support excellent teaching, as well as their ability to recognize and correct teaching that is inadequate. As administrators work with others—teachers, parents, other administrators—to provide leadership in schools, they need to develop ideas and ways of thinking about mathematics, learning, and teaching that are more aligned with today's view of best practice.

Part I of this book addresses this issue in two chapters. The first describes what it means to understand elementary mathematics and then examines the work of three elementary principals who have different views of the nature of mathematics and different amounts and kinds of mathematics knowledge. In this chapter we show that both the depth of principals' mathematical understanding and the way they hold their knowledge can affect their exercise of instructional leadership. The second chapter examines what three principals understand about how mathematics learning occurs. Once again, we show that what these principals think about the nature of mathematics learning affects what they think instruction should look like and the degree to which they are able to help teachers in their schools improve their instruction.

Principals' Knowledge of Elementary Mathematics: Knowing Where You're Going

E LEMENTARY PRINCIPALS do not have expertise in all school subjects. They often are specialists in one subject area but consider themselves generalists in others. Yet the question of sufficiency often surfaces: How much knowledge in any particular subject—and of what kind—is enough for administrators to be effective instructional leaders, especially with regard to decisions regarding instruction in that subject? This question is especially pertinent in elementary mathematics because many principals do not have mathematics backgrounds and readily admit that their mathematics knowledge is weak. In this chapter we first examine what it means to understand elementary mathematics and how principals call upon this knowledge in their work with teachers. Then we analyze the work of three principals: one who has indicated to us that he has developed a more conceptual understanding of elementary mathematics and uses that knowledge to shape his instructional leadership; another who we consider to have good conceptual knowledge of mathematics but who has not yet fully worked out how to use that knowledge in her administrative practice; and a third who acknowledges that her mathematics knowledge is mostly procedural, without strong conceptual understanding. We show how the nature of principals' mathematics knowledge very much affects what they are able to appreciate about mathematics instruction in their schools, and affects the avenues for intervention that are available to them.

KNOWING ELEMENTARY MATHEMATICS

Before we can examine the effect of mathematics knowledge on instructional leadership, we need to examine what is meant by "knowing elementary mathematics." This question has been answered in different ways at different times.

For much of the twentieth century in America, "knowing mathematics" has meant mastery of mathematical facts and procedures for computation, interspersed with periods in which there was also a focus on children's understanding of mathematical ideas. For example, during the Progressive Era a focus on the meaning that students would make of ideas appeared. The new math movement of the 1950s and 1960s focused on having students understand the structure of mathematics and its unifying ideas. During this period Piaget's research also influenced American education, as did the educators who developed and promulgated the use of concrete manipulatives such as Cuisenaire rods. More recently, the cognitive revolution in psychology that began in the 1950s has powered the discipline-based reform movement of the present. However, these movements were often not widespread and, depending on where administrators were educated and where they taught, they might well have experienced mathematics education as fundamentally based on memorization of mathematical facts and facility in computation (Cohen, 1988; Elmore, 1996; Kilpatrick et al., 2001; Romberg & Carpenter, 1986; Wilson, 2003).

In general, the debate has been about whether it is sufficient for children to know the basic facts and procedures of mathematics, relying heavily on memorization, or whether it is also necessary for children to develop a more conceptual understanding of mathematical ideas and processes and problem-solving abilities. Following the National Council of Teachers of Mathematics (NCTM) and the National Research Council, we take the view that mathematics is a system of mathematical ideas and concepts that students learn through their own investigations of problem situations. "Knowing mathematics," in this view, means having a strong conceptual understanding of mathematical ideas and processes so that one can reason one's way through a mathematical situation (NCTM, 1989, 2000; Kilpatrick et al., 2001). Mastery of mathematical facts and procedures for calculation is also important because conceptual understanding and the mastery of facts and skills are interdependent. Conceptual understanding "makes learning skills easier, less susceptible to common errors and less prone to forgetting. By the same token, a certain level of skill is needed to learn many mathematical concepts with understanding . . . [because] the attention students devote to working out results . . . [can] prevent them from seeing important [mathematical] relationships" (Kilpatrick et al., 2001, p. 122).

Examining a simple mathematics problem will help clarify what this conceptual view of knowing elementary mathematics means. Consider the problem

25 + ? = 42.

Students of different ages might solve this problem in different ways. Young children might start at the number 1, count to 25, and then keep counting until they reach 42, noting that it took 17 additional numbers to go from 25 to 42. Alternatively, they could start at 25 and count from there to 42. This is known as *counting on*. Older children would realize that the question was asking them to find the difference between 25 and 42, and they could subtract the first number from the second.

If students were to do this problem using the standard subtraction algorithm, they would have to know techniques for subtraction with *regrouping* (what many of us learned as *borrowing*). They might say something like, "You can't take 5 from 2, so cross out the 4 and write 3, then put a 1 in front of the 2. This makes 12. Five from 12 is 7. And 2 from 3 is 1, so the answer is 17." This is the kind of solution method that is ordinarily expected when computation only is emphasized.

However, many people, including children, might decompose the numbers to make the subtraction easier, indicating a conceptual understanding of how numbers are constructed. For example, a student might say, "Subtracting 25 from 42 is hard, so I will make it easier by taking 2 away from the 42 and putting it back later. So I subtract 25 from 40 and get 15. But I have to put the 2 back, so I add 15 and 2 to get 17." Solving the problem this way entails knowing that the distance between 15 and 40 is two units smaller than the desired answer, because the student made the 42 into a smaller number for computational convenience. He has to add those two units back on to the answer he gets when he subtracts 25 from 40.

Alternatively, a student might understand how the subtraction with regrouping algorithm uses important features of our place value number system. This student might understand that when she crosses out the 4 and writes 3, then puts a 1 in front of the 2, making 12, she is actually seeing the 4 as 40, subtracting 10 to leave 30, and adding the 10 to the 2 to get 12. Five from 12 is 7; 20 from 30 is 10; 10 plus 7 is 17.

Thus doing even simple problems can involve conceptual understanding of the way the number system works if the problem is done from the perspective of making sense of the mathematical ideas and processes involved, and not just relying on an algorithm. While it may be quicker simply to use an algorithm, many algorithms tend to mask what is happening in the problem conceptually. Without access to the conceptual structure of the problem, children may simply memorize the steps of the algorithm and often forget where they are part way through or make calculation errors that they would not make if they understood conceptually what was happening in the problem. Once children understand conceptually what is happening with the numbers, any algorithm that they can use efficiently and accurately is mathematically acceptable (Russell, 1999).

This general, conceptual orientation toward what it means to know elementary mathematics is not sufficient in itself; the definition must include the particular topics and "habits of mind" that comprise competency in mathematics. For a list of topics and habits of mind, we draw on current policy documents provided by the National Council of Mathematics Teachers and the National Research Council (Kilpatrick et al., 2001; NCTM, 1989, 2000): the several kinds of numbers that comprise the number system (whole numbers, negative numbers, fractions, and decimals); how the four basic operations (addition, subtraction, multiplication, division) work in each of these number domains; how the domains relate to each other; and basic ideas in such areas as geometry, measurement, probability and statistics, and algebra. These should not be viewed as a set of isolated topics; rather, it is important that children's understanding of these topics and operations develop in a connected fashion.

By "habits of mind," we mean that knowing elementary mathematics entails becoming comfortable with and proficient in several modes of mathematical thinking, including choosing representations for numerical situations, mathematical reasoning, problem solving, proof, and communication (i.e., sharing one's ideas, justifying one's reasoning, asking questions, listening to others). These modes of reasoning are not only ways of thinking mathematically but also processes for learning more mathematics.

This is a very rich definition of what it means to know elementary mathematics, deriving in part from mathematicians' views about what mathematics is and in part from the findings of cognitive psychology about how children's mathematical thinking develops. Research in cognitive psychology has shown that children build their own knowledge, using experiences and information from the world around them. Competence in mathematics depends not only on storing knowledge in memory but also on building mental representations of ideas and organizing those representations in ways that reflect the structure of mathematics itself (Bransford, Brown, & Cocking, 1999; Kilpatrick et al., 2001; Resnick, 1981; see Chapter 2 for a more detailed discussion).

Attaining such mathematical understanding for all students is a very ambitious goal. For many years the mathematical understanding described above was held as a goal only for those who planned careers based on mathematics; others were thought to be sufficiently well served by procedural arithmetic (Resnick, 1987). Now this goal is being adopted for all students. Specific goals in mathematics education for all students have become heightened since the passage of the federal No Child Left Behind legislation, which stipulates that all students in a school must make adequate yearly progress in mathematics.

Because many current school and district administrators were educated (and did their teaching) at a time when knowing mathematics was thought to involve largely memorizing facts and procedures and reproducing them when required, the mathematical knowledge of many administrators is largely procedural. Of course, some principals have always found mathematical ideas interesting and have maintained that interest, even if the instruction they received in school was largely procedural. Some liked mathematics quite a lot, took advanced courses in it, and may even have been mathematics teachers before becoming principals. But, for the most part, the mathematics knowledge of elementary principals is much like that of the general public—procedural.

Having conceptual knowledge of mathematics, however, affords elementary principals many advantages in their work as instructional leaders. For example, when doing classroom observations, principals whose mathematics knowledge is conceptual are more able to follow students' mathematical thinking as they work on mathematics problems, make judgments about its validity, and judge if the teacher is adequately handling student misconceptions. They also are in a good position to help teachers progress in their teaching.

In the rest of this chapter we examine how knowledge of elementary mathematics shaped the professional judgment of three different elementary principals. Peter Nash uses his conceptual mathematics knowledge to design a learning experience for his faculty in which several ways of understanding a math problem are explored—illustrating heterogeneous grouping in mathematics classes. Marianne Cowan's conceptual knowledge of mathematics enables her to follow children's mathematical thinking in her classroom observations. And Libby O'Brien sets new goals for mathematics instruction at her school after becoming aware that students may think about mathematical ideas in individual ways. The nature of each principal's mathematics knowledge and his or her ability to use it to examine students' mathematical thinking affect what they value in mathematics instruction, how they interpret what they see and hear in mathematics classes, and what they consider it important to do when working with teachers.

DOING MATHEMATICS WITH TEACHERS: PETER NASH

Peter Nash is the principal of a small K–3 elementary school in an affluent suburban school district. When we studied his work, he had been principal of the Linden School for 5 years. He brought to his administrative practice a long-standing commitment to equity in education, a concern for how educational practices can advantage some students and disadvantage others, and a long history of working with ideas from constructivist learning theories.

Mr. Nash's mathematics training as a student had been fairly typical. "[It was] primarily memorization. So, there was nothing that was scary about it, because memorizing I was pretty good at," he said. While he especially liked geometry, he "got stumped" in Algebra II and didn't pursue any serious mathematical study in college. Mr. Nash's most significant mathematics learning occurred when he became a teacher in the early 1970s. Like a teacher described by Schifter and Fosnot (1993) who learned mathematics while teaching it, Nash was finally able to go beyond his basic knowledge of mathematics. As he described it,

> When I first started teaching at the elementary level, and had to teach mathematics for the first time, . . . I really became interested in it and excited about it. I felt as though . . . I was learning it for myself for the first time. Really learning it. . . . I was seeing the patterns and making connections, and thinking about how a system of knowledge . . . is put together and how different people put that together.

This more conceptual relearning of mathematics happened because his school was engaged in a series of weekly workshops with Caleb Gattegno. Gattegno was a mathematician, psychologist, and educator who met Georges Cuisenaire in 1953 and thereafter was an active promoter of the use of Cuisenaire rods in elementary mathematics instruction. Cuisenaire rods are a collection of 10 rectangular rods, each a different color and length, starting at 1 centimeter and increasing by 1 centimeter. Students use these manipulatives to explore mathematical ideas in different mathematical areas, including whole numbers, fractions, and geometry. Gattegno believed that the rods put children in direct contact with the basic mathematical characteristics of the number system, the four basic operations, and algebra.

This more conceptual orientation toward mathematics teaching and understanding informed many aspects of Mr. Nash's work. In the example related below, Mr. Nash was working with his faculty on the issue of heterogeneity and mixed-ability grouping in mathematics classes. At the time of our study, Mr. Nash's district was preparing to select a new elementary mathematics curriculum. The district had a policy of ability-grouping students for mathematics in Grades 3–5, in which students left their regular classrooms and had different teachers for mathematics. Mr. Nash was ambivalent about this practice and thought that the piloting of candidate mathematics curricula could open up an opportunity to examine the grouping policy more carefully.

An Episode from Administrative Practice

Mr. Nash scheduled two faculty meetings for discussion of heterogeneous ability grouping in mathematics so that teachers could have the opportunity to consider what advantages there might be in heterogeneously composed classes. At the first meeting, the faculty and Mr. Nash discussed an article on heterogeneous grouping that he had circulated. At the second meeting, the faculty worked together on a mathematics word problem that Mr. Nash designed. He told us that his intent was for the faculty to experience mixed-ability grouping firsthand by working together on an open-ended mathematics exploration. They would then discuss what constituted good teaching in heterogeneous classes. He said he hoped the teachers would appreciate how different ways to solve such problems might indicate different ways of understanding mathematical ideas rather than simply indicating that some students understood more than others.

The mathematics word problem that Mr. Nash constructed for the teachers to work on was as follows:

> Recently Paul learned how to construct small rafts with Popsicle sticks. Each raft is made with 5 Popsicle sticks. Paul bought five packages of Popsicle sticks and there are 11 Popsicle sticks in each package. How many rafts will Paul be able to construct?

The answer to this word problem is 11 rafts of 5 Popsicle sticks each. This is essentially a factoring problem. In concrete terms, there are 55 Popsicle sticks altogether, which are first bundled into five packages of 11 sticks each, and then into 11 rafts of 5 sticks each. In abstract terms, $5 \times 11 = 55$, and $55 \div 5 = 11$.

The teachers were to work on this problem in pairs and explain their reasoning to each other. Some teachers' strategies were quite concrete:

- Figure out how many rafts you can make with each package: two rafts and one [Popsicle stick] left over. Add up the leftover Popsicle sticks to make one additional raft.
- Add up all of the Popsicle sticks and divide by 5.
- Make five bundles of 11 sticks, put them all together into one pile, and then count out by fives.

Another group talked more abstractly about how they were multiplying and dividing by the same numbers. They explained that they multiplied five packets times 11 sticks only to divide by 5 sticks. One teacher, Dana, explained how she and her partner saw it:

> If we had been less rigid, we would have seen right away. We would have seen that if each raft is made of five Popsicle sticks and there're five packages, then however many is in the package must be the answer, and we didn't need to multiply the 5.

Ron, a third-grade teacher who had a reputation for being one of the best math teachers but was considered by Mr. Nash to be traditional because of his teaching methods, offered his strategy:

> Basically I knew intuitively that I was going to multiply and divide at the same time, since 5 is the same number, and since the operations were inverse. I basically canceled the 5s and the answer is 11.

Dana and Ron were working with the numerical structure of the problem. Once they realized that you multiplied the number of sticks in a package by 5, and then divided the total number of sticks by 5, the number of sticks in the package was the answer.

One teacher, Ann, took this idea further, proposing that in a mixed-ability class the teacher could develop extensions for advanced students by changing the numbers:

> I think one way to stretch this a little bit . . . might be to [ask] what would happen if there were 36 possible sticks in a bundle. And then they'd . . . do it and they'd realize, oh, the answer is 36. And then you'd say, "OK, what would happen if there were 52?" And then you'd say . . . "Why are you getting the same number [in] bundles equals the same number of rafts? What's happening?" And then they would . . . have to answer why this pattern exists.

The students in this teacher's hypothetical class would substitute 36 sticks in a package for 11, but still multiply and divide by 5. In such a case there would be 180 Popsicle sticks in all, first combined as five packages of 36 sticks each and later combined as 36 rafts of 5 sticks each. Similarly, they might substitute 52 for 11, and multiply and divide by 5. In all of these cases the students would be getting "the same number in bundles as the number of rafts" and have to explain this.

In this faculty "math class" the teachers' solution methods varied quite a lot, from very concrete, physically based methods to more abstract methods that focused on the factoring of the larger number and the inverse relation between multiplication and division. These teachers were indeed experiencing a heterogeneous mathematics class.

They then discussed the implications of having such an array of strategies opened up in public in a mathematics class, in particular what students might learn from hearing strategies other than their own. Mr. Nash drew the meeting to a close with a reflection on what teachers needed to be able to do if they were to pull out the mathematical potential of such open-ended mathematics tasks:

> How important it is . . . that [we, as the teachers] have in our minds some notion about where this could go. . . . It isn't just the messing around and . . . discovering. . . . You also have to have in reserve this idea of what significant new kind of learning can occur once they do have these little breakthroughs. . . . You need to be ready then, once that door is open, to walk through [it] with them.

Analysis

In this example, Peter Nash shows how he could use his conceptual knowledge of mathematics to figure out what kind of experience he wanted for his teachers and to design an activity to achieve that experience. Not only was his practical judgment attuned to the value of having teachers do mathematics together but he had the mathematics knowledge to design a mathematically intriguing investigation.

He was able to provide his teachers with the opportunity to explore the complexities of a seemingly straightforward mathematics problem to see that a number of different solution strategies were possible. They were able to explore how, even though some solutions were more mathematically sophisticated than others, each represented a subtly different way of interpreting the problem. Teachers had the chance to examine the mathematical structure of the problem, explore extensions, and experience what it would feel like to be a student in such a class. They experienced how the range of interpretations could stretch the understanding of everyone. As Mr. Nash had suggested, in this heterogeneous "class" it wasn't just that some "students" knew more than others, but that they saw different things in the mathematics. Further, the teachers had the chance to discuss the nature of the knowledge and skill that it would take on the part of the teacher to manage such a mathematical activity.

By having teachers do mathematics together, Mr. Nash offered a way for the teachers to shift the heterogeneity discussion from a relatively narrow debate about the district's current grouping practices to considering the variety of mathematical ideas that might emerge in a heterogeneous class. He also drew their attention to what teachers have to know in order to ensure that such explorations have a mathematical focus. Further, in running the faculty meeting as a mathematics-doing community among teachers, Mr. Nash added open-ended intellectual exploration in mathematics to the range of ways that the teachers and he could interact together.

Mr. Nash's work provides an example of what a good conceptual understanding of mathematics makes possible for a principal. However, his work with teachers does not make visible a further aspect of mathematics knowledge that is important for observing teaching and helping teachers improve their instruction—using one's understanding of mathematics to sort out what students are understanding and what they might be having difficulty with.

UNDERSTANDING STUDENTS' MATHEMATICAL THINKING: MARIANNE COWAN

Marianne Cowan is the principal of the K–5 Clinton School in the small city of Hillsville in the Northeast. Although she had been an elementary school principal for 14 years, the year we studied her work was Mrs. Cowan's first year as principal in this district. In the project she did with us she conducted a number of classroom observations at different grades to explore the degree to which teachers at the Clinton School adapted their mathematics instruction to meet the needs of all children in their classes—those who were performing below grade level, at grade level, and above grade level.

Mrs. Cowan brought to this work a reasonable comfort level with elementary mathematics and, from what we discerned from watching and listening to her, a basic conceptual understanding. She described her history with mathematics to us:

> It wasn't until I was in fifth grade that I really understood anything about math. I was an excellent math student. I memorized everything I was supposed to memorize. I did all the examples. My mother drilled me on the multiplication tables. . . . Little did I know there were all these connections. And I had a wonderful fifth-grade math teacher who was a math major in college. And she understood math and she could explain it. And there were so many ah-ha's as she was explaining how decimals and fractions are related, that's just one

example, and percent. . . . All of a sudden I understood. . . . But, what an amazing thing to have made it that long.

She told us that she was good in geometry but found both algebra and trigonometry hard. She didn't take another mathematics course until college when she was required to take a yearlong course to become a teacher. Although she felt that she wasn't necessarily strong in math, she credited her fifth-grade experience with allowing her to make sense conceptually of the mathematics she had known until then only by rote.

The episode we will examine here came from the observation of a fourth-grade lesson on equivalent fractions. When children move from working with whole numbers to working with fractions, one of the things that is often confusing to them is that the value of a fraction depends on the whole of which it is a part. A fundamental idea about fractions is that *fractions* are equal portions of a *referent whole. Equivalent fractions* can be understood as the same amount of the referent whole expressed in different numbers. For example ²⁄₄ or ³⁄₆ of a pizza is the same amount as ½ of the same pizza. Understanding equivalent fractions entails understanding both the idea of a referent whole and different ways of representing the same size piece—½ is the same as ²⁄₄, ⁴⁄₈, and so on. Equivalence also has geometric dimensions. Fractional pieces of a pizza can be equivalent (the same amount of pizza) but not congruent; that is, they can be differently shaped. Finally, it is important for children to learn that the size of two fractions (relative to the same referent whole) can be compared.

An Episode from Administrative Practice

In the fourth-grade class that Mrs. Cowan observed, each student was working with a copy of a teacher-made manipulative called a "fraction fringe," which was designed to show the relationships between certain equivalent fractions. The fraction fringe was constructed of a stack of small rectangular pieces of paper stapled together at the top. Each piece of paper except the bottom piece, which denoted the whole, was partially split. The piece of paper next to the bottom was split into two halves, the next split into four quarters, and the last split into eight eighths. Students could use this to see, for example, how many fourths would be equivalent to one (the whole). For the portion of the class in which they used the fraction fringe, students also used a worksheet on which they were asked to identify two or three equivalent fractions for each of a set of given fractions. For instance, if they were given ³⁄₄ on the worksheet, an equivalent fraction on the fraction fringe was ⁶⁄₈. If they were given ²⁄₄ on the worksheet, they would find ½ and ⁴⁄₈ on the fraction fringe. The fraction fringe manipulative did not raise the issue of the referent whole, which was fixed at one. It offered the opportunity to explore the relations between a small number of fractions related to each other by the fact that each denominator was a power of two of the prior—halves, quarters, eighths.

In observing her at work, we saw how Mrs. Cowan drew upon her mathematics knowledge to notice things that had happened in the class and discuss them later with the teacher in a way that was far more detailed than would be possible for many elementary principals. For example, in the postobservation conference with the class teacher Mrs. Cowan and the teacher discussed the mathematics work of one of the students in considerable detail. The teacher had brought along Josie's worksheets on equivalent fractions and said that something interesting had happened. She explained what had happened:

> Josie is kind of way out there and a little bit on the slower side. She didn't finish the paper. . . . But the reason she didn't finish, . . . she was thinking about [32nds]. She brought this out to the whole class the next day. She said, "You know what I noticed," and she went right to the board and she wrote it out that "if you multiply 8 × 2 you get 16, [and] if you multiply 16 × 2 you get 32 . . . and then you could just keep doing it. [And] you know that ¾ is the same as ⁶⁄₈ because it's 3 × 2 and 4 × 2." And she went right down the list [of fractions on the worksheet] and she made a whole bunch.

In this example, Josie did two different things. First she extended the pattern of the fraction fringe, beginning with eighths and constructing additional fractions that were the next consecutive powers of 2—16ths, 32nds. She then essentially developed her own definition of equivalence, saying that you could know that two fractions were equivalent if both numerator and denominator were multiples of the same number (¾ is the same as ⁶⁄₈ because 3 × 2 = 6 and 4 × 2 = 8).

Their discussion of Josie continued:

> TEACHER: And she was sitting there [while the class was working on the fraction fringe worksheet] and I could see her, you know, kind of, she was kind of like way out there and to me, like she has her pieces right in front of her. These are her answers right on the fraction fringe and she's trying to pull them out of midair. This was what she was doing in her mind. She was making a discovery.
>
> MRS. COWAN: Which meant the fraction fringe couldn't help her with that; . . . there were no 32nds [on the fraction fringe].

TEACHER: But she was making the discovery about multiplication and she didn't even finish [the assignment] because she was off on something else and this is something we'll eventually get to but we weren't there yet. We're on the real concrete, hands-on kind of part of this and she was getting way up there. . . . The next day [she] was willing to get right up on the board and she showed everybody how that worked and I thought, Wow. . . . And we didn't have pieces that small. So this was something that she, that clicked in her mind and she went with it. So she kind of fell behind on this particular lesson, but went further, you know.

MRS. COWAN: Sometimes children like this . . . [are] not doing exactly as you expect. Sometimes those kids turn out to be some of the better mathematical thinkers. . . . I mean, that's wonderful that she was into the 32nds.

Analysis

In this snippet of dialogue, we see how both the teacher and Marianne Cowan were surprised by the apparently anomalous performance of an otherwise average student. Josie, who appeared not to be attending to the lesson, in fact was finding equivalent fractions that were not on the fraction fringe, and developing a definition of equivalence.

What we feel is notable in this example, however, is how neither Mrs. Cowan nor the teacher moved from describing what Josie did to analyzing what Josie was exploring about equivalent fractions and multiplication—what these ideas looked like from Josie's point of view. It appeared from their ability to discuss the example that they had sufficient mathematics knowledge to follow and be intrigued by Josie's work. But teaching well (and observing teaching well) is not just a matter of knowing the mathematics. Like teachers, principals who are observing mathematics classes can benefit when they can use their mathematical knowledge to hear the mathematical meaning in students' attempts to explain half-formed ideas, and think about mathematical content in ways other than their own (Ball, 2000). Doing so rests on the ability to open up one's own, adult, mathematical understanding and take apart its constituent elements in order to recognize the elements of, say, equivalent fractions, in a student's thinking (Cohen, cited in Ball, 2000).

It is not surprising that Mrs. Cowan did not delve into Josie's mathematical thinking with the teacher, since classroom observation has not generally been understood to be subject-specific and this kind of mathematical exploration is not something that principals are typically trained to do. We have discovered in our other research that quite often principals who score well on independent measures of their mathematics knowledge, as we suspect

Mrs. Cowan would, do not appear actually to use that knowledge when interpreting what is going on in a classroom (Nelson, Benson, & Reed, 2004).

In order to explore what Josie was understanding about equivalent fractions, Mrs. Cowan and the teacher might have analyzed the variety of mathematical ideas that are embedded in the topic of equivalent fractions and discussed the variety of things Josie *might* have been thinking about. Mrs. Cowan and the teacher might have developed some questions the teacher could ask Josie: what she was doing, why she multiplied both numerators and denominators by 2, what she thought about equivalencies that did not follow her rule of multiplying by 2, and so on. The answers to such questions, as in a clinical interview, would illuminate the conceptual structure of Josie's mathematical knowledge. While both principal and teacher were fascinated by Josie's generalization of the pattern on the fraction fringe, they did not—and perhaps were not ready to—take this fascination to a next level.

Mrs. Cowan appreciated the generativity of Josie's thinking, and our data show that she reinforced with the teacher her view that mathematical tasks should have open-ended possibilities to give children the opportunity to show what they can do, which may be beyond what the teacher had previously seen. Had Mrs. Cowan helped the teacher use her own mathematical knowledge to explore the ideas that Josie was working with, she might have moved forward toward her goal of helping teachers differentiate their instruction for students with different levels and kinds of mathematical understanding. The teacher would have been in a position to base her work with Josie on specific knowledge of Josie's ideas about equivalent fractions. This is one of the ways that teachers can fine-tune their teaching to meet the needs of all students in the class.

The image of Mrs. Cowan working with the teacher to do a detailed analysis of Josie's ideas about equivalent fractions may seem more like the work of a math coach than a principal. Indeed, many math coaches would work with teachers in just this way. By creating this image we do not mean to suggest that all elementary principals need to be able to function like math coaches. However, in most elementary schools it is the principal who mentors teachers, and most have specific ideas about what constitutes good mentoring. We do suggest, therefore, that principals' knowledge of mathematics and their curiosity about students' mathematical thinking can form the basis of a different form of mentoring, one that is particularly appropriate in mathematics classrooms that focus on student thinking.

While the work of Mr. Nash and Mrs. Cowan provide images of what is possible when principals have good conceptual knowledge of mathematics, many principals are not so comfortable with, or knowledgeable about, mathematics. This discomfort or limited knowledge can significantly affect what they value in mathematics instruction, what they are able to appreciate about mathematics instruction when they visit classes, and how they help teachers improve their instruction. The last principal whose work we will examine is Libby O'Brien who, at the time we studied her work, was just beginning to understand that mathematics consists of ideas and concepts as well as facts and procedures. She was also new to the idea that teachers can benefit by listening carefully to how students make sense of these ideas. Her work illustrates how having a beginning conceptual understanding of mathematics makes it possible for the principal to have new goals for teachers and classrooms but may not be enough to allow a principal to help a teacher in his or her professional growth. We have chosen to discuss Ms. O'Brien's work because the progression of her learning about mathematics education is quite typical. Many principals take beginning steps much like Ms. O'Brien's and have struggles similar to hers.

LISTENING TO STUDENTS IN A MATHEMATICS LESSON: LIBBY O'BRIEN

At the time of our work with her, Libby O'Brien was in her sixth year as principal of the McGovern School, a K–4 school in a medium-sized industrial northeastern city. Historically, students at the school had done well in computation but hadn't been as successful with word problems and mathematical problem solving. This difference in attainment on standardized tests had not been an important instructional issue for the staff until the state mathematics test began to emphasize mathematical thinking. Then the staff became increasingly concerned about students' limited capacity to work with word problems and mathematical problem solving. This change, and our work with Ms. O'Brien, took place several years before the passage of the federal No Child Left Behind Act, which requires that schools whose students fail to show enough progress for 5 years must be restructured, with control handed over to new managers.

Certified in elementary and bilingual education and with a master's degree in educational management, Ms. O'Brien brought to her principalship 10 years of experience in school administration in three different schools. Prior to working in administration, Ms. O'Brien had spent 8 years as a teacher in bilingual elementary classrooms and as a second language supervisor. She had not been trained in elementary mathematics education, nor was she comfortable with mathematics herself. She described the reasons for her limited mathematics background:

> I always hated math. I knew that I would never go further in math when in fifth grade I was trying to figure out some kind of a problem

> ... and I just could not get it. [I was] getting very embarrassed at the board ... and I can remember [the teacher] saying, "You have a mental block about math." ... From then on I just shut right off with math. ... Any time in high school when I had a choice between doing math or something else, I picked the something else.

In spite of her unfortunate mathematics experiences as a student, Ms. O'Brien was very concerned to provide the best possible mathematics education for the students in her school. The year before our study of her work began, Ms. O'Brien had taken part in a yearlong course, *Lenses on Learning: A New Focus on Mathematics and School Leadership* (Grant et al., 2003a, 2003b, 2003c) in order to have a context for thinking about how to improve mathematics instruction in her school. In that course, Ms. O'Brien was struck by the images she saw of children's mathematical thinking on videotapes of mathematics lessons, in examples of students' written work, and in teachers' written descriptions of the mathematical thinking of children in their classrooms. These were images of children working on mathematics problems much like the one discussed earlier in this chapter.

Ms. O'Brien was especially taken with the variety she saw in children's problem-solving strategies and connected this observation to her memory of having had difficulty conforming her thought to the way her fifth-grade teacher wanted her to solve mathematics problems. She noted that, as a child, she could see patterns and relationships in numbers but had always had trouble "following somebody else's formula and [getting] the right answer." Her experience as a learner helped her appreciate that children have many different ways of conceptualizing mathematics problems, which can lead to a variety of methods of solution, and that "math with kids does not have to be [only] about one right answer." As a result, she became persuaded that mathematics instruction in her school would improve if children had more opportunity to articulate the way they were thinking about math problems, and if teachers listened more attentively to their students' thinking instead of focusing only on whether or not students had the right answer or used a particular method of solution.

However, in our observations of her, Ms. O'Brien did not appear to understand *what* it is important to listen to in students' mathematical discourse. Our sense was that this was because her knowledge of the complexity of the ideas involved in the elementary mathematics curriculum was still limited. Like many principals, she focused more on ensuring that students had opportunities to talk than on making sense of the mathematical ideas that they raised in their talk.

An Episode from Administrative Practice

In the year that we studied her work, Ms. O'Brien observed a mathematics class taught by Jeremy Jones, a fourth-grade teacher in his third year of teaching at the McGovern School. Ms. O'Brien had become concerned that Mr. Jones should talk less in his mathematics class and listen to the students more. As she put it,

> He's very eager to do well. But, as I keep on trying to tell him, he needs to stop talking. He needs to talk less and listen more. . . . That way he's going to learn more about how to be a better teacher.

This assessment of Mr. Jones's teaching dovetailed with Ms. O'Brien's new interest in listening to children's thinking. It would make sense that, if a teacher wanted children to talk more in order to listen to their ideas, he would need to talk less.

The Mathematics in Mr. Jones's Class. Before turning to the actual classroom observation, we need to look at the mathematics that the students worked on in Mr. Jones's class as background for examining how a limited understanding of mathematics shapes an observation in particular ways. Figure 1.1 shows the problem that students worked on. Mr. Jones took this problem verbatim from the previous year's fourth-grade state mathematics test. To an adult, this task may seem straightforward. The pattern involves add-

Figure 1.1. Mathematics Problem to Solve Using Patterns

Use the information in the chart below to answer the questions below.

Week	1	2	3	4	5	6	7
Amount	$1.50	$3.00	$4.50	$6.00			

Label each answer on your chart paper.

a. Complete the pattern for weeks 5, 6, and 7.
b. Use numbers or words to describe the pattern.
c. Use the pattern in the chart to write a story problem about money. Be sure your problem asks a question.
d. Write a number sentence to go with your story problem. Be sure to include the answer in the number sentence.

---

ing $1.50 each week. The amounts for Weeks 5, 6, and 7 would be $7.50, $9.00, and $10.50, respectively. One type of story problem that incorporates this pattern might involve asking how much money there would be at the end of 7 weeks:

> Marilyn puts aside $1.50 of her allowance each week to buy books. How much money for books will she have in 7 weeks?

Two number sentences that go with this story problem would be

$$\$1.50 \times 7 = \$10.50$$

and

$$\$1.50 + \$1.50 + \$1.50 + \$1.50 + \$1.50 + \$1.50 + \$1.50 = \$10.50.$$

An alternative story problem might emphasize the number of weeks:

> Marilyn wants to buy a book that costs $10.50. She saves $1.50 a week. How many weeks will it take her to save enough money for the book?

The number sentence that goes with this story problem would be $10.50 \div 1.50 = 7$. While the two story problems above emphasize accumulating money, a student might imagine a real-life situation in which the money is being spent:

> Theo buys a package of baseball cards each week. One package costs $1.50. How much money will he spend on baseball cards in 7 weeks?

These examples illustrate ways of addressing each of the points in the test question. The mathematical ideas at play in this problem are the discernment of mathematical patterns and writing story problems for "naked number" calculations—that is, understanding the numerical relationships well enough to show how they would work in a real-world situation.

Patterns are a central feature of mathematics, which is fundamentally about regularities: repeating patterns, growing patterns, geometrical patterns, numerical patterns, and functions. As early as kindergarten and throughout the elementary grades, children work with the idea that a pattern is predictable and is made up of units that repeat. One of the goals of exploring patterns is for students to learn how to make generalizations that help them predict unknown information and address issues of proof (i.e., will it always work?). In the problem given in Mr. Jones's class, the pattern is the amount per week, which increases at the rate of $1.50 per week. Once students recognize this pattern, they can find the amount for the next week by adding $1.50 to the last amount. Building on the notions of generalizability and predictability, students might notice that amounts for any even week are whole dollar amounts and amounts for odd weeks have half-dollar amounts. Recognizing this would allow them to say whether the amount for any week in or beyond the chart would be a whole dollar amount or also include a half-dollar amount. Students might also notice that for every even week the whole dollar amount is a multiple of 3—3, 6, 9—and that the odd-week amounts are made up of a multiple of 3 plus half of 3 (or 1.50).

In being asked to write a story problem that reflected the chart, students were being asked to imagine how this pattern might actually appear in real life, which is another way of showing how they understood the mathematical relationships that were described on the chart. Such word problems also lay the foundation for the idea that two very different real-world situations can have the same mathematical structure and thus be the same in important ways.

What Happened in the Preobservation Conference. Prior to observing in Mr. Jones's class, Ms. O'Brien had a preobservation conference with him. The discussion focused primarily on ways in which Mr. Jones might talk less as a means of giving opportunities to students to talk more. For example, Ms. O'Brien suggested that he "give [students] some more time to think, then they might be able to come out with some of those ideas that you were trying to get at anyway." Ms. O'Brien invited him to plan "any lesson of your choice," and suggested that he "try and work on the notion of expanding kids' minds about mathematical thinking." She suggested that the "problem of the day" be a real-life situation and that the students work in groups. Students could either come up with a group answer or share with one another how they arrived at their individual answers. In thinking about having students share their strategies, Mr. Jones was concerned that students might not be able to explain their strategies, and that he might not be familiar with all the strategies they would generate.

What Happened in the Class. Mr. Jones began by describing the mathematics problem and explaining how he expected students to work together. Thus he focused primarily on explaining the directions but did not talk with the class about the mathematical ideas they might explore. From a mathematical standpoint, however, one might have expected him to introduce the activity by discussing some aspect of the mathematics that they were going to explore, such as how they might encounter different kinds of money patterns when they save or spend money.

Students then worked in six groups of four students each. While they worked together, both Mr. Jones and Ms. O'Brien circulated among the groups, interacting a bit with students, ensuring that students were on task and were interpreting the directions correctly. Mr. Jones then gathered the class together to share their work. As each group reported its work, Mr. Jones would ask follow-up questions, most of which focused on group process. For example, he asked one group, "How come your group didn't get that far?" He also asked questions about the accuracy with which groups followed directions and about who used pretend money to help them get the answer. There was little discussion of the mathematics of the problem itself. Mr. Jones noted how well the story problem that each group created related to both the pattern and the chart. In one case, a student offered the following problem that his group made up: "Josh had $9.00. He wants to know how many quarters it takes to get to $9.00. It takes 36." Mr. Jones responded that this was an interesting problem, although he wasn't sure that the answer was correct. A student from another group confirmed the calculation: "It is. 40 quarters makes $10. If you take off 4 quarters, you get $9.00." Mr. Jones then responded, "It's a great problem. But if I were correcting the state's high-stakes test, there'd be a problem because it doesn't go with the chart."

What Happened in the Postobservation Conference. As a participant in the *Lenses on Learning* seminar, Ms. O'Brien had started to rethink what she looked for in her classroom observations and what she talked about with teachers in postobservation conferences. She told us that before she took the course, she had focused on more general, process-oriented classroom practices such as what the flow of lesson was, whether or not interruptions were minimal, and whether or not students seemed motivated to learn. She also said that she had tried to attend to whether or not the teacher was a facilitator of instruction who checked for understanding in a variety of ways.

During the year of our study, however, she decided to focus her observations on mathematics itself and to shift her orientation to content-specific issues. She devised a set of questions, drawn from ideas she had encountered in the course, to guide her observations and postobservation meetings with teachers:

- How is this lesson connected to a long-term agenda you have for your students' mathematical thinking?
- What are you hoping students will get out of this exploration?
- What mathematical ideas are students trying to make sense of?
- Having taught this lesson, what have you learned about your students' understandings and misconceptions, and what are the next steps for this investigation?

Nevertheless, during the postobservation conference, the discussion remained quite general. Ms. O'Brien asked several of her questions but did not use them to stimulate a more detailed discussion. For example, when she asked Mr. Jones what the mathematical ideas were that the students were trying to get hold of, he responded that they were working on patterns, using money as a manipulative, writing a story problem, and showing evidence to support their answer. Ms. O'Brien did not ask any follow-up questions to this response but moved instead to ask about some emotional dimensions of teaching and some management issues, such as how he gave directions and how much time he spent doing so.

While there is no evidence about why Ms. O'Brien kept the postobservation conference at such a general level, it is likely that at this early stage in her learning about mathematics education she did not yet understand how to engage with the content of the mathematics itself. Her general discomfort with mathematics was likely an impediment to moving in this direction, and her largely procedural knowledge of mathematics would have made it difficult for her to work with the mathematical content of many mathematics lessons in a conceptual way.

We can see evidence of Ms. O'Brien's limited mathematics knowledge and its consequences in the postobservation conference. As noted above, Mr. Jones had been concerned that students might bring up ways of solving the problem that he didn't understand himself. This is a common concern among teachers who are beginning to focus their teaching on students' mathematical ideas. Over time Mr. Jones would likely learn the most common ways that students solve these problems, but it would always remain possible that in any particular class one or more students would have a way to think about and solve a problem that he had not seen before. Had her mathematics knowledge been stronger, Ms. O'Brien might have thought to go back to his concern and discuss specific solutions that students did generate, depending on how they were making sense of the problem. She and Mr. Jones could then have talked about what each of these indicated about the students' understanding of patterns in general and the pattern in this problem in particular.

Analysis

Libby O'Brien had had important insights in the *Lenses on Learning* course when she recognized that mathematics was about ideas, not just facts and procedures to be memorized; that children had their own ways of thinking about mathematical ideas; and that these informed how they solved problems. These insights led her to encourage teachers to talk less and listen more, and to organize their classes in ways that would make it possible for students to articulate the way they solved mathematics problems. These were important steps to take. But at this point in her learning, we surmise that Ms. O'Brien did not yet understand that in classes where mathematical reasoning is the focus, she needed to encourage teachers to focus on the mathematical content of students' talk, assess its validity, and think about the next teaching move. Given her admitted discomfort with mathematics and her limited conceptual knowledge, it was likely that she would have to learn more mathematics herself before she would be able to help teachers do this.

Ms. O'Brien is typical of many principals who begin to explore new roles as instructional leaders in mathematics. They begin to recognize that students have important ideas to share and that listening to students is critical to teaching and learning. For these principals, a valuable next step would be to start learning what is involved in listening to students' ideas and making sense of them. Because Ms. O'Brien had shifted her focus from process-oriented classroom features to content-specific features, she might now be poised to consider her own content knowledge and the way it affects what she notices in a classroom. For instance, if professional development resources were available, she might focus next on understanding what students say when given the opportunity to talk and what might be reasonable responses for teachers, given the ideas that students are working on.

CONCLUSION

Recent innovations in elementary mathematics instruction, prompted by the National Council of Teachers of Mathematics policy documents (1989, 2000) and by the consideration of many mathematicians and mathematics educators of what it actually means to do and know mathematics (cf. Kilpatrick et al., 2001), have called the attention of many teachers and researchers to what students are actually understanding conceptually when they do mathematics in school. This focus on students' conceptual understanding—and not just their facility with procedures for calculation—has led to the conclusion that teaching entails attending to individual students' mathematical thinking and making interventions that help students develop rigorous and valid mathematical understanding (see Chapter 2 for a fuller discussion of such instruction).

Defining mathematics as the conceptual understanding of mathematical ideas as well as the mastery of procedures of calculation is a richer and fuller view of the nature of mathematics than many principals had access to in their own educations. Therefore, as teachers begin to act on this larger definition, as instructional materials have it embedded in their design, and as high-stakes tests begin to measure it, principals with largely procedural knowledge may be limited in their understanding of what is happening in the classrooms they observe and the practical judgment that they exercise. Further, they may be less able to help teachers improve an instructional practice that is rooted in this more complex view of mathematics.

In Peter Nash, we saw a principal who understood that the ideas embedded in a mathematics problem can be quite complex, that different people will approach them in different ways, and that the basic ideas that underlie a mathematics problem can be extended and connected to other mathematical ideas. He was able to use his knowledge of mathematics to establish a mathematics community among his teachers, illustrating a point that Marianne Cowan also cared about, that if attention is paid to students' mathematical thinking, mathematics classes can be heterogeneous and instruction can be tailored to each student's mathematical understanding. Like Mr. Nash, Mrs. Cowan knew a substantial amount of mathematics and could examine a student's mathematical work in some detail. But she did not analyze the ideas that were part of her own mathematics knowledge in order to explore in more detail the nature of a student's mathematical understanding. This is an important strategy for meeting the needs of all students in a class—Mrs. Cowan's goal—but she was unable to help the teacher develop this strategy. Finally, Libby O'Brien was able to develop new goals for mathematics instruction in her school, but her limited conceptual mathematics knowledge hampered her efforts to assist a teacher who was eager to move his instruction in the very direction she wanted.

Each of these principals is energetic, thoughtful, and committed to providing the best mathematics instruction possible in their schools, but their mathematics knowledge and how they were able to use it varied widely, with significant consequences for the nature of teaching and learning in their schools. While mathematics knowledge is a critical component of an instructional leader's knowledge base, it is not sufficient. Principals also need to understand how students learn mathematics, so that they can go beyond the surface features of instruction to discuss with teachers what needs to happen for real learning to occur.

PRINCIPALS' IDEAS ABOUT LEARNING AND TEACHING MATHEMATICS

SCHOLARS' VIEWS of the nature of learning are always evolving. With occasional exceptions, behaviorist theories about how mathematics is learned have dominated in twentieth-century America (Bransford et al., 1999; Cohen, 1988; Gardner, 1985). In this view, knowledge is fixed and objective; learning is a matter of absorbing and accumulating this knowledge, element by element; and teaching is a matter of telling students about this knowledge, giving them opportunities to practice new skills and providing reinforcement (Romberg & Carpenter, 1986). For more than 3 decades, however, research in cognitive psychology has supported a view of children's learning commonly called *constructivism*, which refers to the idea that children actively construct mathematical knowledge for themselves through interaction with the social and physical environment and through the extension and reorganization of their own mental constructs (Marris, 1975; Piaget, 1977; Romberg & Carpenter, 1986). In this view, children are not passive recipients of mathematical knowledge. They generate it, put structure into it, assimilate it in light of their own mental frameworks, and revise existing mental frameworks to accommodate new experience. The development of constructivist theories of learning marked the willingness of researchers to attend to students' ideas and not just their observable behavior. While there are many varieties of constructivism, which have developed as scholars from many fields worked with the idea (Phillips, 1987; Wood, Nelson, & Warfield, 2001), the basic tenets stated above are generally accepted.

Even more recently, educational researchers have come to view students' sense making as occurring in specific contexts which have material and social characteristics (J. S. Brown, Collins, & Duguid, 1989; Greeno, 1998; Greeno, Collins, & Resnick, 1996). In this perspective, which we will call socioconstructivist, knowing how to participate in the social processes of the classroom or other learning situation—for example, participating in mathematical problem solving or the discussion of mathematical ideas—is an important aspect of learning and affects what is learned.

Each of these theories of mathematics learning, and its view of teaching, has its truth. As research on learning has moved from behaviorist to constructivist and then to socioconstructivist views of learning, each school of thought has expanded (and redefined) the range of activities analyzed, and increased the explanatory power of learning theory (Spillane, Reiser, & Reimer, 2002).

Elementary principals' ideas about the nature of learning and pedagogy are very important aspects of their identities as instructional leaders and affect the practical judgment they exercise as they do their work. Different theoretical positions about the nature of mathematics learning become enacted in actual processes of administrative practice because administrators' beliefs about the nature of mathematics learning have the effect of shaping what they value and attend to. Beliefs about learning affect how principals understand policy documents, what they see when they observe in classrooms, what they think a good elementary teacher should know and be able to do, and what they think a good elementary curriculum should provide for teachers and students. They also affect what actions they think it important to take in their work as instructional leaders.

Different positions about the nature of mathematics learning also affect administrators' views of the nature of instruction. Within the behaviorist view, *direct instruction* was the name given to a set of teaching functions that in the 1970s and 1980s were thought to be the appropriate instructional methods to use in well-structured domains, such as the teaching of arithmetic facts, mathematical computations, and solving algebraic equations. Direct instruction included the following components:

- Begin a lesson with a short review of relevant prior learning.
- Begin a lesson with a short statement of goals.
- Present new material in small steps, with student practice after each step.
- Give clear and detailed instructions and explanations.
- Provide a high level of active practice for all students.
- Ask a large number of questions, check for student understanding, and obtain responses from all students.
- Guide students during initial practice.
- Provide systematic feedback and correction.
- Provide explicit instruction and practice for seatwork exercises. (Rosenshine & Stevens, 1986, p. 377)

These teaching functions had been identified through the process-product program of research on teaching, and it was expected that they would be modified for different grade levels and student ability levels

Instruction based on a constructivist view of learning consists of gauging what students currently understand and creating social and material environments (problems to be solved, investigations to be undertaken, discussions to be had, etc.) in which students think through new ideas and build ever more complex knowledge structures. Such teaching requires that teachers know the subject well, and understand how children's knowledge of it develops (Ball, 2000; Bransford, Brown, & Cocking, 1999; Shulman, 1986).

The socioconstructivist view of learning leads to a focus on providing students with the opportunity to learn to participate in classroom discourse that is characteristic of a subject matter domain and to use the representational systems and tools of the domain—formulating and evaluating questions and problems, and constructing and evaluating hypotheses, evidence, arguments, and conclusions (cf. Lampert, 2001). Also characteristic of this view is project-based learning, where students engage in complex, real-world tasks in which subject matter concepts and principles are embedded in the activity setting (Greeno, Collins, & Resnick, 1996).

Each of these views of the nature of mathematics learning is true to some degree and under some circumstances. As our thinking about mathematics learning shifts from one paradigm to another, ideas from the previous paradigm are included but reinterpreted in light of the new paradigm's larger and different frame of reference (Spillane, Reiser, & Reimer, 2002). For example, memorization of mathematical facts and procedures and practice in their use—learning that generally proceeds according to behaviorist principles— is important. However, research shows that practice with facts and procedures is most effective when it follows substantial initial experiences that support understanding. Rote knowledge of facts without conceptual understanding produces very fragile knowledge that does not serve students well in the long run. Computation and understanding need to develop together and reinforce each other (Kilpatrick et al., 2001).

Direct instruction has been the mainstay of many administrators' view of instruction for many years, in part because many current administrators were educated before constructivist and socioconstructivist theories of learning were commonly accepted and these therefore were not part of their formal training. However, elements of constructivism are increasingly becoming part of many principals' work. (For interesting analyses of how these ideas have moved between the research and practice communities, see Gardner, 1985; Romberg & Carpenter, 1986; Shulman, 1986.) Principals are finding now that many policy documents, contemporary mathematics curricula, and professional development programs for teachers are based on constructivist or socioconstructivist views of learning. Some of these curricula and professional development programs appear in the cases examined in this book. For many administrators, though, developing their understanding of these newer ideas and how they integrate with behavioral theories entails fundamental conceptual changes and takes considerable time. (Nelson, 1998).

In this chapter we examine the ideas about mathematics learning and teaching held by three elementary principals and the effect that these ideas have on the practical judgment they exercise as they do classroom observations in their schools. We also consider briefly the importance of principals' ideas to the kind of accountability represented by the No Child Left Behind legislation.

We observed each principal at a different point in his or her learning trajectory. Sheila Diggins believed that children are continually working to make sense of mathematical ideas and that teachers need to understand each student's thinking in quite subtle ways if their instruction is to be effective. Libby O'Brien had come to believe that students have individual and unique ways of understanding mathematical ideas that need to be acknowledged in the classroom, but could not yet picture what teaching that focuses on students' ideas might look like. Rob Bouvier was struck by his observation that students who can solve mathematics problems procedurally may lack conceptual understanding of the very same problem; this insight began to affect his expectations for classrooms and assessment. These principals' beliefs about the nature of mathematics learning significantly influenced what they attended to when doing classroom observations and how they talked with teachers in postobservation conferences and worked with them in faculty meetings.

MATHEMATICS LEARNING AS SENSE MAKING: SHEILA DIGGINS

Sheila Diggins is principal of a primary school in a large northeastern city, which uses the *Investigations in Number, Data, and Space* curriculum (Russell & Tierney, 1998), a set of instructional materials built on constructivist principles about children's mathematics learning. At the time of this study Ms. Diggins understood mathematics learning to be a process of *sense making*. This phrase is usually used to convey that in learning mathematics the student's task is to understand what the ideas, facts, and problems of mathematics mean, how they relate to each other, and how they relate to the everyday world. Ms. Diggins believed in a constructivist view of learning, which she contrasted with two other views, the behaviorist and the romantic, as she labeled them. According to Ms. Diggins, the behaviorist view of learning was based on the delivery of information from teacher to student: "You stand and you drill, and people learn because you said so." The romantic view of learning was where children invent ideas for themselves in an unstructured environment: "You give the kids all the tools and the right environment [and] they figure it out. You know, free play, free play." And the constructivist view of learning was not as structured as behaviorism nor as unstructured as the romantic school of thought. As she understood the constructivist theory of learning, it required teachers to understand what students already understood and what they needed to learn, and then to ask questions or pose mathematical tasks that would engage them with the ideas they needed to grapple with:

> It's about giving kids all of the tools and giving them an opportunity to experience them and giving them support in figuring out how they all work. I think there's not enough support [in] the romantic train of thought where . . . you give it to them and watch them grow. And there's too much information or support given . . . in the behaviorist kind of thought. [In the constructivist view] . . . kids are putting things together in their mind[s], and teachers are helping to support them put things together by understanding what they already know and what they need to know and creating situations that are a little bit beyond their reach, to keep them moving along.

In fact, whereas Ms. Diggins focused on the *amount* of structure and support in these different views of learning, it is the *nature* and *form* of structure and support that vary. For example, instruction based on a behaviorist view of learning provides structured information and problems to be solved; support may take the form of reteaching something a student has not understood or offering additional opportunities for practice. Instruction based on a constructivist view of learning provides mathematical tasks that help students restructure their mathematical ideas, and support may take the form of asking a mathematical question designed to stretch their current conceptualizations.

Nevertheless, implicit in her definition of constructivism was an important and correct idea that would be very useful to her in her practice—the idea that students are naturally, and continually, learning by thinking. A corollary of this idea that Ms. Diggins stated is that teachers should propose mathematical tasks or questions that are "a little bit beyond [the students'] reach" so that by thinking about those mathematical tasks or questions students will continue building their mathematical knowledge.

An Episode from Administrative Practice

Ms. Diggins's view of mathematics learning as a sense-making enterprise and mathematics teaching as creating situations that encourage students to reach a little further mathematically, informed her practical judgment as she conducted classroom observations. She was very interested in visiting mathematics classrooms in her school because she liked to see the *Investigations* curriculum "in action." She had studied the text, but visiting classrooms gave her the opportunity to see students' responses to the mathematical investigations that the curriculum posed. One classroom she observed was Ted Davis's first grade. The lesson was from a unit designed to develop children's intuitive sense of numbers—"learning about how our number system is structured and the relationships between numbers" (Kliman & Russell, 1998, I-18). In this unit students also begin to explore addition and subtraction of small numbers. On the day she observed the class, the children were working in small groups, engaged in one of several games or activities that gave them the opportunity to investigate combinations of numbers up to 10—Counters in a Cup, Tower of Tens, Double Compare, and On and Off from *Building Number Sense*, Investigation 2 (Kliman & Russell, 1998).

While Ms. Diggins paid attention to many aspects of this classroom, we single out her attention to two children engaged in one of the lesson's mathematical activities because it is an indication of her view of what was important in mathematics learning. Ms. Diggins focused especially on two children who were playing Counters in a Cup. This game is played with 10 counters and an inverted empty cup. One child takes some of the counters and puts them under the cup, leaving the remainder in view. The second child is to figure out how many counters are under the cup. This game requires children to work out a variety of number combinations that total 10. It involves keeping track of and coordinating three amounts: the total number of counters (10), the number visible, and the number hidden (Kliman & Russell, 1998). When Ms. Diggins observed the children playing the game, she noted that these particular children were doing far more than "just playing the game": they were engaging in the activity "as intended—understanding that they were taking the numbers apart and recombining them." She also noticed that each of the children did the calculations differently, indicating to her that they were at different stages in the development of their ideas about how numbers could be combined. Further, while she watched, one of the students began to use the other student's more advanced method.

The methods of counting used by the children reflected how children develop their counting skills. As children learn to count, saying each number while referring to an object, they gradually begin to relate the last counted word in a series as also referring to the size of the counted group as a whole. This is called the *count-to-cardinality shift*. Later, they can use a still more efficient method, counting on, in which they begin with the cardinal number and continue counting from there (Fuson, 1992). Seeing different counting methods play out before her eyes was very exciting to Ms. Diggins. Here is her description of the event:

> I particularly enjoyed those two children in Mr. Davis's room who were really playing the game the way it was intended. I was like, "Whoa." And they were there for a long period of time playing the game the way it was intended. And . . . I saw the things that we talk about. . . . They were playing with the [counters], and they were counting. [The boy] was actually counting on, and the other one [a girl] had to count from the beginning to the end. By the end of that session, the little girl had begun to count on because there were certain numbers that she started recognizing as a group. . . . The little boy consistently counted on from the beginning to the end, and I saw her, she did it with the number 5 and she did it with the number 3. You could sort of see a little light bulb go on as she watched him. He said, "That's 5," and then counted on. And then the next time, she did the same thing and started counting on. And she hadn't been doing that at the beginning of the game. So, I got to see it really work. I believed that it worked, but I hadn't seen it in action. . . . I got to see the different levels. I knew that there were levels of understanding, and I could see the different levels in that classroom. Boy oh boy!

Ms. Diggins was attending to the way in which the two students made sense of the mathematical task before them. She observed not only that both students were able to combine and recombine numbers totaling 10, but that each did it in a different way, indicating what they understood about how numbers could be counted. She believed that the girl, who initially began with 1 every time, did not yet understand that a set of numbers could be clumped together, labeled, and considered a group, and that you could start counting from there. The boy did appear to understand this.

Later, when she talked with Mr. Davis about the lesson, Ms. Diggins focused on what he understood about the thinking of the children in his classroom. At one point in her conversation with him, he said, "They were getting it, they were getting it." Ms. Diggins asked him if he had been trying to figure out what they knew. He replied,

> I just wanted to watch them play, and then maybe ask them some questions if they needed a little more clarification . . . if they could figure out what the numbers meant in the roll of dice, if they could add them together, if they could break them up. If they'd know what to do if they went over 10, if they could bring them back down, if they could figure out that 10 might be smaller than the 12 and be able to explain it.

Ms. Diggins was not entirely satisfied with this answer, in which he focused largely on the children's strategies. She was not sure "how much information he takes away around their understanding." She told us that she was not sure if Mr. Davis was yet able to see exactly what mathematical ideas the students were working with, what they understood, and what they were still working on, as she did when observing the boy and girl.

Analysis

At this point in the development of her ideas about mathematics learning and teaching, Sheila Diggins viewed children's mathematical learning as making sense of ideas and working with them in situations that are "a little bit beyond their reach" in order to build their knowledge. She characterized herself as firmly holding a constructivist view of learning. However, she was not yet really clear on the nature of structure and support in constructivist-oriented instruction as distinct from instruction based on a behaviorist view of learning or what she called "the romantic train of thought."

The sense children make of mathematical ideas was most important to Ms. Diggins and led her to pay attention to students' mathematical sense making when she observed in Mr. Davis's classroom. She had seen that counting on was initially "just a little bit beyond the reach" of the girl, who saw the other child counting on and later was able to use that strategy herself for some numbers. Ms. Diggins had witnessed learning happening. Attention to how children learn new ideas from observing the strategies of other children in the class is in line with Vygotsky's (1978) notion of the "zone of proximal development," which is the arena in which a student can do something with help but not yet on his or her own. From a slightly different perspective, it also illustrates the social and interactive dimensions of learning analyzed by those scholars who hold the socioconstructivist position and look at classrooms as "communities of practice" (c.f., J. S. Brown et al., 1989; Cobb et al., 1991; Lampert, 1990).

Ms. Diggins also expected teachers to be able to listen to the mathematical meaning that children are making when they do their work or describe their thinking, in order to be able to design the next task or question that will be "just a little bit beyond" their current understanding.

MATHEMATICS LEARNING AS THE PROCESS OF ARTICULATING IDEAS: LIBBY O'BRIEN

Attending to the content of students' mathematical thinking when doing a classroom observation and expecting teachers to do the same, as Ms. Diggins did, requires a subtle shift in attention for many elementary principals, who are more accustomed to attending to teacher and student behaviors. In order to explore the significance of this shift, we look again at the work of Libby O'Brien. In Chapter 1, we looked at Ms. O'Brien's mathematical knowledge and how it affected what she saw when she observed in classrooms and how she could help her teachers. In this chapter, we examine her ideas about mathematics learning.

At this point in the development of her ideas about mathematics learning and teaching, Ms. O'Brien strongly believed that children have their own individual ways of solving mathematics problems and that mathematics classes should be run in such a way that students have the opportunity to articulate and discuss their ways of solving problems. In this chapter we show that she had come to value some of the classroom behaviors that are characteristic of instruction that is based on a constructivist view of how children's mathematical knowledge develops, but she did not yet appear to understand why a constructivist view values those instructional behaviors. Consequently, she was satisfied with less than she likely would be if she understood more.

An Episode from Administrative Practice

As mentioned in the previous chapter, Ms. O'Brien is principal of the McGovern School, a kindergarten through Grade 4 elementary school in a large northeastern city. Recently she had come to believe that mathematics instruction in her school would improve if teachers gave students more opportunity to articulate their mathematical ideas—if teachers "listened more and talked less." We examine here another observation of Jeremy Jones's fourth-grade class to consider what Ms. O'Brien's beliefs prepared her to see in the class and value instructionally.

This observation took place in February. Mr. Jones had been working with his students for some time on applying different strategies to the mathematics problems they worked on. These strategies were listed on the wall and included the following: Make a table; use logical reasoning; look for a pattern; and use objects and act it out. In this particular lesson, Mr. Jones was focusing on using a table as a problem-solving strategy. He assigned his students to work in small groups on the problem shown in Figure 2.1.

This problem had been taken from the statewide assessment test and contained data with an unexpected complexity. The original problem, taken from an actual sunrise table, gave the time of sunrise on August 8 as 4:43 and on August 9 as 4:45, a 2-minute interval. The larger interval between August 8 and August 9 caused some confusion among the students in Mr. Jones's class. When it came to his attention, Mr. Jones assumed he had made an error in copying the problem and changed the numbers to those in Figure 2.1, which is the version the students actually worked with. How-

Figure 2.1. Mathematics Problem to Solve Using a Table

Sunrise in Boston

Jonathon wants to start fishing with a friend at sunrise on August 25. He found this information in the newspaper:

Date	Sunrise Time
August 1	4:36 A.M.
August 2	4:37 A.M.
August 3	4:38 A.M.
August 4	4:39 A.M.
August 5	4:40 A.M.
August 6	4:41 A.M.
August 7	4:42 A.M.
August 8	4:43 A.M.
August 9	4:44 A.M.
August 10	4:45 A.M.

ABOUT what time will the sun rise on August 25? Use pictures, numbers, or words to explain your answer.

ABOUT how much later will the sun rise on August 25 than on August 10? Use pictures, numbers, or words to explain your answer.

---

ever, this incident illustrates the difficulty of using simplified or excerpted versions of real scientific data for school mathematics problems because the patterns may be more complex than is immediately apparent.

After introducing the problem, Mr. Jones started moving among the small groups, first listening and watching and then asking such questions as "How do you know that?" and "Can you make a nice, organized chart?" With one group, he proposed using another strategy along with the creation of their table: "How about using Guess and Check at the same time as continuing to make a table?" When it appeared that some students were trying to calculate mentally what the time on August 25 would be, Mr. Jones said, "You predict it's going to be 5:00. Let's write it down and see if it's what you get when you continue the chart." Then he added, "Why do you say that?" Mr. Jones seemed to be consciously working on his exchanges with students, often quite successfully making them open-ended and inviting the students to express themselves.

Later in the lesson Mr. Jones called the class back to the rug at the front of the room. He asked for volunteers to come up and show their work, instructing the others to "look and listen." He sat on a chair and listened intently. One student explained that their group had added the times up, by ones, from 4:36 to 5:00 in the morning: "We knew the time when the sun rises on August 25 will be 5:00 in the morning, because we continued the pattern." Next the student said that the sun would rise 64 minutes later than on August 1, "because we subtracted 5:00 and 4:36." Mr. Jones responded, "That was excellent. I like how you explained why, and how you got your answer. It's important to explain it in words." Then, referring to the second question, he said, "The only thing, they subtracted 4:36 from 5:00. What about 64 minutes?" Several students murmured tentative thoughts. "Time is tough," Mr. Jones said. Another student volunteered an answer:

STUDENT: We got 24 minutes.
MR. JONES: You got 24 minutes, the other group got 64 minutes. Think about why 64 minutes can't be possible. (He asked them to think back to earlier work they'd done with days, weeks, and hours.) Why is 64 minutes not possible?
STUDENT: 64 is 1 hour and 4 minutes.
MR. JONES: Has 1 hour and 4 minutes passed between the first and the last number? Prove it to me if it has, or if it hasn't.
STUDENT: 60 minutes hasn't passed.
MR. JONES: What would the time be if 1 hour passed?
STUDENT: 5:36.
MR. JONES: When you did the time, from the beginning to the end of doing something, what's the time in between called?
STUDENT: Elapsed time.
MR. JONES: That's the time in between.

Next Mr. Jones moved away from discussing the exact number of minutes that had elapsed in order to affirm students who had solved the problem by using subtraction:

MR. JONES: How many of you at least did a subtraction problem? (Most hands went up.)
MR. JONES: Why did you subtract? Why did most of you use the operation of subtraction to find the answer?
STUDENT: It's the easiest way to answer.

MR. JONES: Why didn't you add? Multiply? Divide?

STUDENT: I used the clue words, how much.

MR. JONES: (drawing the other students' attention to the poster with clue words for addition and subtraction that he had put on the wall) The words in the problem are similar to the clue words for subtraction . . . "later." For all who subtracted, great.

After soliciting sharing from a few other groups, Mr. Jones returned to the earlier discussion about problem-solving strategies. He asked, "How did making a table help you? What did it help you do?" They discussed ways in which a table helped them organize their thoughts, and ways in which this strategy is different from making an organized list. Mr. Jones then apologized to the students about the mix-up that had occurred in the numbers and handed out a multiplication practice sheet.

In talking with him later about this lesson, Ms. O'Brien showed the level of detail at which she attended to the content of the lesson, bringing up a specific student's thinking about the difficulty that the 60-minute hour created in this problem.

I had to ask the [small] group [I was observing], I had them subtract it and . . . I said, why don't you use your mental math? . . . That's when they got it. I said 64 seems off . . . [and I asked] what is 4:36 around, and they said 4:30, and then 5:00, and they said it's about a half hour, and then Algernon, I think, was able to come up with exactly 24 minutes.

Mr. Jones responded:

Well, he did it instantly, actually, and I should have thought of him when we did report out because when I was meeting with them he instantly said it was 5:00; he said it's 15 minutes later because he said between the 10th to the 25th is 15 days, it's one minute, so he automatically got 15 minutes actually right away.

After this brief exchange about individual students' approaches to the mathematics problem, Ms. O'Brien brought the focus of the discussion to Mr. Jones's own instructional strategies and her concern that he talk less and listen more. She said,

something that we've been working on over the year and that I continually tease you about is your question and answering, and giving students a chance to answer. I saw that it was really very well done, and the questions that you gave them [did not require just] one-word kinds of answers, but they were "what does that mean?" and you would say sometimes, "can you restate that?" ... Then you would check back and you said, "Okay, so an organized list is what we're doing there. That means what?" and then you would ask someone else. So you're asking someone else to repeat what someone else said but in different ways. ... That's the thing I was looking at, was the questions and answers. You didn't fish for the right answer, but you accepted many answers and many different responses and you went from there, which I thought was really a nice way to lead the discussion.

Analysis

In the observation of this lesson, Libby O'Brien noticed, valued, and discussed with Mr. Jones some aspects of the classroom that would support learning from a constructivist point of view but did not discuss with him other aspects of his teaching that a constructivist view of learning would indicate were important. To examine how Ms. O'Brien's beliefs about learning affected what she observed and discussed with Mr. Jones, we look first at the mathematical thinking that the students in the class did and how Mr. Jones taught the lesson.

The data from this classroom show that students reasoned about the time of sunrise on August 25 in several different ways. One student extended the pattern to August 25, another counted the minutes of every day from August 1 to August 25. Algernon used his knowledge of mathematical facts—that 25 is 15 larger than 10—to conclude that if the sun rose one minute later each day, therefore the sun would rise 15 minutes later on August 25 than it did on August 10. For the second part of the problem, how much later the sun would rise on August 25 than on August 1, most students subtracted the time on August 1 from the time on August 25, though some got confused because an hour has 60 minutes, not 100. Algernon seemed to know instantly that the answer was 24 minutes. Mr. Jones was not surprised, citing Algernon's ability to use math facts to reason about the second part of the problem, rather than counting the number of minutes.

Teaching decisions are very complex and based on a great deal of information about the children in the class and the intent of the lesson. Without interview data from Mr. Jones, we cannot know why he made the teaching decisions he did. But we can describe what he did and analyze the advantages and disadvantages of having made those particular teaching moves. In his teaching, Mr. Jones chose to listen for the presence of different problem-solving strategies, which had the advantage of legitimating the thinking of many students in the class and allowing all students to see that there were methods other than their own that could be used. He chose not to discuss with the students what was mathematically significant and valid in each strategy—why it worked and how effective it was. For example, one student used a counting method, extending the chart until it reached August 25 and then simply counting the minutes. This is a straightforward method that requires knowing how to complete the chart and being able to count accurately. But it might not work well if the chart was to be extended by a very large number of items. Counting every item would be time-consuming, and counting errors could easily creep in. Employing a different strategy, many students extended the chart and then subtracted 4:36 from 5:00. This, too, is a valid method but requires attending to the fact that there are 60 minutes in an hour—that is, knowing that there can be different numbering systems and which one must be used in order to make sense of the problem. Demonstrating yet another strategy, Algernon used mathematics facts that he already knew to compute the intervals in question. This method was very efficient—"he got it almost instantly"—but students have to know the mathematics facts and how to apply them in particular situations. If Mr. Jones had discussed each method, the mathematical reasoning that made it work, and its pros and cons, it would have had the disadvantage of taking more class time, but the advantage of moving the discussion from a simple description of strategies into the realm of mathematical reasoning.

We also cannot know why Ms. O'Brien made the supervisory decisions she did, but we can analyze what they were and what apparent effects they had. By and large, in her conference with Mr. Jones, Ms. O'Brien did not focus on the mathematical ideas at play in this classroom and how they were worked with, but rather on the teacher's behavior. She was very pleased to see that Mr. Jones was asking open-ended questions—such as "What does that mean?"—that gave students the opportunity to say more about their mathematical thinking, and that he was asking students to paraphrase each other. She was pleased that he didn't appear to be fishing for the "right" answer, but accepted many answers and responses. However, while she was able to follow the students' problem-solving strategies, and even prompt them, in her conversation with Mr. Jones she did not go beyond valuing the existence of students' strategies and the fact that Mr. Jones had allowed them to emerge in the class. Unlike Ms. Diggins, Ms. O'Brien did not discuss students' strategies as a particular "take" on the mathematical ideas embedded in this problem, nor did she comment on the validity or sophistication of the students' mathematical reasoning or expect Mr. Jones to do so. Having lots of student ideas out on the table seemed sufficient for Ms. O'Brien.

It is not surprising that Ms. O'Brien would focus her observation on Mr. Jones's instructional behaviors rather than attend to students' mathematical thinking. As noted earlier, during the period when many current administrators were educated, the process-product program of research on teaching was affecting the design of textbooks and training programs in teacher supervision and the design of classroom observation instruments (Darling-Hammond & Sclan, 1992; Reitzug, 1997). Process-product research identified observable teacher behaviors that were correlated with student outcomes, measured by standardized tests, and aggregated at the classroom level. Dimensions of teachers' behavior included, for instance, the pacing of instruction, the presence of wait time after asking questions, the structuring of lessons, frequency of praise or criticism, and use of lower or higher order questions (Brophy & Good, 1986). Observable behaviors associated with positive student outcomes were taken to be "good" teaching and were often incorporated into checklists for use in the supervision of teachers (c.f. Hunter, 1984).

When she observed Mr. Jones's classroom, Ms. O'Brien appeared to be looking for a list of desirable teacher behaviors. Perhaps on the basis of what she had learned about mathematics instruction in the *Lenses on Learning* class she had taken with us, Ms. O'Brien may have developed a new list of teacher behaviors and classroom structures: having students think about mathematics problems in their own unique ways and describe their thinking, listening to student strategies without fishing for the right answer, asking open-ended questions, and so on. However, there is no evidence that at this point in the development of her ideas about constructivist learning Ms. O'Brien understood the nature of the intellectual work on the part of students that these classroom structures and teacher behaviors were designed to support. As children work through mathematics problems in their own ways, they are using the mathematics problem as a context for exploring mathematical ideas—trying to use their current understanding to solve the problem or trying to stretch their knowledge so that they can work on the new problem. That is, when students are thinking through mathematics problems they actually are constructing new mathematics knowledge in their minds.

There also is no evidence that Ms. O'Brien yet understood that, in a constructivist view of learning, when teachers listen to their students' mathematical explanations, they need to be paying attention to the mathematical validity of what the children are saying and what their ways of working on mathematics problems show about their mathematical understanding. Teachers also need to be thinking about the next questions to ask, or problems to pose, that will help the students develop firmer and more valid modes of mathematical reasoning. Supervisors can help teachers like Mr. Jones pay closer attention to what was mathematically valid, or invalid, in the students' thinking and generate the specific mathematical questions that would have helped the students think more rigorously about these interesting and puzzling matters.

Enjoining the teachers in her school to "listen more and talk less," had been a big step forward for Ms. O'Brien toward a constructivist view of mathematics learning. This behavioral change on the part of teachers might indeed make more space in the classroom for children to express their mathematical ideas. At this point in her learning about constructivist views of mathematics learning, however, Ms. O'Brien did not seem to see that such a behavioral change on the part of teachers would not, in and of itself, ensure high-quality mathematics instruction. Nevertheless, with her belief that children had their own mathematical ideas and her conviction that these should be more central in mathematics instruction, Ms. O'Brien was poised to take the next steps of attending to the mathematical content of students' ideas and wondering, with Mr. Jones, what a student might be understanding when he explained his mathematical thinking.

FOLLOWING RULES VERSUS CONCEPTUAL UNDERSTANDING IN MATHEMATICS: ROB BOUVIER

Principals like Ms. O'Brien, who want mathematics instruction to make room for students' mathematical thinking, may be looking for a new set of teacher behaviors that they expect will give more importance to students' ideas. Yet, making the shift to looking at the content of students' mathematical thinking can be emotionally charged, as in the case of Rob Bouvier.

Mr. Bouvier is principal of the Whitestone School, a suburban East Coast school of 650 students in kindergarten through sixth grade and 31 teachers. The school is in a high-achieving district in which students are consistently expected to perform at high levels. Parents are very active in school life and regard their children's performance in mathematics as an indicator of their prospects for attending an Ivy League college. They expect their children's mastery of mathematics to be quick and expect the mathematics itself to be rigorous and above grade level.

Mr. Bouvier had been a social studies teacher and developer of social studies curricula before he became a principal, and he tended to use his image of the good social studies class, where students are actively engaged in working on real-life problems, as the touchstone for what would count as a good class in mathematics as well. For example, he had this to say about a mathematics class:

> The reason I thought that this [mathematics] classroom experience
> was very strong was that it resembled a social studies class. . . . The

same qualities that I saw as being attractive in a social studies class [were] happening in this math class. . . . The common base was kids talking to each other and solving real-world problems.

His own experiences as a mathematics learner had been quite traditional, and the mathematics he had learned was quite disconnected from any practical application, which he regarded as problematic. As he described it to us,

> My math instruction was based . . . in memorization and not under-standing the connection between what was being discussed [and] the outside world. . . . It was all vertical. You needed to learn this before you could do this. You needed to know that before you could do that. Very little problem solving. It was all arithmetic and formu-las. . . . And I think in my own learning, I never learned a second way to do anything. It was always one way. And then if you learn it only as one way, when you apply it to problems that have little twists and turns, you can't do it.

For some time Mr. Bouvier had believed that in mathematics classrooms students should share their ideas with each other, build their ideas together, and work on real-world problems. He had strong ideas about how classrooms should be set up and how teachers should interact with students in order to give students good opportunities to share their thought processes. He described for us what the mathematics classrooms in his school—all of which encouraged students to share their thinking—looked and sounded like:

> Every classroom in this building has groups of kids together. There are no rows. So very quickly visually you see . . . that kids are seated in such a way that they can face their peers and have a discussion, eye-to-eye contact.
>
> If you went through this building you'd see a print-rich envi-ronment. You would see kids' work up, you would see challenging problems displayed, you would see a lot of chart paper recording students' input. By publishing that input, you're giving a strength to it. By having it just continuing to be verbal and oral, you lose power. . . .
>
> You'll also see overhead used a lot in this building, . . . along with overhead instructional pieces. Teachers have overhead pattern blocks, overhead geo-boards, overhead calculators. There's an impression when you're using an overhead that this is a sharing experience.

> And . . . you hear a lot of questioning. A lot of discussion. A lot of side discussion with kids. A lot of open-ended questions. Very quickly I tune my ear to that.

Further, in his view it was when the teacher took a back seat and allowed students to share ideas that children could construct their own understanding and learning could occur:

> I'm convinced that children develop their own learning when they have the opportunity to share their thought process, when the teacher keeps his or her mouth shut for a while, and allows and promotes kids to talk to each other.

Mr. Bouvier also believed that children needed to "manipulate their own mathematical ideas, develop their own thinking" if they were to develop conceptual understanding. He valued classrooms in which the teacher did not tell students what to think; rather the teacher supplied some information and allowed students to do their own thinking and come to their own conclusions. He described for us a second-grade lesson on estimation that he taught. Using an overhead projector, he projected a handful of beans onto the screen and gave students 5 seconds to estimate how many there were. Initially, their responses were way off and covered a wide range. He then showed them what a group of 10 beans would look like on the overhead and gave them another chance to estimate how many beans there were in the whole group. This time their responses fell into a smaller range. In summing up the incident, he said,

> That to me [was] an example of kids developing their own thinking. . . . When the teacher structures information and [the students] take the information and they start to apply it to what's being requested of them to consider. . . . It was the kids that said, "Now that I've looked at a group of 10, I can see that gee, it's more in this range." "So this bit of information helped you with that?" "Yes." So children creating their own thinking or their own understanding requires time and opportunity and application. . . . I think all lessons should do that.

Episodes from Administrator Learning

Prior to joining our study, Mr. Bouvier had become quite interested in one aspect of mathematics learning, namely, the idea that children can know a procedure for solving a mathematics problem but not have an accurate conceptual understanding of the underlying mathematics. He had encountered this idea in the *Lenses on Learning* course that he took, where he viewed videotapes of mathematics educators conducting clinical interviews with children in which the interviewer asked the child to explain what she was thinking as she worked on a mathematics problem in an effort to understand the child's mathematical thinking. Mr. Bouvier described one such experience in the course and his subsequent experiment in his own school as follows:

> [The interviewer on the videotape] was asking the child different questions that queried the level of understanding the child had about mathematics. And after the first one or two [questions], [when the interviewer was] getting beyond arithmetic [procedures] to . . . look at the understanding, the child had no base or foundation at all. That was an emotionally charged discovery for me. So what I did very quickly is go into a third-grade math class and mimic the same kind of questioning strategies. Low and behold, I found a lot of our students in that class had not established a basis of understanding, but had established a series of rules. "Why do you do this?" "Because that's what I was told." "Why is the one there?" "Because that's what you do to solve the problem."

Now, children who have not had experience in explaining their mathematical thinking may not answer such questions very well the first time they are asked, and the children Mr. Bouvier interviewed might have understood more than they were able to say. Nonetheless, Mr. Bouvier had made the distinction, for himself, between procedural knowledge and conceptual understanding in mathematics, and he was coming to value both. He was dismayed to find so little evidence of conceptual understanding on the part of the third graders he talked to.

Not only did Mr. Bouvier's belief that children should develop a conceptual understanding of mathematics as well as a procedural one affect his ideas about what children should have the opportunity to do in class, it also began to influence Mr. Bouvier's thinking about what teachers can assume their students understand by looking at the mathematical procedures they use in their written work. For example, at a faculty meeting at which members of the math curriculum committee were discussing guidelines for administering the end-of-the-year math tests, the topic of what kinds of math information it would be helpful to provide about a student from year to year was raised. Several committee members voiced the opinion that, in mathematics, the only information of real value to them was how a student did in the overall assessment; this would give teachers a good enough sense of where students were mathematically.

In an interview following this meeting, Mr. Bouvier disagreed with this view, explaining that he did not think it was possible to quickly ascertain what a student does and does not understand mathematically. He had a different understanding of this issue:

> I think that, to somehow think that the assessment of a child's true understanding of mathematics can be done in this quick and dirty way, smacked of, "[If you] do these 15 problems and you get a 100, I will assume you know [the mathematical ideas covered by those problems]." And I know through my experiences through the [*Lenses on Learning*] course, [where we viewed] Marilyn Burns video tapes, that when you start asking the first and second layers of questions of what the child really understands about it, that the understanding falls apart like a . . . house of cards. So I disagree. My vision is that math portfolios should be very similar to language arts portfolios. I think it's very important to show the learning process of mathematics and we can do it with particular benchmarks. I think that looking at a child's math progress from September to June [on a written test] tells only a fraction of a story. For example, when a fourth-grade teacher looks back at how a child's thinking has developed over the course of the year, there's a lot of valuable diagnostic information. And I don't think it's more work. I don't think—so I disagree violently with it.

Analysis

Like Ms. O'Brien, Rob Bouvier had taken the first steps toward coming to understand constructivist ideas about mathematics learning. He had developed an appreciation for the importance of children's having the opportunity to articulate their mathematical ideas and listen to each other's thinking. He took action to ensure that classrooms in his school were set up to encourage the sharing of ideas among students, both in terms of the physical layout of the room and in terms of the instructional materials that were available.

Also like Ms. O'Brien, Mr. Bouvier felt that teachers should not talk so much in class but leave room for students to talk with each other. As we noted earlier, providing the opportunity for students to talk about their ideas is an important aspect of instruction that is based on a constructivist view of learning. However, it is only part of what needs to happen. Students also need teachers who listen carefully to what they say, assess its validity, and then ask questions or design tasks intended to help students address things they might not yet understand. With their interest in having students have the opportunity to articulate their thinking, Ms. O'Brien and Mr. Bouvier had taken the first steps toward developing an image of what classrooms based on a constructivist view of learning might look like. And their interest in students' thinking may later lead them to think about what teachers should be attending to when they listen to students' mathematical thinking and what kind of interventions they should make.

In the episodes from his work that we examined here we could see that Mr. Bouvier was struck by the disconnect between the ability of a student on a videotape to use the appropriate procedures to solve a math problem and that student's lack of conceptual understanding of the same problem. He moved quickly to see whether that was happening in his school as well and, in paying close attention to the content of what the students he interviewed said, was dismayed to find evidence of students who did not have conceptual understanding of problems they could solve procedurally. Later he drew the corollary that in assessing students' mathematics knowledge at the end of the year, it would be important to assess conceptual understanding through "math portfolios" as well as assessing their problem-solving ability on paper-and-pencil tests.

Mr. Bouvier said that discovering that procedural knowledge of mathematics does not necessarily entail conceptual knowledge was "an emotionally charged discovery for me." While he did not elaborate on the nature of this emotional charge, other administrators also have made this comment to us. For principals who have assumed that procedural competence is what it means to understand mathematics and who have believed that if students could do the problems they understood the mathematics, it is often quite a shock to see how fragile the conceptual understanding is of some students who are competent procedurally. These principals often say that such students would have been considered quite good mathematics students in their schools, but now they see that they might not do very well on high-stakes tests that focus on mathematical understanding. This realization often comes as quite a jolt, and the emotional charge is not only the discovery that mathematical understanding is more complex than the administrator had thought it to be, but also the challenge of now figuring out how to change mathematics instruction so that it provides both procedural and conceptual understanding.

Mr. Bouvier had discovered for himself some central tenets of the cognitive view of mathematics learning. He recognized how mathematical ideas at all levels are complex and that students' mathematical understanding develops slowly, over many years. He was beginning to see how, at any given point, students' understanding of a particular mathematical idea might be partially correct and partially incorrect. And he observed firsthand that students who have memorized rules for problem solving can produce written work that masks the true nature of their understanding. Such insights positioned Mr. Bouvier well to begin to attend more carefully to students' mathematical thinking and consider what teachers in his school would need to know, and know how to do, if they were to provide instruction that focused on students' conceptual understanding in mathematics.

CONCLUSION

In this chapter we explored the importance of principals' beliefs about the nature of mathematics learning when they observe mathematics classrooms, think about student assessment, and exercise practical judgment in assessing instruction and working with teachers. These principals' beliefs about mathematics learning illustrated several different orientations toward learning as behaviorist, constructivist, or some combination of the two.

Sheila Diggins said she was firmly constructivist in orientation and thought that mathematics learning was essentially a process of sense making. When she did the classroom observation we described, she focused in great detail on the mathematical thinking that specific children were doing, observing that the girl and the boy counted numbers differently, and believed this was based on differences in their understanding of how numbers could be combined. Libby O'Brien also had a constructivist orientation toward mathematics learning, believing that mathematics was about ideas, that children think about them in different ways, and that mathematics classrooms should give children the opportunity to articulate those ideas. However, she did not yet understand that, in the constructivist view, children need opportunities to articulate their mathematical ideas so that the teacher (and perhaps other students) will know how they are thinking and be able to help them think through aspects of new ideas that may still be confusing. While Rob Bouvier initially thought of mathematics instruction as entailing students manipulating their own mathematical ideas and sharing their ideas with each other, he came also to believe that it was important to distinguish procedural from conceptual knowledge and that one did not necessarily entail the other.

What these principals thought about mathematics instruction also varied in relation to their ideas about the nature of learning. Ms. Diggins believed that teachers should understand quite precisely how each child understood mathematical ideas and processes, like number and counting, and should be able to ask the next question or pose the next problem—one just a little bit out of reach—so that the child's understanding would be stretched and challenged. Ms. O'Brien believed that teachers should talk less and listen more, so that students would have the opportunity to articulate their problem-solving strategies. However, she didn't yet understand what the teacher should be listening for, nor the kinds of mathematical questions that would help students continue to build their mathematical understanding well. Mr. Bouvier believed that teachers should physically structure their classrooms to make it easy for students to share ideas with each other, should have instructional supplies (like chart paper and overhead projectors) that support the public display of student ideas, and should provide information or ask questions that allow students to work with, or "manipulate," their own ideas. His insight that students might not have a conceptual understanding of mathematical ideas was leading him to believe that classrooms and assessments also should provide more opportunity to gather information about students' conceptual understanding.

The major difference between these three principals' views of the nature of mathematics learning is the degree to which they saw it as a matter of students making sense of mathematical ideas and teachers attending to their students' mathematical thinking and asking questions that would prompt students to stretch their thinking. The focus on students' mathematical thinking rather than on teacher and student behavior is an essential shift implied by a constructivist view of learning. Principals whose beliefs about mathematics learning include constructivist as well as behaviorist elements are likely to see and appreciate more of what is happening in mathematics classrooms than principals who hold a behaviorist view of mathematics learning alone.

This shift in principals' beliefs about the nature of mathematics learning and the affect of their beliefs about learning on what they attend to and value when doing classroom observations is significant to those concerned about accountability issues in instructional leadership, especially as these are heightened by the No Child Left Behind legislation. Through the process of classroom observation and teacher supervision, elementary principals serve as the arbiters of instructional quality in their schools. In visiting classrooms and talking with teachers, principals come into direct contact with instruction, judge its adequacy, and decide what help a teacher may need. If schools are to consistently provide high-quality mathematics instruction, what principals recognize and value as excellent instruction is central.

Principals' Use of Knowledge
in Their Work

I N THE PREVIOUS two chapters we focused on the differing kinds of ideas
that elementary principals might have about the nature of mathematics
and the way it is learned and best taught. In order to explore the effects of
these ideas on administrative practice, we showed several principals in action: doing classroom observation and teacher supervision, and designing and
running faculty meetings. In the second part of this book we continue our
examination of elementary principals' administrative practice.

In examining administrators' work, we have found it useful to consider
the concept of practical judgment, which is concerned with the reasoning
and judgment involved in taking practical actions. As we noted in the introduction to this book, there are competing views of practical judgment and
how it is, or ought to be, exercised. We draw primarily from the view articu-
lated by Nussbaum (1990) and Wiggins (1978) and specified for the context
of teaching by Pendlebury (1990, 1995). In this work, which is based on
Aristotle's writing on practical judgment, the changeability, indeterminacy,
and particularity of the practical world come to the fore; how one chooses
to act may rest as much on an interpretation of the particulars of the situation as on general rules of action. In this view, *how* one pays attention in
practical situations, and *to what* one pays attention, are critical in the exercise of practical judgment. Wiggins explains it this way:

> A man usually asks himself "What shall I do?" . . . only in response to a par-
> ticular context. This will make particular and contingent demands on his moral
> or practical perception, but the relevant features of the situation may not all
> jump to the eye. To see what they are . . . may require a high order of situ-
> ational appreciation, or, as Aristotle would say, perception. (p. 144)

The construct of practical judgment calls our attention not only to the
choices and decisions that administrators make but even more fundamentally

to the critical features or facts of a situation to which they are paying attention. What do they value as the facts of the situation that matter? What do
they seem to not notice or at least not value or appreciate?

The construct of practical judgment also invites us to ask what is influencing administrators' sense of the facts that matter? In our work with administrators in the area of mathematics education we have found that they
come to their work with ideas about the nature of mathematics, learning,
and teaching that affect the practical judgment that they exercise—that shape
their sense of the facts that matter. Some of these ideas are based on a transmission view of learning and teaching, others on a constructivist view; many
are an amalgam of both orientations. These views influence administrators'
orientations toward such practical tasks as doing teacher supervision, providing professional development for teachers, assessing students' and teachers' achievements, and interpreting and responding to parents' concerns about
mathematics instruction. They also influence the kinds of actions it seems to
them reasonable to take (Nelson, 1998, 1999; Nelson & Sassi, 2000).

In Chapter 3 we examine the work of three principals as they attempt
to help teachers improve their instructional practice. We show that it is a
principal's ability to connect to the particulars of practice, which in turn
requires specific knowledge of the subject of instruction and how students
in a classroom are thinking about it, that makes them truly effective at
mentoring teachers. In Chapter 4 we consider several assessment processes
that come under the purview of elementary principals—issuing report cards,
assessing instruction, and evaluating teachers—and discuss how principals'
ideas about mathematics, learning, and teaching affect how they use the forms
and records designed for these formal accountability processes. In Chapter 5 we examine the process of communicating with outside stakeholders—
parents, central office staff, and school committees. In these activities educational values intersect with political considerations, and we show how
several principals resolved this tension and consider the effectiveness of those
resolutions.

WORKING WITH TEACHERS:
SITUATING IDEAS IN PRACTICE

T EACHING ELEMENTARY SCHOOL mathematics well requires that
teachers know the mathematics they are teaching in a conceptual and
flexible way so that they can hear the mathematical ideas in their students'
discourse and judge their validity. They also need to know how to structure
mathematical tasks and ask mathematical questions that provide their students with the opportunity to stretch and strengthen their thinking. Further,
they have to be able to recognize the difficulties that many students have with
particular mathematical ideas and the variety of ways that these difficulties
can be overcome. Shulman (1986) has called this body of practical knowledge, "pedagogical content knowledge"—knowledge of mathematics adapted
specifically for teaching.

While teachers profit greatly from preservice education and professional
development courses and programs that focus on these aspects of mathematics
instruction, inevitably much of this learning must occur in the classroom itself, in listening to what children say and watching what they do. Consequently, this learning is never finished. That is, continuing to improve their
understanding of mathematics, and learning about the ways in which students think about mathematics, are intrinsic to the work of teaching, not just
a prerequisite that can be achieved and then set aside. No matter how familiar
teachers are with the ways that students typically think about mathematical
ideas, there is likely always to be a student who has a new "take" on an idea
or a way of expressing his thinking that is challenging to understand. Further,
the mix of students in any particular class will be unique, making the mix of
mathematical ideas to be dealt with, and the intellectual resources available
(including the students' own ideas), highly variable from class to class. Finally,
as teachers' knowledge becomes more developed they are likely to appreciate
subtleties in student thinking that had escaped them earlier. Thus their learning must be continuous and generative (i.e., self-propelling). If teachers are to
genuinely engage with the mathematical ideas their students are exploring,

and develop a community of mathematical exploration in the classroom, a stance of inquiry about student thinking and instruction is central to their work (Ball & Cohen, 1999; Franke, Carpenter, Fennema, Ansell, & Behrend, 1998; Russell et al., 1995).

Principals are uniquely situated to help teachers engage in learning in and from their practice. Elementary principals have two roles with respect to teachers, roles that are often in conflict. One of these is their responsibility to evaluate teachers' performance. Very often the frequency and form of such evaluations are stipulated by union contracts. The other role, on which we focus here, is their function as mentors—supportive colleagues who can help teachers continue to learn in the context of their practice. For many principals, however, their formal role as teachers' evaluators is always in the background and dramatically colors their capacity to mentor. The evaluative nature of the relationship often makes it difficult for teachers to see principals as potentially helpful, to acknowledge that they still need to learn, and to name particular areas of their practice in which they would like help. The elementary principals with whom we have worked find this a frustrating state of affairs. Many enjoy their mentoring opportunities—they are among the few occasions when principals can still teach.

In this chapter, we consider how principals might create opportunities for mentoring, despite their responsibility to evaluate teachers. In observing classrooms and talking with teachers about their instruction, principals are in a position to call teachers' attention to salient features of children's mathematical thinking and their own instructional practice in ways that can open those practices to reflective inspection. In our experience, if principals are to work with their teachers' instructional practice in ways that make examination of that practice educative for teachers, principals not only need sufficient subject matter knowledge, and knowledge of how it is learned and taught (Stein & Nelson, 2003), but they also need to be able to attend to the particulars of teachers' practice and help teachers cultivate a certain kind of attention to their students' thinking (Sassi, 2002). That is, principals must be able to connect ideas about learning, teaching, and subject matter to particular events in teachers' instructional practice. If principals are going to help teachers develop their mathematics teaching, they need to focus in considerable detail on what teachers and students say, what they do, and what the mathematical and pedagogical significance of these actions is. How principals navigate this terrain can affect the ways in which they can help teachers continue learning in the context of their instructional practice.

In this chapter we examine the work of three principals whom we have discussed earlier: Peter Nash, Sheila Diggins, and Libby O'Brien. This time we will look at their work from the perspective of how they are able to help their teachers continue to learn in the context of their mathematics teaching practice. Through these examples we explore what principals need to know in order to connect their ideas about mathematics, learning, and teaching to teaching practice, how fine-grained that knowledge needs to be, and what the connection is between helping teachers change their instruction and helping them learn from their practice.

USING AN EXAMPLE OF PRACTICE IN ORDER TO REFLECT: PETER NASH

In Chapter 1 we described how Peter Nash developed a mathematics exercise through which he expected the teachers in a faculty meeting to explore the possible advantages of heterogeneous grouping in math classes. In a prior faculty meeting Mr. Nash had opened the consideration of heterogeneity in math class by asking his faculty to read a paper by Margaret Riddle, "Beyond Stardom: Challenging Competent Math Students in a Mixed-Ability Classroom" (1996). Riddle, a fifth-grade teacher at the time that she wrote the paper, describes her rationales for supporting mixed-ability classrooms and provides several vignettes that illustrate how more able learners can do well in them. In this chapter we examine how Mr. Nash used Riddle's article to ground his faculty's discussion of heterogeneous, or mixed-ability, grouping in concrete images and stories from instructional practice, thereby framing the ideas that he wanted teachers to consider in a way that made them accessible, real, and connectable to the teachers' own instructional practice.

Mr. Nash believed that instruction is imbued with, and informed by, teachers' ideas about mathematics, teaching, and learning. He told us that by structuring a discussion based on an article in which one teacher described the ideas that lay behind some of her instructional practices, he intended to make those ideas accessible to his teachers and open for discussion. He explained his intentions to the faculty:

> [T]his is a report from a colleague about what made sense to her. And we're using that . . . as a way to shape our own thinking and to discover some of our own beliefs . . . about how to . . . answer the questions that are the premise of her article.

In reading and discussing Riddle's paper, which contained extended examples of students' mathematical thinking, the teachers also were learning to attend carefully to the details of student thinking in classrooms and ground their pedagogical choices in that thinking.

While he did not want his teachers to know the details of his own thinking about heterogeneous grouping in mathematics classes because he wanted them to think the issues through for themselves, Mr. Nash had very clear ideas and deeply felt commitments about the issue. Although he worked in a small affluent community, his concern for equity had its roots in his own socioeconomic background. He came from a working-class family and hadn't had the opportunities that his students had. In our first interview with him, he explained how his background affected his viewpoint:

> I always think of myself . . . even as a child, as being kind of disad-
> vantaged culturally, socially, economically, and so I was always
> mindful about which doors were open to me or not open to me. . . . I
> think it was always there in my teaching experience as far as wanting
> to teach in places where we weren't ranking kids and we weren't
> sorting them that way, [and we were] giving all kids opportunities.
> That's always been my own personal ethic.

Mr. Nash went on to describe a poignant experience early in his teaching career that exemplified the cultural mismatch he felt between his own child-hood experiences and those of the students in his classes:

> I didn't have books when I was a kid, and I was discovering children's
> literature for the first time [when I was teaching]. So I would say to the
> kids, here are the books we're going to read next week, and I was
> astonished to learn not only that they had already read them but that
> . . . they *owned* those books. They would tell me, "I have a copy of
> that." And that knocked me away. I was never given books as a
> kid. . . . And so that . . . helped me get these antennae about kids who
> don't have those advantages.

From his personal and professional experience, Mr. Nash had developed a well-articulated view of equity in education in general and the advantages and disadvantages of homogeneous, or similar-ability, grouping in mathematics classes in particular. The advantages of homogeneous groups that he saw accrued largely to the school or district: All children could be kept engaged; all groups could be doing the same content, with the lower groups spending more time on particular issues while the upper levels did more extensions; and the district would not need to develop a more structured gifted and tal-ented program. The disadvantages that he noted accrued largely to the stu-dents themselves and rested on his view of what it meant to understand and learn mathematics. He believed that grouping is typically based on a limited conception of mathematical ability and of what mathematical prob-lem solving is, and reinforces that view of mathematics. In his view, the determination of homogeneous groups for mathematics was based largely on evaluations of students' speed of computation, but since this is only one dimension of mathematics, such grouping does not allow some students' strengths—for example, the ability to use visual representations of mathematics problems to explore their structure—to be identified or developed. Mr. Nash was also concerned that such homogeneous grouping contributed to what he called the "de-skilling" of teachers, who, in his view, needed to be able to teach a wide range of children.

These ideas were what he wanted the teachers in his school to consider as they thought through the issue of homogeneous grouping in mathematics classes. His challenge was to find a way for the teachers to encounter concrete images of what instruction that brought out a variety of students' talents and strengths might look like and to be able to consider what skills teachers would need in order to teach in such heterogeneous contexts. He found that Riddle's article presented just these images.

An Episode from Administrative Practice

Margaret Riddle wrote from the perspective of a fifth-grade teacher who worried every year about the most competent students in her class. She worried that if they were bored in math class, or found it "too easy," they were missing some of the intellectual richness that mathematics had to offer. She worried about how to provide them with this.

Riddle's paper presents her dilemma through the description and analysis of two instructional episodes in her classroom. In the faculty meeting, Mr. Nash chose to focus on the episode that chronicles Nate, whom Riddle describes as the "math star":

> A quiet, responsible boy with a quick, straightforward mind, Nate entered class in September in active pursuit of right answers. He was competent at problem solving and accurate in computation. Nate was almost never stumped in math and seemed to have unending self-confidence. He had a wonderful way of setting his own agenda in activities—working as hard and completing things as well as he wanted to for himself. . . . He was also generally kind and respectful of his classmates. [But] Nate was completely uninterested in working with classmates to solve math problems. When he was assigned to work with a fellow student, Nate typically would choose to go ahead on his own, checking neither his thinking nor his answers with his partner. He often finished his work early, and the look on his face was one of resigned boredom. (p. 138)

Riddle decided to pair Nate with a student who was neither quick at figures, good with facts, nor capable at computation, but who had some skills Nate lacked:

Like Nate, Brian was kind, respectful, and extremely well liked by his class-mates; but, unlike Nate, he felt he was a poor math student who usually didn't understand much. He was a strongly visual learner who was also artistic, ath-letic, and extremely persistent. Brian's strength was in being able to visualize a problem and to use pictures and manipulatives to work his way through it. He would solve problems by making the math fit his pictures and his common sense understanding. . . . Brian had some real strengths, and they were different from Nate's. (pp. 138–139)

Riddle tells the story of the developing partnership between Nate and Brian in some detail. She describes how they worked together on a complex multiplication problem, which involved figuring out the amount of different kinds of fruit that would be needed to make 14 fruit baskets, given the amount of each fruit that would be in a basket (2 bananas, 3 apples, 4 oranges, 8 dates, and 6 figs, plus 25 nuts and 10 peppermint candies). "This problem is a wonderful opportunity to investigate the concept of multiplication," Riddle says. "When manipulatives are used to approach it, patterns, combi-nations, and relationships emerge visually to make it quite fascinating. Sim-ply computing the answers does not reveal the mathematical structures in the same way" (p. 141). Both Nate and Brian contributed to their eventual understanding of this problem. She describes their individual approaches:

Brian was . . . trying to make sense of the problem using . . . 14 scraps of paper to represent the 14 baskets. He had started by placing 2 buttons on each scrap to represent the bananas, then added a third button for the apples. Nate, mean-while, was sailing ahead, relying strictly on his computational skills . . . and unaware of Brian's alternative methods. (p. 139)

As they began to work together, Nate was able to see Brian's ideas in a way he found exciting. Working together, they were able to combine Nate's flexible sense of how to work with numbers with Brian's concrete and visual sense of what the problem actually meant. For example, they agreed that, in figuring out how many dates there would be, they could "'just double the answer we got for oranges . . . because 8 is the double of 4.' . . . Later they explained to the class that they had simplified the process [of finding the num-ber of nuts] to make one button stand for 25 nuts. They had then grouped their baskets into 4's and counted by 100's to find the number of nuts that were needed" (p. 141). Both of these strategies (doubling the number of or-anges to get the number of dates, and using the fact that $25 \times 4 = 100$ to easily calculate the number of nuts) made use of the structure of the number system and the nature of multiplication.

Riddle found evidence for her contention that heterogeneous classes are good for gifted math students in Nate's experience:

Gradually, Nate became more and more open to working with other students, and he also maintained his interest in finding alternative ways to do problems. Sometimes he would even work on problems long after the class had moved on, looking for different solutions and patterns. He stopped being "finished" when he got an answer. . . . The bright look on his face and his intense concentration led me to believe that his mind was always working and that the natural curiosity he had about mathematics was becoming fully engaged at school during math class. . . . I suspect that if Nate had simply been advanced in math or had participated in a pull-out enrichment program, he might not have learned to use his mind as flexibly as he did when he struggled to understand what Brian was thinking with his manipulatives. The richness of mathematics might have remained buried treasure as far as he was concerned. (pp. 141–142)

Riddle's paper was full of all the ideas that Mr. Nash wanted to make available to his teachers for their consideration. It provided them with vivid and detailed images, grounded in classroom life, of what students with different mathematical strengths can see in a mathematics problem. It pointed out the limitations of one-dimensional grouping practices based on computational speed alone, and illustrated how students with computational and visual strengths might learn from each other. Finally, it provided an image of the kind of teacher orientation toward mathematics, attention to students' mathematical thinking, and creative pedagogy that would work well for students who, like Nate and Brian, are in different places. A rich meaning of heterogeneity in a math class emerged from examining the particulars of Nate and Brian and their work together.

Analysis

When Peter Nash used this paper with his faculty, it functioned, pedagogically, like a case. Images of the possible were presented, events were situated in real classrooms that teachers would find credible, and the motives and dilemmas of the main actors were made accessible (Shulman, 1992). Mr. Nash knew enough about what mathematical problem solving could be, and how it drew on a number of different cognitive strengths, to see that ideas he cared about were embedded in this story of practice. We surmise that he recognized that the reader actually has to engage with the specifics of Nate's and Brian's thinking about the mathematics of the fruit basket problem—attending to what they said and what they did, as the case provided the opportunity to do—in order to understand what students with different kinds of mathematical skills can learn from each other. In providing this case for discussion, Mr. Nash gave his teachers the opportunity to practice attending to student thinking in this way. For example, one of the questions he asked his teachers was, "How would Riddle explain why Nate was not bored?"

Further, he evidently realized that this article could provide a valuable example of how mathematics instruction that doesn't support such diversity in approach is *mathematically* limited. That is, it was in attending to the particulars of practice—the way Nate and Brian worked on the mathematics and talked about it—that it was possible to see how different ideas about what it means to do mathematics are situated in relation to each other.

Mr. Nash was able to use a story that was grounded in practice to free up ideas, and questions, about heterogeneity in mathematics classes, which his teachers could think about and connect to their own practice. He did this by providing a set of questions, which he gave out with the article prior to the meeting, that asked teachers to think about Riddle's underlying assumptions about why "stars" and "less able" students are best served by working together; what she thought were the mathematical strengths not often evident in math "stars"; what competencies she seemed most interested in developing in her students; and what characteristics of her teaching promoted learning in this heterogeneous math class.

In Chapter 6 we will see that Riddle's paper did, indeed, provide Mr. Nash's faculty with a productive opportunity to identify and discuss important ideas about heterogeneous grouping in mathematics classes. Among the things they commented on were characteristics of Riddle as a teacher, noting that she knew her students' abilities, validated their different strengths, and was highly thoughtful and reflective about the individual growth of each student and her ability to deepen their conceptual understanding. The teachers were interested in how Nate became stimulated by Brian's thinking, and wanted to know more about how that worked. They also wondered what Riddle's goals for her class were—"to bring kids to higher levels of math" or "to help them to [be] rounded math people?"

Mr. Nash's use of Riddle's paper illustrates his appreciation that a detailed, contextual account of a teaching situation can help teachers cultivate the kind of perception they need in order to attend to student thinking in their own classrooms and ground their professional judgment in that thinking (Sassi, 2002).

Mr. Nash's view of mathematical problem solving as multidimensional, requiring several different kinds of cognitive skills, and his sense of what his teachers could learn from the story of Nate and Brian told through Riddle's eyes, illustrates a principal who sees the ideas about mathematics and mathematics teaching that are embedded in practice. Mr. Nash was able to both see the ideas that were embedded in Riddle's practice and use an examination of the details of that practice to make possible a discussion of those ideas. However, Mr. Nash's work does not show what is entailed for principals in using their knowledge of mathematics learning and teaching to help teachers learn in the context of their own classroom teaching practice.

HELPING A TEACHER HONE HER QUESTIONING SKILLS:
SHEILA DIGGINS

In order to explore the level of detail to which principals may need to attend in the mathematics classroom and the degree to which their ability to engage with mathematical discourse contributes to their ability to help teachers learn in their own classrooms, we consider again the work of Sheila Diggins, who expressed a well-developed sense of both how children develop as mathematical thinkers and how a teacher's questions can promote that development. In Chapter 2 we saw that Ms. Diggins, who was the principal of a primary school in a large northeastern city, could articulate a view of mathematics learning as a sense-making enterprise. She felt that teachers need to be able to listen to the mathematical meaning that children are making when they do their work, or analyze their thinking in order to design the next task or question that will be "just a little bit beyond" the students' current understanding.

We also saw that Ms. Diggins was able to describe in great detail the mathematical thinking of the students in the class she was observing. In the professional development program she attended she had begun to learn about the process by which children's mathematical understanding develops. And, in the episode we examined earlier, she noticed that a student who was not yet able to "count on" began to do so when working with a partner who did.

By her own admission, however, she was not very knowledgeable of, or comfortable with, mathematics. She had not liked mathematics as a student, though she had been able to memorize what she needed to know:

> It was like, okay, I can multiply, because I can memorize. But I cannot figure out what you're talking about when you want me to divide, using this little procedure that I don't even get. So the one thing that I learned very quickly was, if I do what the teachers say, then nobody is going to really give me any problem. I was the one in the back of the room that . . . could get their work done and then talk.

In a professional development program she was reintroduced to the ideas of the elementary mathematics curriculum from a conceptual point of view, and this time it was more palatable. When asked why, she explained,

> It's been established [in this program] that it's okay to make mistakes. It's been established that I don't know everything, and that I can learn from somebody else. But now I also have permission to take on a strategy and develop it myself and take the time to figure it out.

In the past you have to do *this* in fourth grade, and you have to do *that* in fifth grade, and whether you understand it or not, you need to be done by June. Now it's like if you don't get it done this year, we'll do work on it again next year. . . . And I like math this way.

Ms. Diggins's school uses the *Investigations in Number, Data, and Space* curriculum (Russell & Tierney, 1998), an activity-based curriculum that encourages students to develop their own mathematical thinking and problem-solving skills. When we observed her work, Ms. Diggins was conducting classroom observations and talking with the teachers afterwards about their teaching. In preparation for each observation, Ms. Diggins asked the teacher which *Investigations* lesson would be taught when she came in, and took the time to read that lesson and the unit of which it was a part before the observation. She explained that this helped her understand the intent of the lesson, what was happening as the lesson unfolded before her in the classroom, and whether or not the teacher had made any modifications in the lesson as written.

An Episode from Administrative Practice

One observation that Ms. Diggins conducted was of a very experienced teacher, Theresa Holloway, who also had participated for several years in the *Developing Mathematical Ideas* (DMI) professional development course (Schifter, Bastable, & Russell, 1999a, 1999b). Using episodes of classroom practice written by teachers, DMI focuses on the development of children's mathematical ideas as teachers see them. This program prepared Ms. Holloway well for the *Investigations* curriculum because it prepared her to attend to and understand the ideas that the children brought to each investigation:

> I have found that [students] have a bank of information that I didn't perceive that they had, prior to using *Investigations*. I thought maybe that they weren't old enough to understand a specific concept, [but I became] more open to asking questions around something that I think they might not know, . . . to see where they are.

Ms. Diggins's classroom observation procedure included a preobservation conference at which she asked a series of questions that focused on the teacher's understanding of the students' mathematical thinking:

1. At this point in the year, what progress have you seen? What are your concerns?

2. What is your long-term agenda for teaching and learning mathematics in your classroom?
3. What mathematical ideas are your students working on?
4. How does this relate to your long-term agenda? What makes this mathematics worthwhile?
5. What aspect of the lesson would you like feedback about?

Ms. Diggins told us she felt that the last question was the hardest because it required teachers to identify an area in which they thought they needed further work. Ms. Holloway gave this response to the last question:

> That is a hard question. But I guess, maybe, listening to how well I really listen to kids' ideas. When we have our sharing time; when I'm going from group to group; how meaningful or how thought-provoking are the questions that I'm asking these children based on what the discussion is, or what their question is to me?

Ms. Holloway's request is more complex than might first appear. When teachers begin to change their teaching to a form that involves listening to students' mathematical ideas and asking questions that can forward student thinking, many wonder how they should ask these questions. However, their concern is often quite general (Sassi, 2002). They may wonder how to ask a question that is not a leading one or does not give away the answer. Or they may experiment with such generic questions as: Can you say more about that? How did you solve that problem? or Does anyone else have a different strategy? Ms. Holloway, on the other hand, was asking for something subtly different. She was asking for feedback on how well she *listened* to the students' ideas and how effective her questions were "based on what the discussion is, or what their question is to me." This request suggests that she recognized that her questions needed to be framed in relation to how she heard a student's mathematical idea. They also needed to be "meaningful or thought-provoking." That is, they needed to be sufficiently specific that they connected to the mathematics that the student was working on. Such questions, we argue, need to go beyond the generic questions noted above in order to be real mathematical questions.

The first-grade class that Ms. Diggins observed was working on Investigation 4 in the *Building Number Sense* unit of the *Investigations* curriculum (Kliman & Russell, 1998). There were four work stations for the children: Five-in-a-Row; Solving Story Problems; Dot Addition; and Triple Compare. These stations gave students opportunities to explore addition and subtraction of small numbers by visualizing problem situations that involved combining and separating numbers, developing strategies for solving problems involving combining and separating, and recording their strategies using pictures, numbers, words, and equations. In her observation of Ms. Holloway's class, Ms. Diggins noted many features of her teaching that she later wrote up in a memo that she shared with Ms. Holloway. She wrote about Ms. Holloway's classroom management strategies and connected them to making a classroom based on the NCTM standards work well. She commented on the displays and tools available in the room, and the kind of homework system that Ms. Holloway had developed. She identified how Ms. Holloway facilitated a mathematical community that allowed everyone respect and communicated the belief that students' ideas were important. She wrote that Ms. Holloway seemed able to value confusion in the class as an opportunity for clarifying ideas and making sense of the work.

Ms. Diggins's notes also contained many examples of student and teacher talk. These notes indicate that Ms. Holloway's questions to the students were quite specific and mathematical: "Can you make it clearer by naming the numbers?" "What is it that you know about 5?" "Is there a different way to build 8?" "So you think 5 plus 4 equals 10? You need to prove or disprove that." Each of these questions or statements both probes a student's understanding and asks the student to extend that thinking. For example, the first suggests that naming the numbers would help in making the student's idea clearer, while challenging the student actually to name the numbers. "What is it that you know about 5?" encourages the child to examine her existing knowledge with the expectation that that knowledge will be helpful. "Is there a different way to build 8?" invites the child to try to solve the problem another way, suggesting that the number 8 can be composed of several different number combinations. "So you think 5 plus 4 equals 10? You need to prove or disprove that" accepts the student's idea as plausible, but then pushes the student to prove the contention, which will likely entail going back over the material and perhaps discovering there has been an error in thinking.

Ms. Diggins believed that simply sharing this list of questions Ms. Holloway had asked while teaching would confirm that she had asked meaningful and thought-provoking questions:

> Ms. Holloway specifically said that she wanted to see if her questions were really thought-provoking questions, and to see them on paper the way that I did it really cleared it up for her. Yeah, they are [thought-provoking].

However, from her comments we don't really get much insight into how Ms. Diggins conceptualized the idea of "thought-provoking." We might hypothesize that, because the questions were very much in line with the type both Ms. Diggins and Ms. Holloway would have encountered in the DMI course, Ms. Diggins interpreted them as "thought-provoking." Further, it is not clear that the list of questions in the memo helped Ms. Holloway in the way that Ms. Diggins believed it had. We can delve a little deeper into these two points.

When interviewed later about this classroom observation, Ms. Holloway did not mention the questions, but was impressed with the level of detail of Ms. Diggins's observations:

> [Ms. Diggins] wrote a very detailed statement, for the amount of time that she did the observation. I was really surprised that she could pick up that much. . . . She picked up a lot of . . . what the kids were saying, what was actually happening. . . . [Ms. Diggins's write-up] was really a good picture of what was happening. [So it was helpful.]

In the postobservation conference Ms. Diggins went further and explicitly referred to Ms. Holloway's request that she attend to how well her questions functioned:

> You had asked me to focus on your questions and what you were saying to children and what went on in the . . . large group, and I thought your questions clearly came from what the children were giving you, and that the continual question[ing] that you did made a difference for their understanding, and how they made the connections.

Ms. Diggins had offered to provide feedback to Ms. Holloway and these very general statements about Ms. Holloway's questioning did constitute feedback and perhaps were reassuring to Ms. Holloway. However, if Ms. Diggins wanted to help Ms. Holloway really explore what it means to ask "meaningful and thought-provoking questions" and whether or not her questions constitute such questions, the feedback she gave would likely have been too general.

In order to help Ms. Holloway improve her questioning skills, Ms. Diggins would have needed to ground her comments more specifically in the particulars of Ms. Holloway's practice and make use of the specific data about Ms. Holloway's questioning that she had gathered during the observation. In other words, she would have needed to explore why Ms. Holloway chose to ask certain questions and then explore how they functioned as "thought-provoking" questions. For example, Ms. Diggins might have asked, "When you asked Jamal whether there was a different way to build 8, I wondered what you had observed him doing in the game with the blocks that led you to suggest to him that there might be another way?" Her attention to the particulars of Ms. Holloway's practice then would have given Ms. Holloway a specific instance of her questioning to think about, and she could then reflect on whether or not her question was based on a substantial mathematical issue and how the question actually functioned in her teaching practice. Ms. Diggins's asking a question about what she noticed a student doing would have further supported Ms. Holloway's inclination to attend very carefully to her students' mathematical thinking and to build her questions on those observations. Had she pursued such a question, Ms. Diggins and Ms. Holloway might have had an extended discussion of what Jamal's block-building activity indicated that he understood and didn't understand about how numbers like 8 are composed.

Analysis

Sheila Diggins was well positioned to help Ms. Holloway improve her questioning skills and to support the learning about children's mathematics that she could do by continuing to attend carefully to her students' mathematical thinking. Ms. Diggins could talk about the importance of children's mathematical sense making, could attend to it when observing in classrooms, and understood in general the role of a teacher's questions in the development of children's mathematical understanding. She reviewed the curriculum before doing an observation to prepare for what she might notice and to make sense of what she observed, and conducted a preobservation conference in which she focused on how the teacher was attending to her students' mathematical thinking. Because she had come to believe that mathematics learning is a matter of sense making, Ms. Diggins believed that she must attend closely to both the children's mathematical thinking to see what sense they are making of the materials and to the teacher's work to see what sense she is making of the students' thinking. After she observed Ms. Holloway's class, Ms. Diggins described her intentions:

> I wanted to see what children's understanding was too, so there were two things that I paid attention to. How her children were working, as well as how she was working. The only way to do that was to get the information from both of them, both her and the kids that she was focusing on.

This was a different focus for classroom observation than she had had in earlier years, and she acknowledged that this was hard to learn to do:

I'm not at a place where I can [do this] expertly without questioning myself. So it's a work in progress all around and we all need to be kind to ourselves about that.

Ms. Diggins had come a long way in developing a supervisory practice that supported teachers who offer mathematics instruction based on a constructivist view of mathematics learning. However, in order to help Ms. Holloway investigate her ability to ask meaningful and thought-provoking questions tied to the mathematics at hand, Ms. Diggins would have had to listen to and analyze an entire interchange between teacher and student. This would have included what the student's conversation had been about, what Ms. Holloway's question was, and how the child responded. She would then have needed to discuss later with Ms. Holloway whether her question had been well-connected to the child's mathematical thinking and whether there was evidence that it had helped the student think further. While Ms. Diggins understood generally that she needed to attend to the interchanges between teacher and student, and was quite able to attend to and record both individual student comments and individual teacher comments, she actually did not capture student-teacher mathematical dialogue or analyze how the teacher's questions were "meaningful and thought-provoking" within the dialogue. By missing the dialogue and the mathematics that underlay it, Ms. Diggins missed a mentoring opportunity.

From examining Ms. Diggins' work we can get a sense of the level of detail at which principals would need to observe in classrooms if their observations were to provide teachers with help in their continual learning about mathematics, mathematics learning, and instruction. In order to do this, Ms. Diggins, or any other principal, would have to be able to explore with a teacher the function of a mathematical question like "Is there a different way to make 8?" She would need to be able to consider how such questions connect to the student's prior mathematical work and what such a question gives a student the opportunity to think about. She would then have to be willing to mentally enter the mathematical discourse between teacher and student and think through the mathematical ideas herself. Given Ms. Diggins's discomfort with mathematics and her relatively recent discovery that thinking mathematically can be interesting, we wonder if she was ready to do this.

Ms. Diggins believed that the refinement of teachers' instructional practice entailed developing their thinking about children's mathematical ideas—learning how those ideas develop and how children's mathematical thinking can be strengthened. This belief allowed her to focus on what we consider the central element of instruction, namely, how teachers listen to children's thinking and then pose questions. However, as this case illustrates, principals who have neither conceptual knowledge of nor comfort with mathematics may be limited in their ability to analyze classroom data and discourse.

THE LIMITS OF RULES FOR PRACTICE: LIBBY O'BRIEN

As our example of Mr. Nash earlier in the chapter suggests, working with particular instances in a teacher's practice is critical in helping teachers become generative learners. Exploring this idea further, we look once again at the work of Libby O'Brien, the principal of an elementary school in a midsized industrial city in the Northeast. She had not liked mathematics as a child, was not comfortable with it, and had a largely algorithmic understanding of mathematical procedures, meaning that she could do the procedures but did not always understand their mathematical logic. However, she was very eager to improve mathematics instruction in her school and had taken a mathematics education course where she saw that children had many ways of understanding mathematics problems, which led to many different strategies for solving them. As a result of these insights, she wanted the teachers in her school to "talk less and listen more," so that children in their mathematics classes would have the opportunity to express their mathematical ideas in their own ways.

An Episode from Administrative Practice Revisited

In Chapters 1 and 2, we saw Ms. O'Brien working with Jeremy Jones on two different mathematics lessons: one about repeating patterns on a table, the other about making a table to solve a problem on the time of sunrise. Both times, she had a conference with the teacher before and after the lesson. For the second lesson, Ms. O'Brien focused on Mr. Jones's questioning behavior, noting with approval that his questions were open-ended, allowed for a wide range of answers, and were not leading (i.e., did not "fish for the right answer"). She also was pleased that he accepted a wide variety of answers and "went from there"; that is, he wasn't hoping for one particular answer that he would then use as the basis for the next step in his lesson, but rather appeared ready to work with the answers that the students provided.

We do not know why Ms. O'Brien chose to focus on Mr. Jones's questioning though we surmise that, like "talking less and listening more," for Ms. O'Brien teachers' asking open-ended questions makes more space in the class for student thinking. Neither do we know why she chose to comment on these particular aspects of his questioning, but we can examine the consequences of doing so.

Ms. O'Brien's orientation toward Mr. Jones's questions appeared to be guided by an adherence to a particular general rule (Sassi, 2002); that is, she seemed to think that, as a general matter, if he talked less and listened more and if he asked open-ended questions, he would create more opportunities for students to express their thinking, would be able to assess what they knew and didn't know, and would become a better teacher. What we did not see in her interactions with him is evidence that she understood how this new norm would need to be exercised in practice. She did not articulate an understanding about how he might exercise judgment about when to ask questions, or that he should think carefully about what the questions should be about, given the content of what the students were exploring. Instead she simply stated the new norm:

> You have to restructure the way you teach so that kids are talking more and you're talking less. . . . you will find out much more what they learned. And if you can do that, you will be an excellent teacher.

Analysis

This rulelike orientation toward teaching is quite common among principals. As we noted in Chapter 2, principals who were trained in the 1970s and 1980s were likely to have been trained in methods of classroom observation derived from the process-product school of research on teaching (Brophy & Good, 1986). In this approach, teacher behaviors that were correlated with high student outcomes, as measured by standardized tests, were considered to be "good" teaching and were often transformed into checklists by the developers of instruments for use in the supervision of teachers (cf. Acheson & Gall, 1980; Hunter, 1984; Joyce & Showers, 1988). Items on these lists, such as the presence of wait time after questions are asked, the frequency of praise or criticism, and the use of lower or higher order questions, functioned like rules and were considered to be good when they occurred, regardless of the specifics of the teaching situation.

Libby O'Brien had received such training in classroom observation and was quite understandably oriented toward attending to teacher behaviors and viewing them from a process-product framework. When she encountered new ideas about instruction in the mathematics education course she took, it made sense to adapt her existing framework for observing classrooms. Now she was looking for less teacher talk, more teacher listening, and more open-ended questions.

In fact, these kinds of teacher behaviors are often surface features of classrooms that function according to constructivist principles of intellectual development. But the behaviors themselves are not the important aspect of those classes. When students' mathematical ideas are at the center of attention, as in classrooms that function according to standards-based principles, the teacher's pedagogical process—the process of helping students develop their subject-matter thinking—is inextricably interwoven with his or her assessment of the content of that thinking itself. In order to have collaboratively investigated with Mr. Jones what is going on in his classroom and make valid judgments about the quality of instruction, Libby O'Brien would have needed to attend to both the mathematical ideas in play and the teacher's behaviors. As we pointed out in Chapter 1, Ms. O'Brien was poised to take a next step—learning to pay attention to what students say—but she would need help learning to listen not just for particular *forms* of dialogue but to the *content* of that dialogue.

Becoming a generative learner requires that teachers (1) have richly structured knowledge, so that new knowledge can be related to, and incorporated into, existing networks of knowledge; (2) apply their knowledge to learn new topics; and (3) see their learning as driven by their own inquiry (Franke, Carpenter, Levi, & Fennema, 2001). That is, teachers' generative learning begins with their own knowledge—about mathematics and students' mathematical thinking—and uses the classroom as a context in which teachers can add to that knowledge through their attention to, and curiosity about, their students' mathematical thinking. Ms. O'Brien had not yet become concerned with how Mr. Jones understood his students' thinking, what dilemmas students' comments might have raised for him, or how he thought about his teaching decisions. Her rulelike precepts for teaching in fact limited her ability to help him learn to attend to the particulars of his students' thinking and think about how to listen and respond to them.

CONCLUSION

If principals are to work with their teachers' instructional practice in ways that make examination of that practice educative for teachers, principals not only need sufficient knowledge of the mathematics at issue, how it is learned, and how it is taught, they also need to be able to attend to the particulars of teachers' practice and help teachers cultivate a particular kind of attention to their students' mathematical thinking. That is, principals must be able to connect ideas about mathematics, learning, and teaching to particular events in teachers' instructional practice.

In this chapter we have examined the work of three principals who have varying degrees of skill at this. First, Peter Nash was able to follow the conceptual content of the mathematics of Riddle's elementary classroom and appreciate that attending to Nate and Brian's work on the fruit basket problem provided a window for thinking about what heterogeneity in a mathematics classroom might entail. He understood that Riddle's engagement with the boys' thinking was essential for the development of effective pedagogical moves. He was able to recognize how Riddle's paper would provide his teachers an opportunity to "listen" to the mathematical thinking of Nate and Brian in order to ground their consideration of heterogeneous grouping in mathematics classes. Next, Sheila Diggins was able to articulate a sophisticated view of the way children's mathematical thinking develops and viewed teacher learning as a matter of the development of ideas as well as the development of new behaviors. However, Ms. Diggins did not use the data she gathered to help Ms. Holloway assess whether her questions to students were truly "thought-provoking." We surmised that Ms. Diggins did not actually know how to delve into the mathematical content underlying the student-teacher exchanges she so thoughtfully recorded. Finally, Libby O'Brien focused on Mr. Jones's teaching behaviors in a procedural way and, in so doing, was not able to help him consider the adequacy of his own mathematical knowledge, his ability to understand the mathematical ideas in his students' talk, or the mathematical appropriateness of his teaching moves.

These stories from principals' work illuminate several general things that may be needed if principals are to help teachers continue to learn in the context of their practice: knowing the mathematics that is being taught in a conceptual and flexible way; being curious about the nature of children's mathematical thinking; being curious about teachers' mathematical knowledge and knowledge about how children learn mathematics; and being willing and able to analyze classroom dialogues in order to explore the mathematical ideas at play.

The evident importance of principals' knowledge of mathematics, how it is learned, and how it is taught, raises the question of how much principals need to know about all subjects of instruction, and whether the kind of mentoring that Mr. Nash and Ms. Diggins engaged in was not more appropriate for a math coach than a principal. This question is similar to questions asked about teachers' knowledge in the early 1990s when documents like the NCTM *Curriculum and Evaluation Standards* (1989) first provided images of mathematics instruction that assumed much more knowledge of mathematics than many teachers currently had. How much mathematics did such teachers need to know? Did they need comparable knowledge in all subjects of instruction? How would this be possible? As a field, we are still working to answer questions like these about teachers' knowledge, and there are beginning to be professional development programs for teachers that provide such knowledge and conceptualizations of teaching as an endeavor entailing continuous learning. Similar research needs to be done on the knowledge needed by elementary principals, and similar professional development programs and conceptualizations of administration as significantly entailing continuous learning need to be developed and explored (see Chapter 6).

There is another approach to this question. Administrators do not work alone, but rather work within complex networks of colleagues that form and re-form around specific tasks or issues. Leadership can be viewed as distributed, or "stretched over" the practice of multiple people: principals and teachers in a school; all of the principals in a district; teachers, principals, and district subject-matter coordinators; and principals and central administration (Spillane, Halverson, & Diamond, 2001). This distributed nature of leadership leads to another resolution of the dilemma about how much administrators need to know about every subject. Where individual administrators may not have the requisite knowledge for the task at hand they can count on the knowledge of others if they know how to recognize who has that knowledge and how they can access it.

ASSESSMENT: SITUATING IDEAS IN FORMAL ACCOUNTABILITY STRUCTURES

I N THE PREVIOUS chapter we looked at principals' work with teachers and considered how principals can help teachers continue to learn in the context of their mathematics teaching practice. Continuing to look at the work that principals do as part of their responsibility as instructional leaders, we now consider the assessments that principals make or oversee in the course of their work. These include assessments of student performance in the form of report cards, assessments of instruction in the course of doing classroom observation, and assessments of teachers in the form of annual performance reviews. These forms of assessment all produce written records, which are used to communicate with those being evaluated (students and their parents in one case, teachers in the others) and which become part of students' and teachers' permanent files. As such, written records formalize principals' assessments and make them part of the formal accountability structure of schools and districts. In this chapter we consider the intersection of principals' efforts to use assessment to foster generative growth on the part of students and teachers with the record-keeping practices that are required by these accountability structures, and examine the degree of fit between the content or substance of principals' assessments and the tools provided for doing them.

This chapter on assessment is being written in a context of heightened attention to using assessment instruments to hold teachers, principals, and schools accountable for student performance. In 2002 the federal legislation known as No Child Left Behind stipulated an array of accountability standards for American schools, including (1) annual standardized testing aligned with state content and performance standards in reading and mathematics for all students in Grades 3 through 8 and at least once in Grades 9 through 12; (2) corrective action for schools that do not meet "adequate yearly progress" targets for all students; and (3) provisions for students to transfer out of schools that have underperformed for 3 years.

Even before the passage of that legislation, many state-level policymakers and school districts were beginning to set standards for student performance, specifying standardized instruments for regularly measuring student performance, and instituting systems of rewards and incentives for teachers and schools to achieve stipulated goals. Such accountability systems relied on well-defined uniform standards and objective measures, such as test scores, rather than on human judgments of quality. They were intended to provide incentives sufficiently powerful to motivate teachers to improve classroom practice (Luhm, Foley, & Corcoran, 1998).

Abelmann and Elmore (1999) have argued, however, that while external accountability systems assume that all schools can be held to the same expectations for student performance, individual schools in fact have their own conceptions of accountability that affect the way they respond to external accountability systems. Their research suggests that schools vary considerably in the degree to which they hold internally coherent expectations for teachers and students, have well-developed internal accountability mechanisms, and consider the responsibility for student performance to be an individual or collective matter. "The world that school administrators and teachers see," they argue, "is bounded by their particular settings, by their own conceptions of who they are, who they serve, what they expect of students, and what they think of as good teaching and learning" (p. 1). School- and district-level assessments in use tend to grow out of and reflect these unique histories and situations and may or may not align well with externally imposed assessment systems. Further, administrators' and teachers' educational values and ideas about what counts as high-quality instruction can influence the degree to which they see external accountability systems as congenial and helpful or counterproductive to achieving their goals.

The research for this book was done before the No Child Left Behind Act of 2002 was passed and just as some state and local standardized accountability systems were beginning to be implemented. Such assessment systems had not fully reached the principals we studied. Their assessment work at the time focused primarily on aspects of classroom life that they needed to understand in order to use student report cards, classroom notes, and teacher evaluations both as learning opportunities for teachers and parents and as part of the school or district's accountability structure.

What is particularly noticeable about principals' work in these areas, especially in light of Abelmann and Elmore's research, is how their knowledge of mathematics and beliefs about how it is learned and taught affect the way they develop and use such records in the domain of mathematics instruction. The forms that districts provide for the assessment of students (report cards, for example) and teachers (teacher evaluation forms) indicate what the district believes it is important to know about student and teacher performance, and constitute tacit "theories of action" about what constitutes adequate learning on the part of students and adequate teaching performance on the part of teachers. Over the past decade we have noticed that principals who are developing their mathematics knowledge and becoming more knowledgeable about mathematics instruction based on constructivist views of learning often find that some of these forms, developed a number of years earlier, no longer reflect their instructional values. The knowledge that undergirds their practical judgment is changing, and they have to work to figure out how to represent what they are coming to see as high-quality (or inadequate) mathematics teaching and learning on forms that were designed to evaluate different aspects of teaching and learning.

In this chapter we examine the work of Sheila Diggins as she wrestled with the structure of report cards, Marianne Cowan as she "scripted" mathematics instruction in a class she observed, and Sheila Diggins again, as she worked to adapt the district's teacher evaluation form to record what she thought was important about a teacher's instructional practice. Both of these principals were working with the ideas about teaching and learning that they believed was central to understanding whether instruction is working well and if not, why not. Their efforts to make the given assessment forms work in the way intended provides a glimpse not only of their struggles with the forms but also of their continued learning about how to use the assessment process to help teachers grow.

MOVING BEYOND TRADITIONAL REPORT CARDS: SHEILA DIGGINS

We have examined the work of Sheila Diggins in Chapters 2 and 3, where we saw her to be a principal with a constructivist view of the nature of mathematics learning who attended carefully to student as well as teacher thinking when she observed mathematics classrooms. We now explore what happened when she discovered the inadequacies of her district's report cards for communicating to parents the subtleties of what their children were learning in math class and, indeed, what it might mean to learn mathematics. Along the way, she realized that her efforts to help teachers learn need not be restricted to classroom observations and postobservation conferences. She discovered that she could use a faculty meeting discussion about report cards to continue exploring with teachers what it means for children to build their own mathematics knowledge.

An Episode from Administrative Practice

Ms. Diggins explained to us that several years earlier, when her school was first established, the district administration did not have a good sense of the kind of developmentally oriented report card that would be appropriate for a school serving very young children—a report card that could communicate to parents the emergent nature of children's mathematical ideas and skills.

> [Up to about 5 or 6 years ago] we had report cards that looked just like the middle school report cards. . . . And principals [and teachers] pushed back and said, "This really isn't working. If we're talking about young children and getting them excited about learning and giving parents clear messages, we need to look at our report card . . . and make it match up with what we're thinking." So the report card was changed so that it was no longer an A, B, C, but so that we talk about emerging skills. . . . [Now we can say things like] "Generally they do something, sometimes [they do it], and not yet."

The new report card allowed teachers to represent children's mathematical knowledge and skills as part of a natural process of development. It allowed them to capture how students might partially understand an idea or execute a skill episodically at one point in time, and then gradually, through experience and increased understanding, hold it as a more solid and reliable aspect of their mathematical knowledge. This is quite a different representation of students' knowledge than that captured by a traditional report card that quantifies knowledge with letter or number grades. This approach to reporting students' progress aligns with that of some scholars who recommend that attention be given to the development of students' ideas over the period of their K–6 learning (Carpenter, Ansell, & Levi, 2001; Schifter et al., 1999a, 1999b).

It is likely that parents appreciated such a revised report card. A study done in the early 1990s, amid early debates about the relative effectiveness of performance assessments of students' knowledge and standardized test assessments, found that parents of third graders in a low- to middle-class district rated sources of information such as talking to the teacher and seeing graded samples of their child's work as more useful than standardized tests for learning about their child's progress in school and even for judging the quality of education provided at their child's school (Shepard & Bliem, 1995).

But once the new report card was in place, with categories that permitted the description of students' developmental progress, it remained for the teachers in Ms. Diggins's school to see what the categories meant and how children's understanding could be described. It was here that Ms. Diggins discovered a new venue for teacher learning. She described an episode in which she was going over the report cards a few days before they were to be mailed out. She discovered that the teachers were not seeing that the children came to their classes with emerging mathematical knowledge and continued to build that knowledge through the activities and discussions they experienced in mathematics lessons. The teachers tended to think of learning as something that happened only as the result of their own direct teaching.

> We've been talking about the report cards off and on all year, and they're going out on Friday. And so I was looking at them, and I saw that [teachers] were really most uncomfortable with the math marks. . . . [The teachers are] . . . marking them only on what they've taught and what they think [the students] know, not necessarily on what [the students] understand or . . . have an idea about. And then they were looking at some of the categories very narrowly, and I'll give you an example. One of the areas on the report card . . . asks about children's concept of time, and they were leaving it blank, and I asked why. I said, "You all teach time." And they said, "Well, we haven't done the clock. We don't do the clock work until the end of the year, until like April." And I said, "But what about the calendar work, and what about [the concepts of] yesterday, today, and tomorrow, and what about [the ideas of] this morning, and this afternoon, and what about the [daily] schedule?" And they were like, "Oh." So they're not looking at the report card around the big ideas [that students are developing]. They're looking at it around topics they teach.

Ms. Diggins was proposing a reconceptualization of what should be reported on the report card. In her view, if children are continually constructing knowledge from their engagement with ideas in a number of different situations, then the report card should indicate the robustness of that knowledge as a whole, not simply what students knew about the particular topics that the teacher had taught. In this example, Ms. Diggins interpreted the topic of time far more broadly than did the teachers, to also include work with the calendar, distinguishing between yesterday, today, and tomorrow, and understanding the day's schedule.

Ms. Diggins came to her realization that there was something puzzling about the report card because of her own curiousity and openness to learning. On encountering blank places on report cards that were about to be mailed out, she asked the teachers why those items were blank and discovered in their answers how differently she and they were thinking about the learning and teaching that was going on in their classrooms and what the report card could say about the development of children's mathematical thinking. She remembered how she came to discover this:

> It took me a little while to . . . sort through because I was looking at these blank spaces on the report card, and I knew that wasn't right. And I was trying to think, "Well, what's wrong with this?" as opposed to, "Fill this in." And [I was wondering] if you fill it in, what are you saying?

Once she understood that the report card presented an array of complex possibilities to consider about what children actually knew and how they knew it, Ms. Diggins realized that she could use the report card as a context for helping the teachers in her school further develop their own understanding about mathematics, mathematics learning, and mathematics teaching.

> When we sat and talked about the report cards, it was another way to think about the work and to maybe even change how you plan, change your agenda, change the way you approach a particular idea. . . . And that conversation happened at the grade-level meeting, and I didn't even have to be in the classroom to have that conversation. Just looking at the reporting to parents gave me an understanding about what they were thinking about.

She also began to realize that parents, too, might have to do some learning to understand the new report card. She remembered thinking about this:

> Maybe we need to have this conversation with the parents before we start marking [the report card] like this because they're not going to get it either. If we didn't get it, how are we going to depend on them to have gotten it too? So that's another piece that we're going to have to take some time working on.

Ms. Diggins's hunch about parents' needs is supported by the study of parents' preferences about assessment cited earlier. That study showed that parents' preferences for standardized tests or performance assessments in mathematics was affected by their beliefs about the nature of mathematics itself. A subgroup of the parents studied in fact preferred standardized tests for mathematics because they felt that "in math there is only one right answer" (Shepard & Bliem, 1995, p. 30). Such parents might need assistance in understanding a report card that was based on a constructivist view of the development of children's mathematical thinking.

Analysis

This episode shows how attuned to the subtleties of students' mathematical learning Sheila Diggins was and how her beliefs about how children learn mathematics affected her practical judgment and administrative action. Her beliefs about the nature of early learning led her in the first instance to push for a different kind of report card for her school, and her beliefs about mathematics learning in particular led her to investigate how teachers made sense of the categories on the report cards and what they needed to know to communicate with parents about what their children knew and were learning. Far from taking the report card as a given, she viewed it as an artifact that could be interpreted and used in different ways, depending on one's beliefs about mathematics learning and teaching. Her orientation toward the report card opened the door for seeing that the teachers had ideas about mathematics learning that were somewhat different from her own and so were using the report card differently than she would have. Therefore, a discussion of how to use the report card could become a new venue for teacher learning.

In effect, Ms. Diggins was treating the report card as part of a system of people, tasks, and artifacts with which she was working to craft the kind of mathematics education she thought important for her school to offer. We can look at this story of Ms. Diggins and her school's use of the report card as an example of distributed leadership (Spillane, Halverson, & Diamond, 2001). From this perspective, leadership is viewed not as the characteristic of a single individual or role but as a practice—a system of activities undertaken collectively, by multiple people, and involving the use of a variety of artifacts, namely, the designed programs, procedures, and policies intended to shape school practice (Halverson, 2003; Halverson & Zoltners, 2001).

In this instance Ms. Diggins and the teachers were sorting out together what it means at that school to say that a child is learning mathematics and then communicate this to parents. The teachers, Ms. Diggins, what happens in math class, the report card, and the parents constitute an "activity system." Ms. Diggins wrestled with how to make the activity system as a whole conform to her beliefs about what it means for the students in her school to learn mathematics.

SCRIPTING A LESSON: MARIANNE COWAN

Next we revisit Marianne Cowan and her observation of the equivalent fractions lesson that used fraction fringe manipulatives (see Chapter 7). We focus here on her method of note taking, known as *scripting*. When she scripted such lessons, she wrote detailed notes about what happened in the classroom and inserted in parentheses a purpose that the teacher's action seemed to accomplish. However, in this episode it was apparent that Mrs. Cowan's understanding of what is important in mathematics instruction had gone beyond the generic data collection instrument that she had been using for many years. Although her understanding of mathematics allowed her to follow students' mathematical thinking in the classroom and discuss their mathematical thinking afterwards with the teacher, the generic process of scripting lessons did not help her make subject-specific notes that could support the subject-specific conferences that she had with the teacher.

An Episode from Administrative Practice

When Mrs. Cowan did classroom observations she brought her laptop computer and sat at the side of the classroom making detailed notes about what was going on. She would give these notes to the teacher after the class, as a stimulus for the postobservation discussion that they would have a few days later. The scripts focused on what the teacher did and said, and imputed a purpose to the teacher's actions. The full script for the lesson we consider here was two single-spaced pages in length and covered the entire hour. Below are the notes for a 12-minute segment of it.

> T: Angie said that ⅖ is equivalent to ⁴⁄₁₆ . . . pull it forward, Joe. (Coaching the use of the fraction fringe) Pull . . . ¼ is equivalent to ⅜ . . . Susan has pulled ahead ⅛, ²⁄₁₆. Is there anything else? (Keeps students open and thinking) . . . *9:12 AM*. This should not be that difficult for you . . . write it down instead of telling me. . . . Take one and pass it around . . . (Provisioning). I'm just going to get the overhead set up while you are doing that . . . (Working). . . . You are getting this more than you think you are. You are not giving yourself enough credit. (Encourages—feedback not specific). *9:22 AM.* I am curious to see the combinations you put on the back of the paper . . . the combinations that you find . . . (Helps David use the fraction fringe with the pencil).

Scripting is something many administrators have been taught to do to provide objective data that can ground subsequent conversations with the teacher about the lesson. Some scripts simply record as much of what was said as the administrator can catch. In this case, Mrs. Cowan also imputed purpose, which she put in parentheses, to the teacher's statements and actions: coaching, keeping students open and thinking, provisioning (making supplies available), doing the work of setting up the overhead projector, encouraging the students, and helping David use the fraction fringe with a pencil. She told us that her training had been "to capture as much as I can about what the teacher says," and that much of what she put in parentheses came from the book *The Skillful Teacher* (Saphier & Gower, 1987), which is "all about the purpose of what teachers do." The script provided the teacher the opportunity for reflection about the lesson, which was Mrs. Cowan's intention.

> [The teacher] liked having the data and the script and looking at that and saying, "Oh, I said that," and "Oh, I remember this," because it brings the whole lesson back to her. So she can reflect further on that lesson. Not because that lesson needs so much work, but because that's how you improve your own instruction is to think about what worked and what didn't.

While the script was meant to foster teacher reflection, Mrs. Cowan told us that she thought the categories in parentheses were more appropriate for beginning teachers because they focused basically on classroom management issues. They were less appropriate, she thought, for an experienced teacher like the one who had made up the fraction fringe lesson, who was "way beyond that, doing higher cognitive things." It is possible that, while Mrs. Cowan still continued using her scripting approach, it had outlived some of its usefulness.

And, in fact, during her postobservation conference with this teacher Mrs. Cowan did not refer to the script or the categories in parentheses at all. Rather, she talked with the teacher about the particular ways in which several students in the classroom had worked on the mathematical task that the teacher had posed. Then she made suggestions about how to help them:

> There were probably several children that were having some difficulty. . . . I'm not sure they were really fully understanding and sometimes having them actually do the representation and some kind of a little drawing locks it in for them rather than have them do more. . . . I think it's better for them to do less and really understand it then they can transfer the meaning . . . later after they get the constructs to do it that way.

Mrs. Cowan told us she was trying to encourage the teacher to design her lessons and the artifacts that students would use—manipulatives, worksheets, and so on—so that the lesson could be differentiated for students who were working at different conceptual levels. For example, students who were struggling with the set of equivalent fractions on the worksheet might be encouraged to draw pictures of the relationship between ½ and ⅘, to help them puzzle out the idea of equivalence. Such students might accomplish fewer of the assigned worksheet tasks but use the time to solidify their understanding of equivalence.

Further, Mrs. Cowan wanted students who were thinking well about the ideas at hand to have the opportunity to extend their thinking, much as Josie had. Mrs. Cowan generated an example for the teacher of how the equivalent fractions worksheet might have been modified to indicate additional equivalent fractions:

> One of the things you could have done is had [straight] lines that would have represented the fractions [on the fraction fringe] that you had been working with and then a little squiggly line [to indicate that] there are others that aren't really what we've talked about, but you [the student] might want to kind of challenge yourself. And some of the kids would have just have done the straight lines across, and other ones would have said, "Oh, there are more, there are more."

Mrs. Cowan said she wanted mathematical activities to signal to students that there was more to explore if they were interested. She described what she meant with an analogy:

> You can be standing in the room, which is the task that was structured by the teacher, but then if there's this window or door that you can look out or go out then that's another place to go. The light's coming through and you know you can go there if you're ready. . . . So if [such an invitation] is embedded in what's available and it's there for the taking, if the child is ready for that, I think that's the beauty of it.

Mrs. Cowan and the teacher also had considerable discussion about the adequacy of the manipulatives that were available for fourth-grade teachers, given the kind of exploration of equivalent fractions that Josie undertook. This discussion focused on the mathematical ideas of the lesson, how students were working with those ideas, and how the teacher could differentiate her instruction for students in conceptually different places with regard to the ideas of equivalent fractions. The script that Mrs. Cowan had written offered little help to this discussion.

Analysis

Developing a script seems like it could very well offer a useful approach for capturing what happens in a lesson and encouraging teacher reflection. We consider here how Marianne Cowan's technique might be modified so that the script would indeed reflect ideas about mathematics learning and teaching different from those she captured in her script. In particular, the parenthetical statements in such a script might comment on the mathematical and instructional significance of the teacher's discourse moves. So, when Mrs. Cowan wrote, "T: ¼ is equivalent to ⅜ . . . Susan has pulled ahead ⅛, ²⁄₁₆. Is there anything else," instead of putting in parentheses "Keeps students open and thinking," she might have written "Invites additional pairs of equivalent fractions, implying that there are more."

Alternatively, the teacher moves noted in parentheses might be tied to the mathematical ideas under consideration. For example, Mrs. Cowan recorded the following sequence:

> T: Is it fair to say ½ is equivalent to ⁴⁄₈? . . . Another way? S: ²⁄₄. T: ½ is equivalent to ²⁄₄. excellent. What if we don't use the ½? S: ²⁄₈. T: Angie said that ²⁄₈ is equivalent to ⁴⁄₁₆. . . . pull it forward.

She categorized the phrase "pull it forward" as "coaching in the use of the fraction fringe." However, she might have put the parenthetical phrase after the teacher's paraphrase of Angie's statement instead and labeled the sequence "exploring different ways of representing ½."

Developing categories related to mathematics and how children learn it, rather than using categories related to generic teacher moves, classroom management, and instructional momentum, would indicate an entirely different interpretation of what was significant. It would highlight quite different aspects of the class for the teacher to reflect on and subsequently discuss with the principal. Categories that focus attention on the mathematical ideas in the lesson and the way students are thinking about them would require (and enable) both principal and teacher to pay attention to the mathematical ideas of the elementary curriculum, the ways that students make sense of them, and the circumstances in which certain teaching moves seem effective. Such a script would provide data through which both teachers and principals could cultivate their perception of mathematics learning and teaching (Sassi, 2002).

At the end of our work with her, we talked with Mrs. Cowan about such possibilities. In particular, we talked about what would happen if, when she did classroom observations, she spent more of her time scripting the details of students' mathematical talk to have more detailed examples of student thinking to discuss with teachers. These examples could both provide them with more data about the thinking of the students in their classes and serve as a model for how attention might be paid to student thinking. While she thought this would be hard to do—students' voices are often soft and hard to hear—Mrs. Cowan also could see the benefit of such a form of scripting:

It would be a wonderful model because right now what seems to drive the instruction is that "This is what I've been told to do by the [curriculum]." Versus, "You know, this is what I've decided to do to find out more about where I need to go with this for this group, this child, this class, depending on what you find when you probe." So, great.

Mrs. Cowan appreciated that the categories she had been using in her scripts focused more on the kinds of classroom management issues that beginning teachers struggle with than the "higher cognitive things" that more experienced teachers faced. She was using a tool that was not well aligned with some of her current goals and values and was not getting the assistance that a well-aligned tool could have provided. While her knowledge of mathematics informed her practical judgment of what to discuss in conferences with teachers, Mrs. Cowan was more successful in these discussions with some teachers than with others. In the case of the teacher of the fraction fringe lesson, the discussion was quite successful. But our data shows that Mrs. Cowan was less successful in having such discussions with teachers who were not already engaged in thinking about students' mathematical thinking. Given her conviction that teachers should attend to their students' mathematical thinking, Mrs. Cowan was well positioned to modify her script to include categories that focus teachers' attention on students' mathematical thinking and their own actions in relation to that thinking. Such a modified form might be of considerable help in calling those teachers' attention to the particulars of their students' mathematical thinking.

WRITING A NARRATIVE TO SUPPLEMENT AN
INADEQUATE FORM: SHEILA DIGGINS

Mrs. Cowan's scripting practice, though no longer well aligned with current goals, was an informal part of her district's teacher assessment system, and the scripts themselves did not become part of the teachers' permanent files. But what happens when a principal's views about the nature of mathematics learning and teaching are no longer aligned with the district's teacher performance evaluation form, which *does* become part of the teacher's permanent record? For this we return to the work of Sheila Diggins and examine how she used her district's teacher evaluation form to record her assessment of one of her teachers, Ted Davis.

We observed Ms. Diggins doing the required formal classroom observations according to a format that had been worked out in negotiation with the teachers union. This entailed annual observations of teachers who did not yet have permanent status and observations of teachers with permanent status once every 3 years. The district required Ms. Diggins to meet with the teacher before the observation, do the observation at an agreed-upon time, and then meet with the teacher again, within a prescribed interval after the observation, to discuss the evaluation. Ms. Diggins was required to use a specified evaluation form and teachers were asked to sign the filled-in evaluation form to indicate that they had seen and discussed it with her.

An Episode from Administrative Practice

The teacher performance evaluation form in use at the time required teachers to be evaluated on eight standards of performance. Four focused on classroom performance: setting the stage for learning; classroom management; effective teaching; and monitoring, assessment, and follow-up. Four focused on professional responsibilities outside the classroom: collaboration with parents; collaboration with colleagues; school responsibilities; and professional growth. Ms. Diggins was to rate the teacher as *satisfactory* or *unsatisfactory* on each of these standards, give an overall rating of *satisfactory* or *unsatisfactory,* and cite specific observations of strength and areas for development in each category.

Ms. Diggins had been using this form for teacher evaluation for many years, but had recently noticed a change in how she used it. For several years she had been coteaching the course entitled *Developing Mathematical Ideas* (Schifter et al., 1999a, 1999b) to the teachers in her school, and that experience had provided her with the opportunity to expand her thinking about how to interact with teachers. The DMI course focuses on the development of children's mathematical thinking and teachers regularly turn in written homework assignments and write brief journal entries at the end of class sessions, which are read carefully and commented upon in writing by the course instructors. The experience of reading teachers' writing, trying to understand the way they were thinking about the ideas in the course, and responding in ways that would help teachers move along in their thinking, changed the way Ms. Diggins undertook the task of writing formal teacher evaluations. Not only did she now have a better idea of what the ideas in mathematics classes were, she also had a better idea of how children learn them, how teachers think about those ideas, and how teachers' learning itself takes place. She also had learned to cite evidence for the observations she made about teachers:

> [In the DMI course] we spend hours responding to people's work, and . . . it really changed my thinking around the write-ups that I do for folks [in the formal evaluations]. . . . It's different than it was in

the past. Certainly, I take more time to reflect on it. It's not as cut-and-dried. There's more evidence that I understand, and I'm able to pick out more evidence in the classroom . . . because I understand the ideas better that teachers are trying to convey to kids, and the sense that they're trying to make for themselves.

. . . I'm sure I would have had a much harder time writing this kind of [evaluation] 3 or 4 years ago, because I wasn't clear about what I should be looking for, and what teachers were thinking. . . . I may have in the past tried to speed people along when I shouldn't have, as opposed to letting them . . . kind of figure things out.

Ms. Diggins's DMI experience had put her in a very different position when she did formal evaluations. Now she tried to attend to the mathematical ideas being discussed, noting how the teacher worked with students' ideas to strengthen them, and she viewed the formal evaluation as an opportunity to help teachers grow in their own thinking. However, the teacher evaluation form that she was required to use was not particularly helpful to her. The page for commenting on effective teaching (Figure 4.1) can serve as an illustration. Two thirds of the page was used for a checklist of teacher behaviors that describe "effective teaching," followed by one inch of space for the principal to write her specific observations of teacher strengths and one inch for her to describe areas for development. There was no space for principals to describe any connections they saw among the eight standards for evaluation. In Ms. Diggins's view, this form

doesn't support this kind of process at all. There are so many examples already. . . . Most of the form is already written. . . . [There's] just a little space there to talk about what you've seen. It also breaks up the information, and I'd rather do it in a straight manner, but then I would be rewriting the form at the same time. So I switch back and forth [going from the small spaces for comment on the form to the back pages where she writes more extensive comments].

Ms. Diggins typically appended a three-to-four-page, single-spaced narrative commentary about each teacher she observed. This narrative described what she saw in the class, with very specific examples of student talk and teacher responses that focused on how the teacher's instruction achieved the desired results. She also was able to show relationships among the performance standards. Consider an excerpt from Mr. Davis's evaluation form:

All of the required materials were located in close proximity; the manipulatives, wipe-off board, student recording sheets, and a "work

Figure 4.1. Excerpt from School District's Teacher Evaluation Form

---

C. Effective Teaching

1. The teacher communicates learning goals and high standards and expectations to students.

—— Regularly tells students lesson objectives and expected learning outcomes

—— Conveys that virtually all students can master a challenging curriculum if taught well

—— Models the skills, attitudes, values, and processes of the subject being taught

2. The teacher uses appropriate instructional techniques that involve and motivate students.

—— Uses a repertoire of effective strategies: lecture, discussion, group work, hands-on, etc.

—— Sparks excitement, enjoyment, and enthusiasm in students

—— Explains concepts using clear and precise language

—— Helps all students learn by having them solve their own problems and make their own discoveries

—— Activates students' prior knowledge while introducing new material

—— Integrates reading, listening, writing, speaking, viewing, and appropriate learning tools

—— Assigns writing, projects, etc., that allow students to apply new concepts and skills

3. The teacher develops students' independence and their higher order thinking skills.

—— Asks questions that stimulate students' critical, independent, and creative thinking

—— Helps students see the relevance of the curriculum to lifelong learning, personal goals

—— Helps students set goals and take increased responsibility for their own learning

4. The teacher creates a classroom environment that is conducive to learning.

—— Maximizes the time students are working successfully with appropriate materials

—— Knows how and when to get students, colleagues, and classroom volunteers in to help

—— Works effectively to carry out educational plans for special needs students

—— Makes optimal use of other professionals to help meet students' special learning needs

Specific observations of strengths:

Areas for development:

---

board" identifying partners and their assigned tasks. . . . One of the important aspects of transition times is organization and setup. All of this was completed with minimal confusion, preparing students for the upcoming learning events. . . .

Mr. Davis has begun to tenaciously adopt teaching strategies that allow his students to construct and explore their own mathematical ideas. The classroom climate was conducive to this type of work. Students were encouraged to take risks and explain their thinking. Mr. Davis demonstrated respect for children's ideas as he made an honest mistake and enlisted a student's support to bring clarity to the group and his own confusion. "I said it backwards but you said it right. Michael, explain what you were thinking."

It was made clear throughout the large group discussion that the children were potential resources to each other. . . . As a result of this strategy there were few questions about how to accomplish the task presented once the work began. . . .

Mr. Davis modeled attentive listening while posing questions about mathematical ideas. He called on students who required support to accomplish tasks in both large and small groups. . . . He was not just after the right answers, but he was able to see and hear how students did their work. . . .

S.: We only need one more to make 10.
T.: What did you say?
S.: We only need one more.
T.: How did you know?
M.: They have 9. One more makes 10 (rolls the number one and puts a cube on the tower).
T.: Now how many altogether?
M.: 1,2,3, , , , , , 10.
T.: Did everyone hear that?
C.: Nine plus one equals 10.
M.: Why don't you count them?

This episode illustrates that not only does Mr. Davis listen but that the students, at various levels of understanding, listen to each other's thinking and build on the ideas as well. It also presented a missed opportunity. Michael's final question was never addressed. How did Charleyne know without counting? Addressing this question may have clarified some ideas and/or identified a new strategy for Michael and others.

It is clear from this narrative that Ms. Diggins attended very closely to what both students and teacher in a math class have to say, and how the teacher responds to what students say. She had indicated by the words "see attached description" on three of the standards of performance on the evaluation form that she intended this narrative to speak to several of the district's standards for evaluation—setting the stage for learning; effective teaching; and monitoring, assessment and follow-up. By constructing a narrative she was able to show the relationship between these categories. For example, she showed how having the physical materials at hand makes transitions less chaotic and thus supports learning. She highlighted the elements of Mr. Davis's instruction that were effective, and pointed to how listening to students' thinking makes assessment of what they understand possible. She also wrote in great detail a snippet of dialogue from the class, noting where the teacher had missed an opportunity to bring out that there are strategies other than counting for reaching 10.

Analysis

A narrative like Sheila Diggins's has very different potential than does the district's form—which is essentially an elaborated checklist—for both capturing the significance of what happens in a classroom and making learning possible for the teacher. In writing her narrative description of Mr. Davis's teaching practice, Ms. Diggins wove together the strands of the event that the district's evaluation form would have required her to pull apart. She showed she was aware of this, when she said,

> [The form] also breaks up the information. . . . There is too much overlap to break [any single] piece out and talk about it. I'd rather do it in a straight manner, so I do exactly what some people say don't do, I do the write-up in the comments section.

Pulled apart and commented on in different sections of the form, the evaluation would be a list of important characteristics of good teaching, but how and why they are important would be obscured. In writing her narrative, Ms. Diggins was able to capture a moment of instruction in which several threads were woven together to make a single fabric, and the significance of the interconnections was clear.

A narrative such as the one Ms. Diggins wrote also captures the contextually embedded particulars of the teaching situation; in this case the fact that the students were talking together in a large group about how to go from 9 to 10. Capturing student-student and student-teacher dialogue, as she did,

allowed Ms. Diggins to present Mr. Davis later with the details of this episode of student thinking and discuss with him what he thought about it. As
we noted in the last chapter, it is consideration of such particulars of teaching and learning that best supports teacher learning.

But beyond the advantages of the narrative form itself, Ms. Diggins's
essay shows that she was paying attention to subtly different aspects of this
class than the district-prescribed form suggested. As such forms go, this one
was quite cognitively oriented. It reflected research done in the late 1970s
and early 1980s on the cognitive psychology of instruction, in which it was
understood that the goal of instruction was not to "put knowledge into the
head of the learner but to put learners in positions that allowed them to
construct well-structured knowledge" (Resnick, 1981, p. 660). In calling the
principal's attention to whether or not students were "solving their own
problems," "making their own discoveries," engaged in "critical, independent, and creative thinking," and "taking increased responsibility for their
own learning," this district form focused on the development of general cognitive abilities and metacognitive skills, processes whose role in learning had
been demonstrated by research on symbolic information processing (Greeno,
Collins, & Resnick, 1996). The form also called principals' attention to instructional practices that information-processing research had indicated
would be effective. For instance, different forms of instruction such as lecture, discussion, group work, hands-on are appropriate, prior knowledge
needs to be activated before new instruction begins, and using new concepts
and skills is an integral part of learning them.

However, Ms. Diggins attended to more than this. For example, for her,
it was not sufficient to note that students were "solving their own problems"
and "making their own discoveries." She also attended to the content of the
students' mathematical thinking, as we saw in the example above when she
captured the student dialogue. Further, Ms. Diggins could conjecture that
the teacher might have missed a mathematical opportunity when he didn't
use the student's question to explore the possibility that strategies other than
counting exist for going from 9 to 10.

While it was cognitively oriented, the district's teacher evaluation form
did not ask the principal to focus on the subject-matter content of the ideas
under discussion. Focusing on the growth of children's understanding in
particular subject domains came a bit later in the history of research on learning. Ms. Diggins's experience in the DMI course, which is based on this later
research, shifted her orientation toward these new ideas with the result that
it was out of sync with the ideas that informed the teacher evaluation form.
Ms. Diggins needed to create a narrative addendum in order to write the kind
of teacher evaluation she now thought was appropriate.

Finally, Ms. Diggins struggled with how to use this form for both professional development and evaluation purposes. The form required that she indicate whether the teacher is *satisfactory* or *unsatisfactory* on each strand of the evaluation and overall. Ms. Diggins faced a dilemma similar to that posed by the older report card discussed earlier in this chapter. For her, teaching well was largely a matter of developing particular attitudes and beliefs toward children's learning, and she didn't feel that teachers whose attitudes and beliefs were still developing should be labeled *unsatisfactory*:

> I really think about adult learners a lot like I think about kids who are learners. We've got to make our mistakes and move along, and get better at what we do. And certainly, I have a certain level of expectation around the teacher's expertise, but I also know that what's being asked of teachers now is different from what we learned in school. . . . People aren't willing to give teachers the opportunity to get better. They want them to be good teachers today, and know it all today, and you really have to grow into it.

While there are major differences between how children learn school subjects and how teachers in classrooms improve their craft, Ms. Diggins recognized that, for both, understanding develops slowly, over time. In effect, Ms. Diggins wanted a "developmental" teacher evaluation form. Because one didn't exist for her, she marked the items *satisfactory* but then wrote a narrative to indicate how there was more learning to be done.

As in the case of the school's report card, Ms. Diggins's beliefs about mathematics learning (and, in this case, her beliefs about teacher learning as well) informed the practical judgment she exercised when she observed Mr. Davis's math class and wrote the narrative report on the teacher evaluation form. In both cases, Ms. Diggins's beliefs led her to a place where the forms provided by the district no longer seemed to her to provide adequate opportunity to record what she observed and to say what she thought needed to be said.

CONCLUSION

As principals' beliefs about how mathematics is learned and taught become more oriented toward how students understand and construct specific mathematical ideas, their sense of what their teachers should be held accountable for often changes. Like Sheila Diggins, they may come to see children's mathematics knowledge as emergent over time and not restricted to what has been explicitly taught in class. Like Marianne Cowan, they may begin to view what happens in mathematics classrooms differently, focusing more on the mathematical significance of what students and teachers say than on the orderliness of students' behavior or on general cognitive processes. And like Sheila Diggins, they may see teachers and students as involved in complex dialogues about mathematical ideas. As their views of mathematics learning and teaching become more constructivist in orientation, what principals attend to and record when they observe in classrooms, how they evaluate the effectiveness of instruction, and what they think should be reported to parents may change in subtle ways.

How principals act on such new views of learning and teaching in the school or district accountability system depends in part on the processes and forms that are available to them and the degrees of freedom that they have to modify these forms. The forms that the district provides (or that principals have obtained in earlier professional development) may be askew of their new beliefs, and they may find it a challenge to use those forms in ways that reflect their current knowledge and values.

Further, the principals whose work we examined here have found that, for professional development purposes, they need data that is quite detailed and attuned to the particularities of each teacher's instructional practice. Each of the principals whose work we examined in this chapter found ways to capture such detailed data. Ms. Diggins used quite specific aspects of instructional life—like the several contexts in which teachers dealt with the issue of time—to explore with teachers the difference between assessing students' understanding of the concept of time and assessing how well students understood the aspects of time that the teachers had taught. Mrs. Cowan was quite detailed in her scripts, providing the teacher with a precise record of what had happened in the class for reflection and later discussion. Ms. Diggins wrote a detailed narrative of what had happened in an observed class, including student-student and student-teacher dialogue, and attached it to her formal teacher evaluation.

Given the assessment forms they were using, however, each had to work hard to make the forms work. Ms. Diggins needed to persuade the district to adopt a more developmentally oriented report card and then work with her teachers to understand that reporting what students were coming to understand about mathematical ideas was not equivalent to reporting how well they understood what the teachers had taught. Mrs. Cowan devoted great effort to providing teachers with a detailed account of what had happened in the class, with generic instructional purposes noted, but she was beginning to consider that this form of scripting might be modified to focus more on the content of the mathematical ideas and how teacher action focused on them. Such a modified form would be more helpful to her in discussing these issues with teachers. And, in the second example of Ms. Diggins's work, she virtually ignored the district's teacher evaluation form altogether, producing a highly detailed narrative that wove together the district's several standards for performance into a description that included attention to the mathematical content of the lesson, ideas that students were working on, and the teacher's attention to those ideas.

These principals' challenge is that they are being held accountable according to standards that no longer seem to them appropriate. Their thinking has grown beyond the ideas that underlie the construction of the forms they are using and they are unwilling not to use their best thinking on behalf of improved instructional quality in their schools.

These principals' efforts to change the assessment forms tend to support Abelmann and Elmore's (1999) suggestion that administrators' ideas about what should be learned and taught, and what is important in particular schools, will affect how external accountability structures are interpreted and used. On the basis of how they turned available assessment forms to their own purposes, we can speculate that these principals will interpret the meaning of the coming external accountability systems in light of how they understand mathematics, learning, and teaching, and will find these systems congenial and helpful to them in their efforts to improve instruction to the degree that they embody a compatible view of mathematics, learning, and teaching.

"Education and Politics Meet at the Crossroads": Engaging Stakeholder Audiences as Learners

IN CHAPTERS 3 and 4, we explored two functional roles of instructional leaders: supporting teachers' professional development and managing assessment within formal accountability structures. In looking at what they do, and how they exercise their practical judgment, we also have considered what instructional leaders need to know in order to do their work well. In particular, we have emphasized the importance of subject matter knowledge, knowledge of how children learn, and beliefs about what counts as effective instructional practice.

This chapter considers one of the more challenging—and politically sensitive—responsibilities administrators have: interacting with stakeholder audiences. By stakeholder audiences, we mean parents and other community members, such as local business people, taxpayers, registered voters, and, of course, the school committee, whose mandate is to represent these constituents. Principals, who have been the central focus of this book, interact a great deal with the parents of the children in their schools. They represent the school to the parents at community events like parents' nights or in one-on-one meetings with individual parents. Principals, especially, often find themselves serving as intermediaries between parents and teachers. They have described this responsibility to us as "running interference."

When we look at the broader context of district-level policy making, administrators such as superintendents, assistant superintendents, or mathematics coordinators often have to take on more explicit roles as public spokespersons for the district. They are frequently required, for example, to make presentations to the school committee or respond to the media, and consequently find themselves more visible and open to public scrutiny. They may indeed be quoted in newspaper articles or even videotaped for the local cable station.

Whether we look at principals' relationships with parents or at district administrators' relationships with school committees and other community stakeholders, there is no doubt that the work takes on a distinctly more political aura than the more school-based work of mentoring teachers and monitoring instructional programs. Even administrators who are deeply committed to shifting the intellectual culture of their schools to one of collaborative learning and reflective inquiry find it challenging to transfer this stance to their work with stakeholders. One assistant superintendent acknowledged the disjunct between the complexities of learning in schools and the need for things to look orderly and under control to the school committee when she described to us what it is like to present to it:

> The reality is that schools . . . are messy. Schools have all kinds of loose ends, and people, and human beings. Individuals interacting with 25 kids every hour on the hour is not neat. . . . I know that [our math coordinator's] work with teachers is messy. . . . But, publicly, you don't recognize that. You look forward and say, "With professional development, we're doing this . . ."

We have witnessed, both through their stories and through observing them in action, administrators' struggles with how to navigate this terrain. In the words of the assistant superintendent quoted above, this is where "education and politics meet at the crossroads."

How, then, can administrators' knowledge of learning, teaching, or subject matter influence how they approach these situations where they are trying to describe learning processes that involve uncertainty and risk, but where any perceived incompetence or lack of control could have serious political repercussions? A principal might lose legitimacy in the face of a parent, or an assistant superintendent could even lose his or her job. We argue that, even at this level of instructional leadership, where risk taking may carry serious potential consequences, pedagogical knowledge and beliefs do matter and can affect how administrators deal with stakeholders.

Three issues confront school administrators as they interact with their constituents. The first is that the rules, norms, and procedures for interacting with stakeholders are likely to support or require a didactic stance rather than one of open-ended, collaborative inquiry (cf. Cohen & Barnes, 1993). That is, within structures like school committee meetings and parent-teacher conferences, administrators may have limited opportunities to generate open-ended discussions, entertain questions in an apolitical way, or engage in reflective conversation with stakeholders. In the first case in this chapter, we examine how administrators Charlotte Jenkins, an assistant superintendent, and Dana Goldstein, a mathematics coordinator, confronted and attempted to overcome this constraint during a presentation to their school committee on the state of mathematics instruction in their district.

A second issue administrators confront is understanding how to shift their own discourse with stakeholders so that it might allow for collaborative learning. Administrators may be far more accustomed to using a more "public" discourse with parents and other stakeholders that is focused on information exchange but is less effective in fostering open-ended discussion of substantive issue (cf. Eliasoph, 1996). In the second example, we revisit Peter Nash to look at how he organized a parents' forum entitled "Images of Good Teaching."

A third issue administrators may find themselves grappling with is how their own set of beliefs about learning translates into practice within this more public realm. Even administrators who are working to shift their understanding of learning and teaching may still believe that implementing policy changes in their district entails presenting clear, concise, and unproblematic policy decisions and not fostering open-ended discussion and learning (cf. Spillane, 2002). In the third case we examine assistant superintendent Joseph Garfield's description of a presentation he and his staff were to make to their school committee about a pilot high school mathematics program. We show how his own beliefs about learning, especially learning in this public realm, helped to ensure that there was little opportunity for the committee members to learn together or even entertain a different vision of working collaboratively.

DOING MATH WITH THE SCHOOL COMMITTEE: CHARLOTTE JENKINS AND DANA GOLDSTEIN

Our first example of administrators engaging with stakeholders involves a presentation about mathematics education to a district's school committee. The data for this example comes from a study group for administrators that we ran as a teaching experiment. (See the appendix, "Research Methodology," for an explanation of teaching experiments.) At this particular session of the study group, participants were asked to think about how they would present some aspect of mathematics education reform to a stakeholder audience. They were to think about what was important about the topic and what their conjectures were about the audience: what the audience knew, what was important to them, and what they thought would be the best way to communicate with this audience.

In this example, Charlotte Jenkins, assistant superintendent of curriculum and instruction in a midsized city in a northeastern metropolitan area, and Dana Goldstein, K–5 elementary mathematics coordinator, told the study group about a presentation they had just made to their school committee. In designing their presentation, they ventured a little beyond the bounds of the typical presentation structure to engage the committee in experiencing what it was like to do mathematics from the perspective advocated by the NCTM *Curriculum and Evaluation Standards*. In order to understand the significance of the modification—which appears small relative to the overall presentation—one needs to understand the usual context for working with the school committee, as these administrators understood it.

As these study group members described to us, presentations to the school committee are quite carefully crafted. In order to keep the agenda moving smoothly along and to maintain the school committee's confidence in the superintendent and other administrators, the work presented to the school committee is portrayed as straightforward and unproblematic. Efforts are made to assure the committee that decisions have been made only after careful consideration, that staff is confident of these decisions, and that, in general, things are under control. According to these administrators, one doesn't acknowledge the complexities of schooling or the inherent uncertainties that make decision making challenging.

In making presentations before a school committee or a school board, image control is essential. One wants to use scarce time efficiently, design the presentation so that it anticipates questions that school committee members might have, and, since school committee meetings are often now broadcast on the community access channels of local cable television, avoid embarrassing anyone. These aspects of school committee presentations were described to us quite vividly by the administrators with whom we worked. One administrator described managing the timing and focus of a school committee presentation as a matter of staying in "the chute":

> I feel like I'm [a] ship that ran aground. . . . You have to sail in a very narrow shipping lane to get ideas through school committee and to get out of it so that the next item gets off and there's no unfinished business. . . . If you do too much or too little you go aground. . . . And if you kind of keep your focus, you go—shwoosh—right through. . . . I think it's a chute. If you don't get into the chute with the right information, it becomes a long presentation and then the chairman and the school superintendent are looking at watches and the people who are behind you on the agenda are furious. . . . So you have to do something structured, clean, clear.

Presentations to school boards typically are highly orchestrated, highly ritualized performances. Often one may have only 15 minutes. Many administrators may see little opportunity for any kind of innovation within such a structure. The stakes are too high to make any mistakes or misjudgments. However, administrators who bring certain ideas about learning, teaching, or content knowledge may be able to use that knowledge to push the boundaries of these settings and create openings for collaborative learning. Thus, in the first example, a small change to the standard school committee format did open up the school committee structure—and possibly even the relationships among members present—if only for a few minutes.

An Episode from Administrative Practice

Dr. Jenkins and Ms. Goldstein, together with another elementary mathematics coordinator and the high school mathematics department chair, were presenting to the school committee a comprehensive view of the district's mathematics program. In their view, the district's mathematics program in the past had been defined by the published materials that the district used. Dr. Jenkins told us that she worried that the district's mathematics education program may have appeared too ad hoc, as a variety of new curricula had become available, were pilot tested, and used at different grade levels. She was concerned that the school community might think that no comprehensive and rational plan to guide decision making was in place. She and her staff, which included Ms. Goldstein, designed this presentation to bring the school committee up to date on the standards and criteria being used to make decisions about the mathematics program. They planned to describe progress to date in the implementation of the plan and to enlist the school committee's aid in monitoring the program development process in the future.

Dr. Jenkins and Ms. Goldstein told us that the presentation was very carefully designed and planned. Together with the other elementary math coordinator and the high school math department chairperson, they had begun months earlier working out what they were going to say and how they were going to do it. They planned a coordinated set of presentations, which collectively took about 45 minutes. Prior to the school committee meeting, they rehearsed the presentation to be sure they knew how long each section would take. They also met with the school committee's curriculum subcommittee the day before, and "they had asked all the hard questions."

Anticipating the community's interest in high achievement, the presenters told us they chose not to rest their description on what was in the curriculum materials, but to describe what was in the district-designed assessments.

> This is what everyone in that room wanted to know—how do we
> measure what students have learned? And we . . . had to demonstrate

to them that we had a document in place that was going to try to do this for all students.

Through examination of the assessments, they said, their intent was to show that elementary mathematics now has some new topics in it, that both new and traditional mathematics topics are now taught in a different way than these adults probably had experienced when they were in school, and that the mathematics itself is hard. That is, they intended to show that the district had high expectations in mathematics and was prepared to assess students' knowledge to assure that these expectations were being met.

Up to a certain point, they said, their presentation before the school committee was just what they had described—highly structured, it anticipated the committee's questions and concerns, and described the mathematics program as well in hand. It was presented with an air of confidence and moved briskly along, staying in "the chute." But at the point at which Ms. Goldstein made her part of the presentation, their strategy changed. In her 10-minute section of the presentation, Ms. Goldstein started by highlighting how the district's new mathematics standards were linked to the NCTM *Curriculum and Evaluation Standards* and the state's Mathematics Curriculum Frameworks. She presented the major goal of the district's mathematics curriculum policy as achieving "a balance between mastery (in the sense of, Can they multiply?) and inquiry [into mathematical ideas]." But Ms. Goldstein had decided to include in her presentation some examples of the assessments for mathematics that had been added to the curriculum since school committee members and parents had gone to school as well as more familiar topics, such as whole number operations. Drawing on her knowledge of mathematics and teaching, she chose to have everyone in the room actually solve and discuss two mathematics problems that were in the district's student assessment instrument. In effect, she broke from convention to transform the school committee room into a mathematics classroom for a few minutes.

Ms. Goldstein described to us how she handed out a statistics and probability problem. The problem was to select from a set of graphs the one that showed the height of fourth graders. The other graphs showed the number of cavities that fourth graders have, the ages of fourth graders' mothers, and the number of people in fourth graders' families. She described what she did:

We handed this out to the entire audience and I said to them, "You didn't think you could get away from me without having to solve a problem?" And, of course, they laughed. They loved this. They absolutely loved this. And I said, "You can work with a partner or can find the smartest one in the room." I mean, they loved this.

After giving them some time to work on the problem, Ms. Goldstein said she called on the superintendent of administration and finance, figuring that he would know the answer and no one would be embarrassed. She was afraid that if she called on someone who didn't know the answer they "might have some trouble." She told the assembled group that students make graphs all the time, but this problem is harder. "It was hard for the adults, too, because the answer isn't evident." She told them that most students in the fourth grade in the district had taken this as an assessment and had been able to find the right answer. "So, it was a real-life situation."

Anticipating the school committee's and parents' interest in whole number operations, she then gave the group a division problem:

> Really, that's all people care about. . . . It's like the SAT scores. All this is wonderful and good, but when are they going to know their facts?

The problem given was 287 divided by 14. School committee members and parents who were attending were asked to think of a real-world situation in which that problem would occur, solve the problem, and as they solved it, record each step of their work so that someone looking at their work would understand their thinking. In the past, most people in the room would have simply solved the problem. But they likely would not have done the additional activities, meant to preserve the meaning of the problem and make explicit the nature of the learner's mathematical thinking.

Analysis

In providing this experience with probability and statistics and division problems, Dana Goldstein gave the school committee, assembled parents, and members of the general public a sample of what classroom mathematics was like for their fourth graders. Her intention was to make the mathematics concrete, so that they could infer how it was similar to and different from what they had done when they were in school. As she described this new way of working on a mathematics problem to our study group, "You do it with other people, you talk things through, you have to think beyond the evident, there are new topics." What is notable is that she chose to communicate this new approach to the school committee not by presenting examples from the curriculum but by having those present actually do two mathematics problems. In doing so, she created a momentary community in which interactions among members weren't constrained by the usual norms of school committee meetings. In this 10-minute "classroom," puzzling about something confusing, working with a peer to think through the issues together, and perhaps not fully figuring it out by the end of the "lesson" were allowed. She effectively offered the school committee a glimpse of a different intellectual culture. By doing this, she provided the school committee and others access to some subtle aspects of classrooms based on a constructivist view of learning—aspects that go beyond curricular topics and teaching techniques. And when they would have to decide if this mathematics program was a direction in which they wanted to go, they might in fact be more deeply informed of what that course would mean for the nature of students' mathematics knowledge.

Creating such a "classroom" in the school committee room required taking some risks and flying in the face of the usual strategy for school committee presentations. By asking the members to work in pairs on the problems and talk about them with each other, she gave over control of the discourse and created a situation in which it was not possible to predict what would happen. The tasks were not presented as ones that were tidy, cleaned up, and in hand, but rather as puzzling situations that needed figuring out. By implication, mathematics classrooms were not intellectually tidy, but full of situations that needed figuring out. Because she could not take the time to discuss the mathematics thoroughly, so that everyone came to some resolution, she had to risk that some people might have been left with a sense of uncertainty about what the mathematics was about and, perhaps, what the district's math program was about.

It is worth noting that these administrators kept their eye on the political horizon all the while and did not flagrantly disregard the accepted norms of school committee presentations. The risks to having the group do mathematics together were carefully hedged by attention to predictable school committee concerns. Specifically, the mathematics program was being described as a coherent, rational K–12 plan. Secondly, the substantive part of the presentation, including the selection of mathematics problems to do, focused on the rigor of the district's mathematics assessment program. And, finally, the problems themselves provided prima facie evidence that school mathematics was hard, albeit perhaps in different ways then when school committee members and parents had been in school.

Yet Ms. Goldstein brought to bear her own beliefs about how people learn together to modify the accepted format of the school committee meeting. Rather than work only within the more didactic format to which presenters were accustomed but by which she felt constrained in this instance, she exercised her own professional judgment to turn her portion of the presentation into an experiential learning situation. Certainly there were no guarantees that the committee members would come away reassured that the mathematics program in the district was on solid ground. But even a small step such as the one she took might have signaled a shift in the accepted modes of policy implementation (Cohen & Barnes, 1993) and the accepted working relationships among committee members (cf. Forester, 1999).

BUILDING POLITICAL CAPITAL WITH PARENTS THROUGH A PARENTS' FORUM: PETER NASH

The example above may seem rather unremarkable in the degree to which it represents a collaborative learning experience. Ms. Goldstein and Dr. Jenkins structured their presentation to their school committee much as they always had, except everyone present actually did mathematics together. What is special about their case becomes clearer in light of another example. In Chapters 1 and 3, we showed how Peter Nash offered strong and intellectually rich instructional leadership within his school. Yet, as we show here, when it came to working with stakeholders such as the parents in his district, he struggled with how to engage them in the reflective and open-ended discourse he so favored.

In Mr. Nash's district at the time, however, his dilemma did not seem unfounded. In contrast to Ms. Goldstein's successful mathematics activity, for example, Mr. Nash described a more disturbing incident: When the high school math department chairperson, who had taken over coordinating the elementary mathematics review, brought manipulatives to a school board meeting to share an activity with members, one of the parent members got very angry and started yelling that she didn't need manipulatives, that her child didn't need manipulatives, and that they were for babies.

Mr. Nash believed that the pressure he felt from parents stemmed from their wanting to maintain practices that had worked for their own children. He felt that his situation was akin to that described by Alfie Kohn in his article, "Only for *My* Kid: How Privileged Parents Undermine School Reform" (1998), where Kohn argues that more affluent parents often support more conservative efforts to undermine detracking reforms. According to Mr. Nash, the issue of grouping students homogeneously for mathematics had become politically charged, and many parents took pride in having their children in the higher groups. He noted that parents with children in the lower groups also supported the grouping practices because they liked having the lower teacher-student ratio.

But, even beyond the grouping issue, Mr. Nash said on different occasions that he felt that he was continually dealing with a group of parents who exerted a lot of pressure on the school and district to maintain the status quo:

There clearly are many parents who, separate from any discussion about their own children, make everyone know that they hope that the system continues to offer challenging work for children who are more successful. . . . More often than not, they mean homogeneous instruction.

[It's] not just about the grouping question. It's also a question of will the new program appear to be as rigorous or will the new program or the new materials give people the same confidence that their children are achieving.

In these statements, we get the sense that Mr. Nash saw the parents in his district as a very real political influence. They could make a difference in, for instance, what policy decisions the district made, what curriculum materials it chose, what actually would be taught, and which students had access to what resources.

He said further that many parents were very vocal and "suspicious that they were not getting their money's worth," saying things like, "I want you to explain to me what you're doing in math. I want you to explain to me . . . what was your reasoning." He added that they were vocal with anyone who would listen to them: "other parents in the class, the teacher. I can't tell you how many times I have to give feedback to parents about taking their concerns to the wrong place." One of his goals in working on the issue of heterogeneous grouping in mathematics with teachers (discussed in Chapters 1 and 3) was to help them articulate their own reasoning better:

It's for [teachers] who say, "That's an idea that seems important to me, I don't quite know how to sell that to people or explain it to people." I think we have a very sharp staff; I'm trying to give them the thinking time and the resources and each other to develop their thinking about that.

While one stated purpose of the faculty meetings was to help his teachers think about the issue of grouping in a nonpoliticized context, another was indeed to support his teachers in the face of what he perceived as demanding and questioning parents.

When asked if he thought the parents generally understood the ideas and reasoning behind school practices when explained to them, he responded,

I feel that [for] most of the things that we have initiated or that are in place that we do explain to them, they do come on board. I do think that some things are harder. And I think this one would be. And I think it's going to be hard enough just having a math program that looks a little more unfamiliar, let alone the grouping practice.

An Episode from Administrative Practice

After the two faculty meetings that he devoted to the issue of heterogeneity in math classes, Mr. Nash told us that he felt that he couldn't have another one. The mathematics curriculum review had been put on hold and a small group of parents were exerting increasingly more influence in having the district reconsider its commitment to curricula that conformed to the *Curriculum and Evaluation Standards* of the National Council of Teachers of Mathematics (1989). Realizing that consideration of the grouping issue would not be on the school agenda that year, he began to consider the idea of offering a parents' forum. He said he was feeling that his energy at this point would best be spent in reaching out to the parents of his school.

A month after the second faculty meeting, he decided to offer a parents' forum entitled "Images of Good Teaching," which he scheduled for 90 minutes during a weeknight evening. This meeting would not address mathematics teaching directly but would be focused on general teaching issues. Shortly before the meeting, he said that he wanted to have an opportunity to talk with parents about values and what counts as good teaching. He reiterated his own concern for how the dialogue around such issues is often reduced to an either-or debate and said that he was going to use the session to illustrate how a lot of issues are indeed linked to some either-or position that ultimately proves not so clear-cut. He wanted to highlight how such dichotomous positions often become a source of tension and political stalemate.

Mr. Nash decided that, unlike the sessions he did with his teachers, he would not structure activities for the parents through which they might experience and then analyze "good teaching." Rather, he would use a presentation format with stories and examples from his personal experiences followed by a time for questions, to share his image of what good teaching entailed. We observed this parents' forum and will look here at the main ideas he set out for the 23 parents who came.

Mr. Nash had organized his talk around six points, which he had posted on a flip chart. He referred to the points as "Nuggets," each of which consisted of a short phrase that summarized a larger point he wanted to make. His talk consisted of elaborating each point. In each case, he shared some experiences from his own teaching to illustrate the point.

In introducing the session, he read a portion of a letter he had written more than 20 years earlier in response to an article that attributed one classroom's success to its physical environment. He was a third-year teacher at the time and in the letter cautioned that "good teaching" could not be measured solely by the amount of paraphernalia—lofts, touchables, murals, and so on—in it. He wrote, "We need more written about what happens in the teacher-student interaction. How do teachers and students talk to each other about the work they do and the way they do it? What do teachers learn when their students don't find an lesson or activity challenging?"

He used this letter to set up the intent of his talk, which was to share some of what he had learned and come to believe about what "good teaching" entailed. He told the parents that he was offering a body of knowledge that he had collected over his years of teaching. After this brief introduction, he turned to elaborating his six key points.

The first point, "Know where you're going," referred to the need for teachers to have a deep understanding of the content, which he referred to as knowledge, and a solid understanding of how to execute the knowledge, which he called "know-how." He also emphasized that students should "know the ropes," meaning they should know what the routines are and know how to navigate in the classroom environment. He included in this category a need for teachers to have a "profound understanding of all the ways in which students construct these ideas."

His second point, "Know the learners," referred to how students are sorted. He recounted historical reasons for sorting students according to ability, noting specifically the application of the industrial model that emphasized efficiency. He pointed out how this historical practice still exerted influence in the ways that schools sort and organize students. Indeed, as he mentioned throughout our work with him, one concern Mr. Nash had with formal grouping practices was that they were done to make teaching more "efficient," but he saw this efficiency as actually contributing to the deskilling of teachers, since they might become expert at teaching only the group to which they were assigned. In discussing this point with the parents, he raised a somewhat rhetorical question: "Are kids with special needs in the same classroom as kids without?" and answered the question by saying, " It isn't an either-or but it has to be both."

In discussing his third point, "Give and take," he made reference to a "riddle" from Piaget: "If the rabbit eats the cabbage, is the rabbit like the cabbage or the cabbage like the rabbit?" He used this idea to raise the question of whether or not the teacher should adapt to the students or vice versa. He said that the dichotomy of "teacher-centered" versus "student-centered" classrooms came into play here but he felt that it was really a moot dichotomy. He showed another overhead that depicted an alternative schema. It had four quadrants, suggesting four types of classrooms. High teacher engagement–low teacher engagement was on the vertical axis and high student engagement–low student engagement was on the horizontal axis. He described each of the resulting four quadrants and ended by saying that the high teacher engagement–high student engagement was what he was looking for in classrooms. He ended his discussion of this point by saying, "We have two loyalties that appear to be in tension: to the students and to society and the discipline."

In addressing his fourth point, "Shape the pattern of talk," Mr. Nash talked about how he had come to appreciate a model of teaching that involved very little talking, which he called the "silent way." He showed an overhead of a triangle in which the top angle was labeled "teacher initiation," the left bottom angle was labeled "student response," and the right bottom angle was labeled "teacher evaluation." He described how this was often the typical discourse pattern in classrooms. He also recounted Mary Budd Rowe's (1986) work on wait time. He told the group that his belief in the "silent way" led him to examine different kinds of discourse patterns in classrooms and he had come to understand how cultural differences matter a lot. He noted that patterns of talk can indicate why some students, especially from different cultural backgrounds, are less successful than other students.

The fifth point, "Know the learning," referred to the role of *scaffolding* as an alternative to traditional teaching approaches that involve correcting students' mistakes. He talked about traditional approaches to writing in which the child is told how to improve the writing: change this word, shorten this sentence, and so on. But scaffolding doesn't directly tell students what to do. He explained how it was a way to intervene that increases students' independence. He also mentioned the role of *disequilibrium* and the ways in which it can help students develop the ability to do things independently.

The last point, "Motivate students," gave him the opportunity to talk about the nature of praise. He said that he used to be extreme in his position that he wasn't going to mindlessly praise students, but he was now coming to appreciate that what was key was not avoiding all praise but avoiding empty praise. Specifically, he felt that it was important to give students descriptive feedback rather than just saying that they did a "good job." He talked about the role of motivation and the dilemma that teachers face of whether or not the motivation should be intrinsic or extrinsic. He shared a quote he used with teachers:

> We view motivation as an attribute of situations and not as a character trait of individuals. No one is "motivated" all of the time, for all kinds of learning.

After he finished describing each point, he went back over them briefly, suggesting the either-or dichotomies that he wanted them to think about: teacher-versus student-centered; indirect versus direct teaching; breadth versus depth; and intrinsic versus extrinsic praise.

Mr. Nash closed his talk by sharing a quote from Peter Elbow (1986) on the need to embrace these contraries and telling the parents that, as they embarked on future decisions "as informed citizens who want a voice," they should join him in talking about teaching practices "not so simply as these either-or's." He then entertained and answered a number of questions from parents.

Analysis

In his talk Peter Nash tried to summarize the ideas about teaching and learning that were so dear to him and central to his own professional identity. He told us later that this was his first attempt to bring together in a concise way all of the ideas that had been guiding his practice as a teacher and principal over the years.

In talking with Mr. Nash the week after the parents' forum about how he thought it went, he started by saying that initially he was disappointed because there were so many things that he wanted to touch on that he didn't get to. He had wanted to use different examples and illustrations to make certain points and he was also a little disappointed that there were certain ways he wanted to make the points and didn't. But some parents had positive feedback for him. Several talked about how they acted differently with their children and had a new understanding of how to work through issues with their own children. Others talked about how they felt more informed about what goes into teaching children. He shared two excerpts from parents' letters:

> I feel so much more informed now about you and about what goes into teaching children. The strategies you explained with us are so interesting in their applications and impact in the classroom and at home. It was a valuable source of information for parents, and should be an annual event.

> The talk confirmed our delight that our children are in the school. The passion, thoughtfulness, and caring about the children came through.

In asking him what he thought was eye-opening for these parents, Mr. Nash commented that he thought that the session might have confirmed what they had hoped:

I think the people who were making these comments are very deliberate and focused people about their parenting. And I think they sort of suspected and hoped that people talked about teaching and felt that way about the teaching that occurred in their children's school. . . . I think it was a good confirmation for them that this occurred.

For Mr. Nash, it was very significant that some of the parents came away with the sense that the decisions that went into teaching their children were carefully thought out and considered. He thought that the forum did indeed help to forward his overall goals:

Well, this is just a hunch, but what I think [the forum] does sort of prepare them, or make them more trusting. If we were to do some innovative project, or if we were to take some direction in the curriculum or program that wasn't immediately familiar to them, . . . they would sort of give us the benefit of the doubt, and sort of stick with us and see that we have been careful in that decision to do that, even if it isn't something that they immediately have confidence in, or know about.

Here, we again see Mr. Nash's concern for building trust and confidence within the school community. Besides educating parents about the philosophy and practices of teaching at their children's school, a deeper purpose of this meeting was to build trust and confidence in the school and in Mr. Nash himself. He was creating, as he later put it, political capital in the form of trust that he could draw on when he needed it. In addition, he was trying to shift the discourse landscape by introducing parents to a new set of ideas about teaching and learning.

There are many reasons why a principal (or teacher) might choose to give a presentation rather than create interactive learning activities for a particular audience or lesson. If they do, audiences and students will likely construct their own representations of the material, in any event. It is just that some structures for lessons make such construction easier. When asked about his choice to structure this meeting as a presentation, Mr. Nash said he had a desire to give the parents a window on his thinking "more than I wanted them to learn about teaching techniques." He admitted that he did have "conflicting purposes" because he had thought about how he would have done this session with teachers, which might have included some interactive activities. But, he felt that such a structure with parents would not have achieved his "bigger purpose" which was to "get across the thoughtfulness of the teaching that occurs at the school, and the thoughtfulness of how teaching is supervised at the school."

Given how thoughtful and reflective Mr. Nash was when working with his teachers, it is also possible that other reasons were at play. We suspect that he was being cautious about opening up the discussion and felt safer presenting to parents rather than facilitating a collaborative exploration. He told us after the meeting that he had been concerned that some parents might be too vocal and would try to turn the conversation to be implicitly about their own children. He also admitted that "there were a lot of people there I didn't want to have a conversation with."

This stance did seem contrary to what we might have expected, given the emphasis Mr. Nash generally placed on discourse and "open, honest dialogue." It is possible that he was not ready to envision different ways of working with parents as learners in this more public realm, especially given his perceptions of a very influential and contentious parent contingent. Mr. Nash's design of the forum may have reflected a more tentative and exploratory attempt to communicate a complex set of ideas. He may have believed that he had to introduce parents to these ideas before he could entertain the possibility of engaging them in a different kind of learning dialogue.

This case highlights the challenge principals may have in putting into practice their beliefs about learning and teaching across all the varied school contexts in which they work. Talking with stakeholders is different from talking with teachers. And, as our final case in this chapter illustrates, for many administrators, the pressure to appear credible and in control may indeed supercede engaging stakeholders as collegial learners.

SCHOOL COMMITTEE PRESENTATIONS AS POLITICAL PERFORMANCES: JOSEPH GARFIELD

Finally, we look at a more typical presentation to a school committee as a way of examining the kinds of assumptions about learning that administrators are likely bring to their work with stakeholders. These assumptions were present in our previous two examples, though perhaps to a lesser degree. This last example will help to bring to light some insights into how an administrator's understanding of learning, teaching, and content knowledge can, in fact, shape his interactions with stakeholders.

The data for this last example comes from the study group for administrators we ran prior to our formal study of principals' practice. In this example, Joseph Garfield, the assistant superintendent of curriculum and instruction in a mixed-income town in a larger urban area, described a presentation that several of his high school teachers would be making to the school committee the next evening. The presentation would describe the pilot year of a new high school mathematics program. Dr. Garfield described the presentation to the study group this way:

> The context is this: the program has been very well received in its first year. We're not trying to make a case for the program. The program has been very well received by parents. It's been very well received by the staff. We had no trouble getting students to sign up for it. It's a year-end report from Year 1. The whole school committee has never had a presentation of this. The subcommittee on curriculum and instruction has had maybe two or three. . . . So, we're not trying to clean up from a mess or something overlooked. This is a routine, garden-variety school committee presentation on a new program.

Dr. Garfield's description of the presentation indicated that it would follow a typical format and would be "a *very* simple presentation about a new math program for the school committee." His central concern with the presentation coming off well was less with parents and more with the general public because the meeting would be videotaped for broadcast on the local cable station.

The presentation would be descriptive. Two high school teachers who taught the curriculum would make the presentation and speak from overheads. Dr. Garfield noted that because he didn't know if the school committee knew what the program was, they were giving the committee "little talking papers." These papers included a statement of principles and philosophy, including equity principles such as greater access to mathematics; a description of how class sections of the program are heterogeneously grouped; and a description of instructional strategies. The presenters would tell the committee that the curriculum was "a problem-centered program, that there are definite content changes in mathematics, and that the students are involved in long-term investigations and projects."

After describing the program, the next section of their presentation would address why they chose it. Reading from an overhead, Dr. Garfield continued:

> That's what it is. Very simple. But, "why is it important for our students?" is the next section. Why does it fit [our town]? . . . Because it's a traditional preparatory college curriculum. That's a very important idea in [our town.] Its use of cooperative groups. Another very important idea in [our town]. That we will start small with 50 students, also a very important concept in [our town], that things start small and safe and that they're well supervised and watched over during the initial year.

He then described the remaining sections of the presentation. The next section would describe what mathematics topics are taught through the program. As he said, "We always want to have a focus on the curriculum to monitor what kids are getting and how closely we're honing our new programs to old programs."

Dr. Garfield then described how the teacher who had led the pilot program would show the committee some sample lessons and noted that the high school mathematics coordinator would speak to how the sample lessons related to the state standards. The district's mathematics coordinator, who was present at the study group, added that it was important for the committee to know that the new curriculum was aligned with the *Curriculum and Evaluation Standards* of the National Council of Teachers of Mathematics and the state frameworks. Specifically, she said that it was important to highlight that the program "asked teachers to address problems where children were engaged in writing about mathematics and illustrating in diagrams and doing graphing of it as well."

Dr. Garfield also noted that the presenters were prepared to show student work. They would first show some work from a geometry problem and then show a problem in which students were asked whether or not they would double the area of a triangle if they doubled its sides. This sample also included student homework "showing students can write about mathematics."

Dr. Garfield then got to what he considered the main point of their presentation. As he said, showing one of the overheads:

> Ta da! The key point. The only point that matters in the whole presentation: How do [pilot program] students' SAT scores compare to students in traditional math programs? Of course we don't have any data yet from [our town] but this is some data that our teacher has gathered [from elsewhere]. [Showed data.] And, you see that they do no worse and maybe a little bit better.

Analysis

From many perspectives, this presentation appears to be thoughtful, prepared, and sensitive to the expectations of the school committee. It came across as well-researched and contained relevant data that the committee had come to expect. Joseph Garfield and his staff honored the norms and time constraints of the meeting and ensured that they could cover their points within their 20-minute time slot.

Yet, as he described this presentation, we were left with the impression that Dr. Garfield actually could not envision how the public context of a school committee meeting might work differently as a learning context. Forester's (1999) observation seems especially apt here:

> Some meetings can be so structured, so predictable, so predetermined that no one learns much of anything new. The designers of the decision-making process may have decided what information shall be explored and how it shall be, and their controlling intentions may make surprise, discovery, and the identification of new issues and opportunities practically impossible. (p. 142)

In the context of the professional study group in which he participated with us and other administrators, Dr. Garfield always brought a thoughtful, self-reflective, and insightful sensibility to the dialogue as well as a desire to learn. He was learning a great deal about what it might mean to understand mathematics, how it might best be taught, and the implications of both of these for the professional development that his district might offer teachers. However, as we will explore more fully in Chapter 6, he acknowledged to us that he had not yet had the chance to experiment with how the new ideas about learning, teaching, and subject matter he had been exploring in the study group might translate into new administrative practices on his part (see also Stein & Nelson, 2003). When dealing with stakeholders, especially the school committee, he worked from a more traditional set of beliefs and norms about what people need to know and how they learn it. The kind of information that Dr. Garfield deemed it necessary to provide the school committee was grounded on certain assumptions about how the committee as a whole learned together and the kind of learning relationship he had with them. He expressed the following view of the committee:

> It's very didactic. And, it's functional. They want functional information. They want information they can use. You know, like the SAT scores. . . . I think they want a couple of big ideas and an example, to latch onto the big idea. . . . And they want to know what it is and how it's the same or different from what we now do. And they also want to know how much it costs and how long it's going to take.

Besides bringing this didactic mind-set to the design of the presentation, Dr. Garfield also exercised certain beliefs about the political need to ensure that the committee was receptive to the presentation. One belief was that the fewer questions the committee had, the more credible he and his staff would look:

> So, basically, what we're trying to do here is answer the school committee's questions before they ask them . . . so that, in the

discussion that follows, there won't be confusing answers to questions. If we anticipate the questions, we can answer them as fully as we think they need to be answered. And the questions won't be posed from a partisan point of view or a political point of view. They'll be posed from an educational point of view.

Anticipating questions (and preparing provisional answers) is itself a politically savvy planning strategy. Not doing so could leave the presenters unprepared and vulnerable to embarrassment, criticism, and verbal attack. Anticipating questions can also be a way to prepare oneself to hear what committee members have on their minds. However, we sensed that Dr. Garfield's desire to anticipate questions came less from a spirit of learning about what school committee members might think, or being ready for the unexpected, and more from a need to minimize surprise and protect credibility. He told us that the school committee would be interested in the following kinds of issues:

> How long have I known about it? [the new pilot math program] Have I lived with it? Have I talked to people about it? Have I gone to [curriculum] meetings? That's all important to them. Do I have a good network? Do the people I trust trust [the program]? And, have I really steeped myself in it, not just by reading but by talking, considering? It's a . . . journey you take with an idea. And no surprises is one of the big things—no surprises.

He added that the emphasis on "no surprises" went both ways:

> And, I don't want to be surprised either. Because I don't want a parent to rise up in the audience and contest my opinion. And the school committee doesn't want to have a proposal that . . . hasn't stewed, with all the juices, and all the flavors, and all the elements that go into a stew. That's very important, no surprises.

Dr. Garfield described this stance as a matter of saving face. In this public forum, not only did he want to avoid appearing to lack any information that the school committee expected, he certainly did not want anyone to stand up and provide information that he or the other presenters did not already know.

Certainly, it is critical that school administrators make policy decisions only after thoughtful and careful consideration and not jump into something without having anticipated the implications. But, following Forester, by structuring out questions and by deliberately avoiding the possibility of being "surprised," Dr. Garfield and the presenters may have indeed closed off the possibility of deeper learning about curriculum implementation, the discovery of new issues that need attention, or the redefinition of relationships among members.

CONCLUSION

The examples in this chapter depict how administrators, be they principals or central office staff, can struggle with interacting effectively with stakeholder audiences. The available structures and procedures favor more didactic approaches such as the strategically prepared presentations we saw in this chapter. Yet, all of the administrators highlighted in the examples— Charlotte Jenkins, Dana Goldstein, Peter Nash, and Joseph Garfield— wrestled in different ways to engage their stakeholders even though they were bound by norms that supported more unilateral forms of learning.

Dr. Garfield illustrated for us the difficulty administrators face in challenging the given norms and procedures for interacting with stakeholders in such high-stakes settings as school committee meetings. We will see in Chapter 6 that he was working to develop his practice in other professional contexts, but he perceived that he was bound here by a need to defend his policy choices and protect his credibility. By his own description, he approached the committee adversarially and thus saw few opportunities to engage in any type of professional relationship with them other than the didactic one he presumed they expected.

The examples of Ms. Goldstein and Mr. Nash offer a glimpse of how, even in a constrained, highly structured, and politically sensitive setting like a school committee meeting or a parents' forum, school administrators can explore ways to open the process. In so doing, administrators may be able to shift the kind of learning possible from solely the transmission of information to developing a deeper pedagogical understanding and an appreciation for what is involved in the task of learning.

Both Ms. Goldstein and Mr. Nash tried in different ways to help their stakeholders understand the work of teaching and learning differently and to shift the relationship they had with them. Ms. Goldstein opened the door for the school committee to experience what it was like to do mathematics as the students in their district were doing it. For the few minutes when they were all engaged in doing mathematics together, the relationship between the school committee and the central staff shifted from the more typically adversarial one to one of collaborative learners. Again, as Ms. Goldstein described the committee's reaction to being told they would do math, "they laughed. They loved this. They absolutely loved this."

Mr. Nash, while knowingly resorting to a more didactic approach, hoped to help the parents who attended the forum think about learning and teaching from a different perspective. He was very focused on the need to shift the adversarial stance he saw embedded in the dichotomous thinking present in so many school policy debates. Unlike Dr. Garfield, who seemed much more concerned with limiting dialogue and the possibility of open-ended conversation, Mr. Nash was interested in shifting the dialogue and changing the discourse so that more reflection and learning could be possible.

From these stories of administrators' work with stakeholders, we can begin to understand how their own beliefs about learning and teaching influence the kinds of openings and possibilities for learning that they see—or carve out—in more public settings. While working with stakeholders such as parents or the school committee may be more politically sensitive than working with teachers, administrators need to recognize how effective political practice itself may require what Mr. Nash had referred to as "open, honest dialogue."

How Principals' Knowledge of Mathematics Learning and Teaching Affects How They Build a Sense of Community in Their Schools

THERE IS INCREASING concern among both those who think carefully about the nature of school administration and those who think about instructional improvement that administrators need to focus their attention on the improvement of teaching and learning more than they often do. These observers note that over the decades the functions of teaching and administration have grown increasingly specialized and less and less interconnected, with teachers, department heads, teacher leaders, and district-level curriculum coordinators focusing primarily on instructional issues and those in the "administrative track" (assistant principals, principals, assistant superintendents, superintendents) focusing more on management issues (Fink & Resnick, 2001; Prestine & Nelson, 2003).

This split between instruction and administration has long been problematic; in viewing the school in quite different ways, the "administrative" and "academic" tracks often focus on different goals and may work in parallel rather than in interaction, not always to the school's advantage. To redress this situation, there are many calls for people in the administrative track to become instructional leaders, focusing more on learning and teaching than they have in the past (Elmore, 2000; Fink & Resnick, 2001; Murphy, 1999; Resnick & Hall, 1998). Prestine and Nelson (2003) go so far as to propose that how we think about learning and teaching should drive how we think about school administration, rather than the reverse:

If the valued activity of school organizations is teaching and learning then it is from this that all else should follow, including the defining of leading, and interactions among adults. In other words, we may now need to start from a learning theory in designing school organizations and constructing conceptions of leadership [rather than starting] from organizational structures and leadership/management techniques. (p. 34)

One solution to the split between instruction and administration proposed by some reformers is the *communities of practice* perspective (sometimes called *learning communities*), in which the school is viewed as a community that centers around learning about teaching and learning, though individual members' responsibilities may entail that they use their knowledge in different ways. Communities of practice is an idea proposed by Lave and Wenger (1991) and Wenger (1998) in which "people who share a concern, a set of problems, or a passion about a topic deepen their knowledge and expertise in this area by interacting on an ongoing basis" (Wenger, McDermott, & Snyder, 2002, p. 4). Communities of practice can occur in a variety of settings—engineering groups in major industries, soccer moms comparing notes on parenting, artists in cafés sharing painting techniques. Over time members of a community of practice develop "common knowledge, practices, and approaches" and often deep personal relationships (Wenger et al., p. 5). Members of a community of practice learn through increasing engagement in shared practices and through talking together about them. Such a perspective entails viewing learning as not just something that occurs in classrooms, but as something that we all do in many aspects of daily life, which social institutions like schools can take advantage of and foster, to the benefit of the learning that takes place in classrooms.

While the idea of schools as communities of practice is a complex one and its utility for supporting desirable educational outcomes is still being investigated, our work with elementary principals suggests that principals' knowledge of subject matter, in this case mathematics, and their beliefs about how it is learned and should be taught can affect two areas related to the communities of practice perspective: the way principals use their leadership positions to create learning environments for themselves and the teachers in their schools, and the way they, as administrators, become engaged with issues of learning and teaching in their schools. (Although principals' views of learning and teaching in other subjects may also be relevant, for this book we are examining their work only in mathematics, except for the case of Mrs. Sampson in Chapter 7, where we examine her work in the development of literacy as well as mathematics.)

To elaborate, as we examine first how principals' ideas about mathematics instruction affect their practice of instructional leadership, we see in some cases that instructional leaders not only lead—that is, develop a vision for their schools and manage the available array of human and organizational resources to move toward that vision—but also engage in leading that is simultaneously learning. They may arrange for learning experiences for students, teachers, and themselves that simultaneously signal that learning is the school's core practice and illuminate important policy issues around which decisions may need to be made. In Chapter 6 we argue that their beliefs about learning and teaching, in this case in mathematics, affect how they do this.

Second, we have observed that principals' beliefs about the nature of mathematics learning can affect what they believe to be the scope of intervention needed for instructional improvement and the nature of their own role in it. Some of these principals believe the nature of the school's intellectual culture is at issue, as well as the instructional strategies being employed in classrooms. We address this issue in Chapter 7.

LEARNING THROUGH INSTRUCTIONAL LEADERSHIP

M OST OFTEN one thinks of instructional leadership in terms of what administrators *do*. For example, they hire and supervise teachers, monitor the quality of instruction in the school, and communicate with parents and others in the district about the school's academic programs. In addition, instructional leadership requires expertise that informs such action —knowledge of subject matter content, knowledge of pedagogy, knowledge of what good instruction looks like, and knowledge of how to lead. However, in our work with administrators we have found that many engage in their practice as learners as well. They engage in instructional leadership from a stance of inquiry, that is, a stance of curiosity about how children learn, how teachers teach, why certain instructional strategies work the way they do, or why the teachers in their schools have such a variety of ideas about instructional practice. Sometimes such inquiries are motivated by very real, but external, pressures such as the need to improve instruction so that students will score higher on high-stakes tests. At other times, their inquiries are motivated by the principal's genuine curiosity about such issues as how learning happens, or what teachers in their school think about the nature of mathematics instruction, or how children of diverse abilities and backgrounds should be taught. In either case, a stance of inquiry can dramatically affect a leader's own experience of leadership, which tends to become richer and more interesting; his or her relationship with faculty, parents, and others; and the nature of the intellectual culture in the school. Different stances toward inquiry also have implications for the development of a school as a community of practice anchored in learning about teaching and learning. Instructional leaders who are curious about teaching and learning can structure situations and build a school culture in which they learn, in which their teachers learn, and in which all learn together.

In the field of educational administration we encounter the notion of learning in the context of practice largely in the internships and field placements of training programs or in courses in which principals write analytic papers about some aspect of their practice. These occasions are viewed as opportunities to develop knowledge in circumstances very similar to those in which it is intended to be used and to learn how to turn theoretical knowledge into practical, how-to knowledge (Leithwood, Jantzi, Coffin, & Wilson, 1996; Milstein, 1990; Milstein, Bobroff, & Restine, 1991).

Research in administration more generally points to the notion that administrators reflect in and on their practice, "surfacing, criticizing, testing . . . intuitive understanding of experienced phenomena" (Schön, 1984, p. 42). Such learning in and from practice entails allowing oneself to be surprised by some aspect of the situation, framing this surprise as a puzzle to be solved, and conducting on-the-spot experiments into what is happening (Schön, 1988). The planning literature highlights the fact that learning through practice requires both a psychological process of conceptual reframing on the basis of experience (Hummel, 1991; Schön, 1983) and learning in the context of engagement with others (Forester, 1999; Hummel, 1991). From careful listening and engagement with others, one "comes to see that what may have seemed unimportant is important, what may have seemed not feasible may be feasible after all." (Forester, 1999, p. 133). Further, research in planning suggests that administrators at different parts of the organization know and learn different things, by virtue of the very fact that they have different roles and different organizational positions: "Organizational design is also the design of conditions of knowledge" (Hummel, 1991, p. 33). In this view, administrators learning in the context of their practice do so in a situated way; in other words, their learning is influenced by the vantage point that their role provides and what they learn is influenced by the social, cultural, and material characteristics of that situation. (See also the literature on situated cognition, e.g., Lave & Wenger, 1991.)

While the idea of administration as entailing learning through practice has been around for a while, usually such learning and reflection has not been understood to be about subject matter content or learning and teaching, but about administrative practice more generally. This reflects the fact that for many years the source of the knowledge base in educational administration has been the social sciences—management, organizational behavior, organizational culture. However, in this era of changing definitions of instructional leadership, which bring it closer to the teaching and learning process, one must ask if instructional leaders also need to be learning from practice about the learning and teaching of the subjects in their schools, and if so, what such learning would look like and how it would affect their administrative work.

We can get some sense of what administrators' learning in practice about the teaching and learning of school subjects might look like from analyses of contemporary mathematics instruction. Scholars analyzing mathematics instruction argue that in addition to knowing their subject matter, the curriculum, and how children learn the subject, teachers need to know about the act of teaching the particular subject of mathematics. They need to know how to encourage children to express their mathematical ideas and how to interpret the mathematical meaning of what children say. They need to learn how to investigate what students are doing and thinking moment by moment in the classroom (see Ball & Cohen, 1999). Teachers need to learn to use such knowledge to improve their instructional practice, and they need to learn how to operate experimentally in response to students and situations, developing hypotheses about what their students are thinking, and testing those hypotheses by asking the next mathematical question (Simon, 1997). In sum, scholars argue that a stance of inquiry about student thinking and instruction is central to the role of teacher (Ball & Cohen, 1999). Such inquiries into student thinking have been called "practical inquiry" to distinguish them from formal research (Richardson, 1994). Researchers also suggest that, because such knowledge is situated in practice, it must be learned in practice (Feinman-Nemser & Remillard, 1995).

Further, scholars argue, teachers who inquire about children's mathematical thinking and why particular instructional moves on their part are successful, who internalize that knowledge and make it their own, and who believe that they can continue to test their knowledge and learn from their students, are *generative learners* (Franke et al., 1998). They continue as self-propelled learners, for whom good teaching requires continual learning about student thought.

If such subject-specific generative learning might become an integral part of instructional leadership as well, one needs to ask specifically what leaders might learn in the context of their administrative practice and what such instructional leadership might look like. In this chapter we will explore these issues by examining the work of two elementary principals and one assistant superintendent.

In Chapters 1 and 3, we saw how Peter Nash was able to use school faculty meetings as learning contexts to think carefully about what was involved in teaching mathematics in mixed-ability classrooms. There was a way in which he was *inside* these events with the teachers, developing joint understandings. As Tharp (1993) puts it, "Joint activity requires dual input, which in turn allows sharing perspectives and the emergence of shared understanding" (p. 277). In this chapter we examine more closely how Mr. Nash was himself a generative learner. While his own ideas about heterogeneity in mathematics instruction shaped the meetings, he was able to employ his own stance of inquiry to learn both about teachers' thinking and about heterogeneity itself.

Marianne Cowan, whom we met in Chapters 1 and 4, used her administrative practice as a context for learning differently by conducting informal studies of topics in which she was interested. We consider here how, in the course of her project with us on teaching in mixed-ability classrooms, she discovered something quite unexpected about teachers' mathematics teaching, which led her to develop new professional development goals for her staff.

Joseph Garfield, an assistant superintendent whom we met in Chapter 5, told us that his ideas about mathematics, learning, and teaching had changed because of the courses he had taken with us, but he suspected that his administrative practice had not. He decided to experiment with a district-level process—the selection of an elementary mathematics curriculum—to see how his behavior would have to change if he wanted to enact new ideas. By examining Dr. Garfield's learning in this chapter, we identify some of the skills required to conduct one's administrative practice in support of conceptual development for both teachers and administrators.

This chapter shows that, while all these instructional leaders learned about the learning and teaching of mathematics in the context of their work as instructional leaders, there were qualitative differences in what and how they learned.

CONCEPTUAL LEARNING IN ADMINISTRATIVE PRACTICE: PETER NASH

One of the features of Peter Nash's practice as an instructional leader was his commitment to fostering what he called "honest dialogue." Finding ways to shape the dialogue that occurred among his colleagues so that it brought out the complexities of issues important to the school was one of the strategies that he used to have influence in his school and on district policies. For his project with us, Mr. Nash structured three such events. He devoted two 60-minute faculty meetings to discussing the topic of student grouping for mathematics instruction and one 90-minute parents' forum to discussing "Images of Good Teaching." We discussed the first of these in Chapter 3, when we examined how he used an article written by Margaret Riddle to make the particulars of a heterogeneous math class salient to his faculty. We discussed the second in Chapter 1, where we looked at how he was able to use his mathematics knowledge to structure a mathematics exploration as part of a faculty meeting. We discussed the third in Chapter 5, where we talked about how instructional leaders communicate with outside stakeholders. Here we will examine how and what Mr. Nash himself learned through discussing Riddle's article.

In brief, Riddle believed that high school "math stars," who were successful at solving math problems quickly, were best served in heterogeneous classes where they could work together with students who were working through mathematics problems more concretely, perhaps using methods different from the standard algorithm. In working with students who were not depending on standard algorithms, the "math stars" had to slow down and try to understand what it was, conceptually, that the other student was doing. In so doing, they often discovered conceptual depths to the mathematics that they had not considered before.

An Episode from Administrative Practice

In preparation for the faculty meeting, Mr. Nash distributed the article with a memo that described the upcoming session and provided some questions to guide teachers' reading of it. He organized the questions into three sets, as follows:

- What are Riddle's underlying assumptions—that appear either explicitly or implicitly in her text—about why "stars" and "less able" students are best served by working with each other rather than separately? Which of the experiences Riddle reports appear to confirm her assumptions?
- According to Riddle, what are the mathematical "strengths" that are often not evident in math "stars?" What are the competencies she appears most interested in developing in her students?
- How would you characterize the teaching practices that Riddle promotes for heterogeneous math classrooms? What knowledge and know-how are essential for someone to teach the way that Riddle teaches?

Embedded in these questions are a number of Mr. Nash's own thoughts about good teaching and what well-run heterogeneous classrooms entail, as he described them to us in an interview. The first set of questions draws attention to what underlies the assumption that it is a good idea to have students of mixed abilities work together. The second set questions the criteria that are generally used to identify "math stars" and how such criteria might mask what such students do and do not know. And, in the third set of questions, Mr. Nash marks the idea that a teacher needs to have certain skills and knowledge to be able to teach heterogeneous classes well.

In his introductory remarks at the faculty meeting he stressed the most immediate questions that they faced as a faculty. As he recapitulated in an interview later,

> My first point was that as a school system, we . . . have begun a review [of potential mathematics curricula]. And as part of that

review we inevitably are going to face questions, lots of questions. . . .
One category of questions has to do with the topics that are related
to [the Riddle] article . . . which is how we challenge advanced
students, whether we do that by having separate groups, whether we
retain the current practice of third, fourth, and fifth grade . . . switch-
ing classes, or whether we change that practice. . . . We need to be
prepared to answer [such questions] in careful and thoughtful ways,
both from the point of view of how we talk with ourselves, with
other faculty at other schools, as well as with the community, parents, and so on. . . . Like just about anything else, it's very easy to
reduce this to oversimplified slogans and answers, and so we've got
to see that it's complicated and think it through.

He acknowledged that everyone tended to "attach [themselves] to a particular system of beliefs" about these issues but said that he wanted the teachers
to use the faculty meeting time to engage in careful dialogue among themselves.
He saw a need for all of them, himself included, to "prepare . . . to talk in a
public way—to talk with parents and other faculty at other levels." He believed that such politically charged issues could be dealt with in part by engaging in thoughtful and reflective discussion about the underlying assumptions
of different positions.

In the faculty meeting, teachers wrote individually for 5 minutes in response to the posted questions and then discussed their writing with each other
in small groups. Then, thinking of themselves as Riddle's "critical friends,"
they talked in their groups about two questions: (1) What was a principle of
good teaching that you saw evident in what Riddle was doing? and (2) What
would you want to know more about—something that didn't ring true, based
on your experience, or for which the evidence Riddle gave was not sufficient?
Finally, teachers had a whole-group discussion of these two questions.

For the first question, the principles of good teaching that teachers identified included the following:

- She validated and verbalized the strengths of the children of different
  abilities.
- She was highly thoughtful and reflective about the individual growth
  of each student and her ability to deepen their conceptual understanding.
- She made thoughtful connections. She knew her students; she knew
  her students' abilities.
- She very gently led her students to a deeper conceptual understanding of mathematics through careful questioning, observation, and
  listening.

In answer to the second question, teachers were curious about the following issues:

- How do you tease out what is the product of really thoughtful teaching and how much depends on the grouping practice? In other words . . . how much of [getting kids to have a deeper understanding of math] has to do with just being a good math teacher, versus how much is related to how you group students?
- How do you deal with both the stars and the weaker students? How do you address the pace of students?
- Were the examples that she had given [in the paper] . . . typical responses in a heterogeneous group? Or [were they] more of an ideal?
- How [did] Nate [the math star] [become] stimulated by Brian's thinking?
- Just what was her math goal? Was it really to bring kids to higher levels of math? Or was it to help them to [be] rounded math people?

Analysis

Peter Nash told us that he had three purposes for this faculty meeting: for the teachers to have an opportunity to develop their thinking about heterogeneous grouping in math classes, for the teachers to have the opportunity to develop ideas and language for communicating about this with parents and others, and for Mr. Nash himself to learn more about the teachers' thinking about heterogeneous grouping in math class. Mr. Nash said that he needed to learn from this first faculty meeting in order to design the second meeting:

> I felt that I just need to think of this session as time to hear them, listen to them talk about the topic, something related to the topic, and to get them to generate some ideas. Now I have something to work with.

In addition to learning about the teachers' thinking, in talking with us later about the teachers' questions Mr. Nash also seemed to be grappling with his *own* questions about what makes for good teaching in a heterogeneous classroom. He commented that he thought that the last question that teachers wanted to ask Riddle—"What is her math goal?"—opened up a new issue for him to think about because, as he said,

> I think it really tells me what would make it difficult for somebody to accept what Riddle is doing. . . . That is, that [the decisions about

grouping students] are all practical decisions. They are decisions that
you just make in practice. And where is . . . [the teacher's] . . .
compass as far as what they see as their really main goal as a math
teacher?

This last question allowed Mr. Nash to see, as he may not have before,
that disagreement about goals might be just cause for rejecting the practical
decisions that Riddle had made in her mixed-ability math class. Conversely,
teachers' questions about instructional practice might also indicate a disagreement about goals. This, he said, was "an interesting thing to work with."
He began to think aloud that part of his teachers' examination of grouping
practices in mathematics instruction might productively include examination
of the question about goals, which would allow teachers to examine what
was motivating their teaching and what their own intentions were for teaching mathematics, and he noted, "we can have reasonable disagreements about
that."

Mr. Nash's approach to structuring this faculty meeting was open-ended
and adaptable. While he set out a very structured set of questions for the
teachers to think about, there was ample opportunity for the teachers to
develop their own thinking and improvisational opportunities for Mr. Nash
to gather information about what his teachers knew. He seemed to grasp
the idea that teaching involves being responsive in the moment and that learning can happen in both directions. As his teachers gained a deeper appreciation of the complexity of heterogeneous classrooms, they helped him learn
more about both the idea of heterogeneity and how they thought about it.

CONDUCTING STUDIES AS A WAY TO LEARN FROM PRACTICE: MARIANNE COWAN

We now turn to Marianne Cowan, whose way of learning in and from her
administrative practice was more individual and less focused on collective
learning. In Chapter 1 we examined how Mrs. Cowan's knowledge of mathematics served her in understanding what was happening in a math class that
she observed, and in Chapter 4 we discussed how she used scripts as tools
for classroom observation and teacher supervision. In this chapter we explore an episode that illustrates how she learned what her teachers understood the idea of mathematical exploration to mean.

Throughout her career as an elementary principal Mrs. Cowan had
regularly conducted what she called "studies" of puzzling issues that were
important to her school. During the year we worked with her, she was conducting a study on bilingual education and in her work with us was turn-

ing her attention to exploring how teachers could adapt their mathematics teaching to reach all students in a heterogeneous classroom. These informal studies were integrated into her daily administrative practice—talking with teachers and students, observing in classrooms, and continually reworking her observing and interviewing skills and tools. The episode we explore here shows her grappling with how to ask teachers questions about mathematical exploration in their classrooms.

An Episode from Administrative Practice

Mrs. Cowan had a lifelong concern for equity in instruction and was interested in exploring for her project with us how teachers could reach "students who were struggling, who were at grade level, above grade level, and well above grade level in mathematics." She proposed to conduct observations of one or two teachers at each grade level, holding a preobservation conference, doing an observation of a mathematics lesson, and holding a postobservation conference with each teacher. She chose classes that had special needs students, regular students, and gifted students to ensure that heterogeneity would be an issue. She planned to focus on the heterogeneous composition of the class and the ways in which the teacher modified instruction to match the needs of all students. She expected that the postobservation conference with each teacher would be about the differentiation of instruction that was or was not present during the observed lesson. She also wanted to learn how to ask open-ended questions of teachers that would help them reflect on the differentiation of instruction in their classrooms.

Shortly into the project, however, her work with teachers took an unanticipated turn and became an exploration of how her teachers understood the very nature of mathematics learning and teaching. This took the form of an extended inquiry into how teachers understood the nature and role of mathematical exploration in mathematics learning.

Following her standard practice of giving a questionnaire to the teacher before the preobservation conference, Mrs. Cowan developed a special questionnaire (Figure 6.1) for this project. She used the questionnaire to signal the areas that she wanted the teachers to be thinking about. In her view questioning was at the heart of supporting teachers' learning:

> Teachers need to reflect on what they are doing and then take the risk of changing. Good questions prompt such reflection.

Initially, Mrs. Cowan did not include a question about mathematical exploration. However, after observing the first class for the project—a first-grade lesson introducing subtraction—Mrs. Cowan commented that she felt

Figure 6.1. The First Draft of Mrs. Cowan's Questionnaire

Math Project
Preobservation Conference
(Draft: January, 2000)

Teacher's Name: Date:

Grade Taught:

- What is the objective of this math lesson?
- Describe the math levels that are found in your class, including below level, at level, above level, and well above level.
- What has preceded this lesson that prepares the students for this lesson?
- Describe the lesson that will be observed. If it is a Mathland* lesson, what changes/adjustments/modifications, if any, have been made to match the learning needs of the students in your class?
- What will follow this lesson to reinforce the math objective?
- How will you assess student learning? What specifics will influence future lessons?
- Is there anything else you want to share? Is there any teaching strategy, student behaviors, or any kind of data you would like collected during the observation?

---

* Mathland was the name of the curriculum in use at the Clinton school.

the teacher prescribed the intellectual structure of the work too much and did not encourage students to explore the ideas or represent them in their own ways. The teacher first had the students enact a subtraction problem by having six of them sit in chairs as if they were on a bus and had two or three of them "get off." The class then figured out together how many students were left on the "bus." The teacher then gave students work sheets with pictures of vehicles on them. Using counting bears and working in pairs, they were to start with a total of 10 people, choose a number less than 10 to represent how many got off each vehicle at a certain point, and then were to figure out how many would be left on the vehicle. They were then to make horizontal number sentences of the subtraction problems they generated. There was no subsequent whole-group discussion of this work.

While this lesson had the advantage of giving children the opportunity to develop and work through their own subtraction problems within the scenario defined by the teacher, Mrs. Cowan saw it as lacking sufficient opportunity for the students to explore mathematical ideas. She told us that she thought this lesson had been too intellectually controlled by the teacher. This observation made her realize that there was no question on her questionnaire that addressed the importance of mathematical exploration:

> I want a question that talks to the exploratory. . . . How were the children empowered? Somehow, it wasn't just that they could get their own slate and go to their own spot. But how were they intellectually empowered?

Because she did not see mathematical exploration, as she understood it, in her first observation and wanted to open up an opportunity to discuss mathematical exploration in subsequent observations, Mrs. Cowan decided to add the following question to her questionnaire:

> What opportunities for math exploration will you provide during this lesson?

She used this question in the next two observations but was dissatisfied when she discovered that the teachers didn't seem to understand the question. For the final observation in this project, she modified it to read as follows:

> What opportunities are provided for students to explore ("play with," "mess around with") mathematical thinking/ideas/concepts during this lesson?

Mrs. Cowan's struggles with this question on her questionnaire took place over several months and reveal what she was discovering about the teachers' thoughts about mathematical exploration. For example, before observing a first-grade lesson in which the students were to use small tiles to explore the relationship between tens and ones, she asked the teacher the first version of the question. The teacher responded, "Children will be working with manipulatives. They will be working in pairs." It suggested to Mrs. Cowan that the teacher interpreted the term *math exploration* to mean "using manipulatives." When Mrs. Cowan pressed further, asking the teacher what the children would actually be doing, searching for where the children would have intellectual latitude and flexibility, she discovered that the children would have flexibility only in the way they recorded the numbers on their work sheets. When she asked if the children had actually explored the mathematical relationship between ones and tens using tiles in previous lessons, the teacher could not remember and said she "didn't have an answer for that." Mrs. Cowan later concluded that this teacher had not understood what she meant by the term *mathematical exploration,* saying,

> It didn't sound like [the teacher] really understood the depth of that question. [It] was more like [she thought] you're moving things around so you're exploring. But what is the mathematical thinking that goes behind what it is that you're doing? That was the next layer that I wasn't sure she understood.

On the basis of this discussion Mrs. Cowan resolved to modify her question:

> I think I need to rework [the question] further. . . . I think I need to be more specific about exploring math ideas or something, because "exploration" apparently can equate [to] manipulatives and that wasn't . . . my intent. It can be bigger than that. . . . I think it's good to have a question that gets at that among my questions, but I'm not sure that this [version] is the best.

> She, herself, was clear that there was a relationship between a manipulative and the idea it represented:

> Messing around, both with the manipulatives and with the ideas, go together. They're not the same thing, but they're related. There's a partnership there.

Mrs. Cowan saw "messing around" with manipulatives as a context for children to test their hypotheses about mathematical ideas. She described this while talking about the fraction fringe manipulative, previously discussed in Chapter 1. She said,

> Let's take the case of the fraction fringe. Let's say [the students wanted to compare] a half and . . . two quarters. They could put them next to each other. They could lay them on top of each other. . . . [The children] are testing what their hypothesis is. Half is the same as two quarters. . . . They can test it. They can take . . . the two quarters and they can put them on top of each other and they prove it to themselves. It's like they test the hypothesis.

While for Mrs. Cowan mathematical exploration seemed to be the process of "messing around" with a manipulative in order to test a hypothesis about a mathematical idea, it was never entirely clear how wide a range of activities in a classroom she would count as mathematical exploration. We do not know, for example, whether Mrs. Cowan would have believed that mathematical exploration could happen in contexts that did not involve manipulatives, such as through classroom discourse or paper and pencil tasks, or how she would determine if mathematical exploration was happening. However, Mrs. Cowan was very clear that she wanted mathematics classrooms at her school to provide students with sufficient intellectual flexibility and latitude that they could test hypotheses involving their own mathematical ideas. In fact, as was apparent in many of our discussions with her, mathematical exploration as the testing of mathematical hypotheses was quite central to Mrs. Cowan's view of mathematics teaching and learning. For her, it was the process by which children individually built meaning for mathematical ideas.

In the end, Mrs. Cowan was quite concerned by her discovery that many of her teachers apparently did not understand that mathematical exploration involved the exploration of mathematical ideas. She saw a difference between them and teachers at her previous school who used the mathematics curriculum *Investigations in Number, Data, and Space* (Russell & Tierney, 1998), which emphasizes mathematical exploration:

> I would bet my boots that there's not one teacher who has been trained in [*Investigations in Number, Data, and Space*] . . . that wouldn't understand that question [about mathematical exploration]. . . . So it's my audience that has changed and I'm trying to figure out how to connect, but it also shows me that there's a lot of work to be done. . . . That's what I was worried about when I [realized that I] needed to add the question [to the questionnaire].

As successive teachers did not understand what she meant by her question even as she refined it, Mrs. Cowan became more and more convinced that there was a professional development task ahead. She told us that she planned to talk with the school's curriculum specialist to see if she could do some work with the teachers on the nature of mathematical exploration and its role in children's learning.

Analysis

We see in this episode how Marianne Cowan engaged in practical inquiry or reflection-in-action in her practice, much as Schön (1988) describes it. She was initially surprised when one teacher did not seem to understand what was meant by the term *mathematical exploration* and went through a series of experiments, wording and rewording a question on the questionnaire, in an attempt to figure out if the teachers she was observing understood the role of mathematical exploration in mathematics learning. She examined the possibility that she simply hadn't worded the question well but, in the end, concluded that her initial concern was well-founded. Most of the teachers at her school did, indeed, need to learn about how the exploration of mathematical ideas serves children's learning.

Her learning was situated in the context of classroom observation and teacher supervision, available to her by virtue of her position as principal. She was able to explore first how teachers were adapting instruction for students of different abilities and then whether or not teachers understood the idea of mathematical exploration. She was open to the quite unexpected turn in her inquiry and subsequently spent considerable energy trying to figure out what teachers understood and didn't understand about children's mathematical learning. Her mathematics knowledge and her beliefs about how children's mathematical understanding develops positioned her to perceive a gap in what her teachers knew and how this affected what they could do in their classrooms.

This learning opportunity, however, was also constrained by Mrs. Cowan's ethical sense of how to conduct postobservation conferences. She believed strongly that in postobservation conferences with teachers she should not ask questions that had not been prefigured in the preobservation questionnaire and this conviction both structured her inquiry and placed constraints on what she could learn from observation conferences. She believed that teachers should know before the observation what she would be attending to; if she noticed something unanticipated she should not bring it up spontaneously, but add it to her questionnaire for the next time.

> If I put [an idea] on the table as a prequestion, then I felt comfortable coming back to it as a postquestion, but if I didn't include it in the preliminary conversation, it was almost like . . . I was introducing something after the fact. . . . So that I could ask the question, observe the lesson, and then come back to the question . . . instead of having it be open season on anything [I] wanted to talk about.

This commitment made it difficult for Mrs. Cowan to inquire spontaneously about something she noticed in a teacher's practice, or explore in an open-ended way what a teacher might understand about teaching and learning. And it constrained what she could learn. As she said near the end of the project, "I'm still trying to find out what the teachers here . . . think that mathematical thinking is."

Mrs. Cowan's highly structured inquiry was one in which she and the teachers learned from a succession of individual interchanges. However, she told us that she hoped that she and the teachers could have conversations "more like partners" rather than as supervisor and supervisee in their postobservation conferences. Given her hopes, a next step for her might be to design more collective learning experiences about the role of mathematical exploration for herself and her teachers, thereby building a community of learners centered around exploring mathematics learning and teaching.

The shift from learning through practice as an individual process, toward learning through practice by creating a community of learners, is subtle but important. The latter puts collective inquiry at the center of faculty and administrative attention. In turn, collective learning requires that the administrator develop norms for reflection, skills of questioning, and the ability to view his own knowledge as provisional, as always susceptible to revision. We get a glimpse of how such skills can be developed from the case of Dr. Garfield, which we will examine next.

TRANSFORMING AN ADMINISTRATIVE PROCESS INTO A CONTEXT FOR CONCEPTUAL LEARNING: JOSEPH GARFIELD

Joseph Garfield had been assistant superintendent of curriculum and instruction in the Avon School District for 8 years when he participated in our mathematics seminars for administrators. Shortly after Dr. Garfield completed the seminar, it was time for his district to select a new curriculum in elementary mathematics, and it was his responsibility to direct the selection process. Based on his experience in the math seminar, Dr. Garfield told us that he rejected as no longer appropriate his district's standard procedure for curriculum selection, which consisted of evaluating candidate curricula against a checklist of criteria (e.g., coverage of a list of mathematical topics or ease of use), rating each curriculum against the criteria on a scale of 1 to 5, and calculating the numerical result. He said he was willing to sacrifice the efficiency and apparent objectivity of such a procedure in exchange for a process that would assess candidate curricula on the dimensions that mattered for mathematics learning and teaching as he now saw them. From his point of view the issue now was how a candidate curriculum supported students in their efforts to build mathematical ideas in their minds:

> I think the shorthand of it would be to move the school system in a way in which we would be known as a school system whose children were mathematical thinkers as opposed to arithmetic practitioners. ... And the vision was really teachers thinking with [students] about mathematics.

The practical challenges of curriculum selection were still salient for Dr. Garfield:

> I can become very concerned with the ease of operation [of the materials in the classroom], because the phone calls that I will get will be about operation, and [about] not having enough of this or not having enough time to do that.

But in the curriculum selection process this time, Dr. Garfield wanted to strike a different balance between consideration of practical issues and consideration of educational ones.

Further, he said that he explicitly wanted to learn how to transform a standard administrative process like curriculum selection, which he saw as practical and political, into a process in which all participants would be learners. He wanted to use the process of curriculum selection as an opportunity to create a community of teachers and parents who examined the ideas about mathematics, teaching, and learning that were embedded in the several relevant standards and frameworks documents and debated about what it meant for students to be mathematical thinkers. He expressed his intent clearly:

> What I wanted to learn was how to take the process that is generally considered high risk and political, that is, choosing a textbook, ... and make it be one that is also a learning experience for me and for the teachers [and parents on the committee].

He recognized that teachers and other administrators in his district tended to interpret the state mathematics frameworks, which drew from constructivist learning theories, through the familiar "transmission" lens on learning. They failed to appreciate how the frameworks represented an altogether different set of "conceptual" lenses on learning that would require reconceptualization of many district practices. (This is a phenomenon also reported by Spillane, 2004, in a large study of school leaders in Michigan.) Dr. Garfield described the current situation this way:

> People are taking "guiding principles," "strands," "concepts" [from the state frameworks] ... and saying, "Well, they will work" or

"They won't work," [and] "They're good" or "They're not good," because of how they shape up in terms of the prevailing view [of mathematics education]. There's no consciousness about taking what we [currently] do and comparing it to the frameworks' [different frame of reference.].

Dr. Garfield began to imagine a new role that he needed to play, namely, helping other school staff examine their assumptions about mathematics learning and teaching, so that working with the frameworks could become an opportunity for transforming the basic premises about mathematics learning and teaching that underlay schooling in his district. This new role, he decided, could develop as he engaged in the process of elementary mathematics curriculum selection.

An Episode from Administrative Practice

Dr. Garfield was responsible for designing the curriculum selection process, establishing the membership of the selection committee, chairing or facilitating the meetings of the curriculum selection committee, recommending to the School Committee the final choice, and implementing the decision over the coming years. We worked with him to design a "consultancy" through which we could scaffold the learning that he wanted to do, providing just enough help so that he could do most of what needed to be done by himself and later do it independently. Analogous to classroom visitations with teachers, the consultancy allowed Dr. Garfield and project staff to examine together the conceptual underpinnings of this aspect of his current administrative practice and provided help for him in looking at daily tasks through new conceptual lenses, reflecting on what he saw, and considering how he might act in light of new insights.

In the 6-month process that followed, we learned from Dr. Garfield's experience that, for him, the development of new ideas about mathematics, learning, and teaching and new practices of instructional leadership were intertwined. Dr. Garfield determined that one of his first tasks would be to develop a set of questions to guide the selection process. He felt that these questions needed to keep committee members focused on a vision of a school system in which children are mathematical thinkers and draw less attention to issues solely about materials management and ease of operation. Dr. Garfield developed these questions himself, by consulting the *Curriculum and Evaluation Standards for School Mathematics* of the National Council of Teachers of Mathematics (1989) and the state's mathematics standards, and with some discussion with us about the kind of ideas it would be important to highlight. The questions that Dr. Garfield developed are presented in Figure 6.2. These questions focused on the mathematical ideas presented in the curriculum, how these ideas were developed over the course of the elementary grades, the ways in which students would encounter and work with these ideas, the kind of professional development that teachers would need, and the resources provided for parents to support their children's learning. In general, they did not probe whether particular topics were present in the curriculum, but rather how they were developed. That is, they focused on the kinds of mathematical thinking that each candidate curriculum would make possible for students. For Dr. Garfield, these questions were central to the committee's deliberative process, and developing the questions had an important effect on his own behavior:

> The exercise of forming those questions . . . gave me the courage, . . . the willingness . . . in each session to say to the [members of the committee] not so much "What does this [mathematical] exercise do?" or "What does this unit do?" but "What kinds of thinkers will this create?"

Centering the discussion on the kind of mathematical thinkers students would be if they were taught from each candidate curriculum allowed Dr. Garfield to stay focused on the central intellectual issues that needed to be addressed and not get deflected by peripheral issues:

> For me the initial experience [of forming the questions] was truly instructive in terms of coming to what I thought of as the essence of the core . . . issues here. I never felt that I got distracted by the [committee members'] interest in the management stuff. I knew at various points that politically I had to worry about that, but . . . that's not how I got channeled . . . because I had a stronger, more powerful idea of mathematics education being central to kids' thinking. . . . "How would the child's math education be different as a result of this program?" That [question] seemed to provoke some pretty interesting responses from [the selection committee].

The analysis of each curriculum afforded by Dr. Garfield's set of questions provided committee members with the opportunity to think about the nature of learning and teaching in mathematics, as well as selecting a text.

Project staff met with Dr. Garfield after every committee meeting and asked him questions about what he had observed at different points in the meeting, what he had intended when he made particular leadership moves, and what he thought might happen if he had made different moves. These questions were designed to prompt Dr. Garfield's reflection about his practice

Figure 6.2. Dr. Garfield's Questions to Guide Elementary Mathematics Curriculum and Selection

---

Questions asked of every candidate curriculum:

General Learning Issues

1. To what extent does the program set high expectations for students?
2. How does the program help students to learn through a variety of strategies and approaches?
3. To what extent does the program foster learning that is based on (a) inquiry? (b) problem solving? (c) application of key issues and concepts?
4. How does the program point to connections between mathematics topics and across the disciplines to other subjects?
5. How does this program support all learners at all levels?
6. How does this program broaden understanding of mathematics in (a) a cultural context? (b) our culture? (c) other cultures?
7. In which ways does the program foster mathematical thinking through technology (calculators and computers)?
8. To what extent is student mathematical discussion and interaction fostered in the classroom? Is discussion essential to learning or is it an added activity?
9. What kinds of teacher mathematical communication and student-teacher interaction are fostered in the classroom?
10. To what extent is writing about mathematics fostered?

Implementation

1. How does this program assist the teacher to understand and manage all of its components?
2. What information is sent home to parents about children's learning?
3. How does the program foster students' application of mathematics learning (a) at home? (b) on their own? (c) with their parents?
4. What transitions from current practice will our staff need to make to teach this program?
5. What kinds of in-service plan would this program require to insure successful implementation?
6. How should the program be introduced? Which grades? In which order?
7. What communication to parents is available to explain this program?

Assessment

1. What assessment practices are used? Are they consistent with instructional practices?
2. To what extent does the program help students understand for themselves what they know and don't know?
3. To what extent does the program offer a comprehensive approach to assessment? (i.e., providing any perspectives to understand students' progress?)

(continued)

Figure 6.2. *(cont'd)*

Summary

1. Is the overall program structure for the understanding of mathematics (a) linear (self-contained lesson after lesson)? (b) a widening spiral of topics? (c) in-depth exploration of topics over time? (d) themes or big questions? (e) other?
2. To what extent does this program offer a complete or comprehensive mathematics education for our students?
3. To what extent does this program prepare K–6 students for mathematics in Grades 7–12?
4. How would our students' mathematics education be different as a consequence of adopting this program?

Number Sense and Numeration

1. How does the program develop understanding of the numeration system (counting, grouping, regrouping, place value)?
2. How does the program develop understanding of the numeration system? ($+, -, \times, \div$)
3. How does the program develop understanding of fractions, mixed numbers, decimals, percents, integers, and rational numbers?
4. How does the program model, explain, and develop understanding of basic facts and algorithms?
5. How does the program build understanding of the representation of numerical relationships on graphs?
6. How does the program give practice in selection and use of appropriate methods for computing: mental arithmetic, paper and pencil, manipulative, calculator, computer, other?
7. How does the program teach estimation to check the reasonableness of results?

Patterns and Relationships

1. To what extent does the program use patterns, variables, open sentences, number sentences, and relationships to explore mathematics?
2. How does the program use tables, graphs, rules, and equations to represent situations and to solve and model problems?
3. How does the program develop understanding of the solving of linear equations, using concrete, informal, and formal methods?

Geometry and Measurement

1. How does the program develop understanding of how to describe, model, compare, and classify shapes?
2. How does the program use the process of measuring and concepts related to units of measurement?
3. How does the program demonstrate understanding of perimeter, area, volume, and angle?

Statistics and Probability

1. How does the program provide experiences in collecting, organizing, describing, and interpreting displays of data?
2. How does the program teach students to make inferences and construct arguments based on data analysis?

in the meeting, calling into question some automatic aspects of his practice that might not encourage conceptual change on the part of committee members and inviting his reflection about other moves that might be more effective.

Our data suggests that over the course of 6 months, Dr. Garfield transformed the curriculum selection committee from a group of individuals implementing a rather procedural, checklist selection process, into a community in which substantive ideas about mathematics education could be explored. This required two significant changes in his practice: first, to value a new intellectual level for the discourse, signaled through the new discussion questions; and second, to cultivate discourse practices that would help teachers and other participants learn how to engage in such conversation. As part of the first change, early in the process he offered the following directions to committee members:

> The heart of your discussion is to say at the end of K–12 with this series, "What would a child think math is, geometry is, be ready to do probability and statistics? As a mathematics learning experience, what does this do for a child's intellectual development?" That's the question you need to be addressing. . . . You're not supposed to talk about the [physical] quality of the materials now. I'm asking you to say, "What would a child think about the base 10 [number] system as a result of this experience?" . . . That's the level of discussion I want you to be having.

In the early sessions, Dr. Garfield kept reminding committee members that they were doing something new. For example, interrupting a small-group discussion, he advised: "The small groups are to talk about the math, not the organization of the text as a whole. That's for later in the whole-group discussion." But as the weeks proceeded, the committee settled into using the guiding questions and the vision of children as mathematical thinkers to structure their assessment of candidate curricula. Dr. Garfield made occasional summary and interpretive remarks to keep the discussion process on course, such as "So our concerns are around all children" and "How does this series ask students to think differently?" Generally, however, his role and behavior had shifted away from advisor, coach, or lecturer and more toward facilitator. He finished the consultancy in the firm belief that his goal of changing the focus of the selection process had been accomplished.

The second shift in Dr. Garfield's practice was a change in the discourse pattern in the committee itself, from one in which he directed the turn taking in the discussion to one in which any member could comment on an idea that had been put forward. When asked, he said that directing the discussion had been his old style of teaching:

> It definitely was an old way of teaching. Yes. And the way I would explain it is this: that the old way of teaching was the students as totally unrelated individuals relating to me. As opposed to my being there in order to let the students relate to each other. To create a way for them to relate to each other.

He went on to explain that he had always wanted his students (and, in this case, the teachers and parents on the committee) to feel safe and affirmed. He worked with project staff to create a process and context in which the members of the committee could talk directly to each other and through which their ideas could be listened to and built upon by others with profoundly affirming effects. He described the differences in approach:

> I hadn't actually thought of the [committee members] wanting to relate to each other ... or their wanting to build on each other's ideas. My orientation is to reward people for their ideas, to congratulate them, thank them, and be warm. As opposed to the school of thought that says, it's about ideas, and we can still be affirming and supportive, but let's put the ideas on the table. . . . What you showed me was that people feel really affirmed and validated and rewarded when their idea goes someplace. . . . It's really a huge sense of accomplishment if your idea has led to another idea. . . . And that was a new idea for me in this sort of environment. Yes it was.

Analysis

Through the modified curriculum selection process, Joseph Garfield learned to focus discussion more on the ideas that were built into each curriculum and less on the practical aspects of using it. He learned how to ask questions that would bring out these ideas, how to listen to the thoughts of the parents and teachers on the committee and help them listen to each other's ideas, and indeed how to make ideas be the center of the discussion. He learned that such attention to ideas could be intrinsically gratifying to members of the committee. He was beginning to do what Peter Nash had done in his faculty meetings, namely, use the administrative function of curriculum selection to provide committee members with opportunities to express their own ideas about mathematics instruction, listen to others' ideas, and think carefully about the assumptions that lay underneath such ideas.

Not only did Dr. Garfield develop new administrative behaviors, reinventing the curriculum selection process as a learning as well as a leading process, but the very act of moving new ideas into practice contributed to his understanding of the ideas themselves. The opportunity to think through ideas about mathematics learning and teaching in the context of curriculum selection provided the opportunity for him to consider the consequences of selecting any particular curriculum—consequences in terms of the amount and kind of learning that teachers would have to do to teach well from these materials, the nature of teacher professional development that would have to be offered, the issues involved in gaining public approval, and so on. Such thinking about consequences shed new light on the very meaning of the ideas about mathematics learning and teaching that were embedded in curricula. In an interview at the end of the study, Dr. Garfield said,

> I got to know [these new ideas about mathematics education] in a new way, by having to put something on the line. It wasn't just talking about it to [someone]. It wasn't conceptual. It was actually having to make some decisions.

In this sense, practice provides a unique venue for learning.

CONCLUSION

We began this chapter by asking what administrators could learn about mathematics learning and teaching in the context of their work as instructional leaders and how they could learn it. We explored what an administrative practice that included learning might look like and how different stances toward inquiry on the part of the principal would contribute to the development of the school as a community of practice. We considered how administrators might structure their work in order to learn about teaching and learning issues in their schools, and showed how faculty meetings, teacher conferences, and special committees all could be structured to afford opportunities to learn.

Administrators also can use their discussions with teachers to further their own understanding of a topic, as Peter Nash did with his understanding of heterogeneity, and as Joseph Garfield did as he explored with the committee how the candidate curricula offered different images of students as mathematical thinkers.

We also were able to get some glimpses of what administrative practice that is also fundamentally a *learning* practice can look like. Among the many possibilities, we saw that it could take the form of conducting studies, as in the case of Marianne Cowan, who used the practice of classroom observation and teacher supervision to learn how her teachers were thinking about mathematics learning. It could also take the form of creating learning communities among teachers, parents, and administrators, as it did in the cases of Mr. Nash, who used a faculty meeting to explore heterogeneity in math classes, and Dr. Garfield, who used the curriculum selection process to create a collective exploration of what it meant for students to be mathematical thinkers.

We can ask if these glimpses of administrator learning in practice tell us anything about how administrators can do such learning. By examining the work of Dr. Garfield, we were able to identify some of the skills that are needed if administrators are to turn typical administrative functions into conceptual learning opportunities for themselves and their faculties. These include listening, creating norms for listening, question-asking, and fostering collective discourse about ideas. While we do not have independent measures of their mathematics knowledge or their beliefs about what it means to learn and understand mathematics, we can see from their work that these administrators did use specific ideas about mathematics and how it is learned to guide their design of learning environments. While we don't know how nuanced her understanding was, Mrs. Cowan knew enough about mathematical exploration to notice that her teachers seemed not to understand its role in children's learning and to explore how extensive that orientation was among her faculty. Mr. Nash had a clear enough sense of the relationship between different aspects of mathematical thinking (e.g., conceptual understanding, use of concrete representations of ideas, use of numerical representations of ideas, use of calculation procedures) to facilitate a faculty discussion of Riddle's hypotheses about what "math stars" and average math students can gain from working on mathematics together. Dr. Garfield understood that it was important to consider not only *what* topics were covered in a curriculum, but *how* they were covered, to develop guiding questions for curriculum selection that focused on instructional means as well as mathematical topics and to keep the committee's discussion focused on those questions.

Further, all three administrators had beliefs about adult learning (teachers' and their own) that guided the way they conducted their inquiries. Mrs. Cowan saw teachers' learning as involving reflection on practice and therefore designed questionnaires that would present teachers with opportunities to reflect on important aspects of their teaching. Mr. Nash viewed collective reflection as important and designed a faculty meeting to support such reflection on the part of his teachers. In the process of learning how to change the curriculum selection committee from a solely administrative process to one that provided participants with opportunities for conceptual learning, Dr. Garfield's own beliefs about adult learning began to shift. He saw it less as a process that occurred between himself and individual members of the committee and more as a process involving the collective discussion of ideas.

We also can speculate about the implications these administrators' stances toward inquiry might have for the development of their schools as communities of practice anchored in learning about teaching and learning. Mrs. Cowan told us that she wanted her staff to know that she was a learner, that they were all learning together, and that she was trying to structure postobservation conversations as a set of partnerships in which she and the teachers were using the observations as opportunities to learn more about mathematics instruction. We do not know if the teachers felt that sense of partnership, but if Mrs. Cowan were successful in attaining this goal such partnerships could be a significant component of a community of learning in her school. Mr. Nash and Dr. Garfield were focusing on collective learning. Both were engaged with posing questions about mathematics teaching and learning, listening to how teachers and others worked with the ideas embedded in those questions, and making the next move in the discourse on the basis of what they had heard. It appeared that a community of learning existed in both of these contexts. We do not know how typical that was of their administrative practice, but it was one context in which administrators and teachers were participating in a community of practice centered on learning about the learning and teaching of mathematics.

In this chapter we have explored how principals can design administrative processes that also support learning for all in their school communities. We examined how three administrators created opportunities for themselves to be in learning relationships, as well as administrative relationships, with their faculties. Such designs for adult learning are one aspect of creating a community of practice centered around learning about teaching and learning. We explore another aspect of such communities of practice in the next chapter, where we examine how principals' ideas about mathematics learning and teaching affect the nature and depth of their own engagement in this community of ideas.

THE ENGAGED INSTRUCTIONAL LEADER: "I'M IN THIS, TOO"

I N TEN YEARS of working with principals as they deepen their own mathematical knowledge, as they explore how children learn mathematics and how it is best taught, and as they come to understand mathematics instruction differently than they had earlier, we have noticed that some principals also come to believe that their own administrative practice needs to change in subtle ways if instruction that focuses on students' mathematical thinking is to flourish in their schools. That is, some principals come to believe that it is not just *other* people—teachers, the publishers of curricula, the developers of tests, and so on—who need to develop new ideas and practices, but that their own ideas and practices are part of the equation.

To understand how and when this happens, we need to examine how principals' beliefs about learning and teaching mathematics link to their views of their own administrative roles. We have observed that as principals come to understand that elementary mathematics classrooms built on a constructivist view of learning focus on mathematical *thinking* as central to learning and teaching, some draw the corollary that the values, norms, and orientation of the school as a whole need to be such that they support learning and teaching as *thinking* enterprises. Values that support learning and teaching as thinking enterprises include respect for people's (children and teachers) ideas and the hard work that they are engaged in when they struggle to understand how a new idea works; appreciation of the risk that a learner takes in pursuing a new idea; ongoing curiosity about the ideas in a subject and how other people (children or teachers) think about them; appreciation for the length of time that it takes students to work through important new ideas and, similarly, the process teachers go through to work through new instructional ideas and practices; and a sense of the power of a reflective community for supporting and amplifying this work. Over time, some principals come to believe that sustaining high-quality mathematics instruction in their schools would require not just technical changes in teaching technique that individual teachers could make, but also a large change in values, beliefs, and administrative structures and practices that would shift the intellectual culture of their schools to one of collaborative learning and reflective inquiry. These principals conclude that because they are part of the school's culture, they too must hold and enact the values that support thinking.

As we noted in the introduction to Part III, the idea of communities of practice is currently in vogue as a way to think about how people in schools work together. From a communities of practice perspective, "people who share a concern, a set of problems, or a passion about a topic deepen their knowledge and expertise in this area by interacting on an ongoing basis" (Wenger et al., 2002, p. 4). Communities of practice can take many forms and it is not the task of this book to thoroughly analyze this complex topic. However, we argue that principals' understanding of the nature of learning and teaching affects their view of what it would mean for the school to function as a community of practice centered on reflection on learning, and also their sense of their own role in such a community.

In this chapter we look at the work of three principals—Louise Sampson, Rob Bouvier, and Costanza Wilson—who are in different places with respect to their ideas about the nature of mathematics learning and teaching. Where they are in this respect affects their sense of the scope of the task of supporting high-quality mathematics instruction, their beliefs about their own role in the work, and the nature of the reflective community that develops in their schools. One principal is fully engaged with her staff in every aspect of school life; one stands back and lets the teachers engage with the issues; and a third learns over time that her own understanding of the ideas that children and teachers are working with is critical.

DEVELOPING A CULTURE FOR PONDERING: LOUISE SAMPSON

Louise Sampson is a principal who believes that learning and teaching are about thinking and that the work of the principal is to support the development of a culture of thinking in the school. Before becoming a principal, Mrs. Sampson had been a bilingual teacher for several years, had worked with colleagues to develop the district's bilingual program, and then had become coordinator of primary education for the district, a position she held for 15 years. She became the first principal of the Port Arthur School when it was founded in the early 1990s, and we knew her during the first 5 years of the school's history, as it grew to 330 students in Grades K–8. The school reflects the general demographics of this small city in the Northeast—about 33% of the students are on free or reduced-price lunch; the ethnic composition is about 36% African American, 10% Asian American, 11%

Hispanic, and 43% White. Nearly 15% of Port Arthur's students receive special education services.

Mrs. Sampson seems to have encountered many of the ideas that undergird a constructivist view of learning in an intuitive way through experiences she had when she was a young adult. As a high school foreign exchange student in France, Mrs. Sampson was immersed in a culture very different from her own, which she struggled to understand. She vividly remembers what it was like to learn French while living in France and what that experience taught her about the nature of learning language.

> [My ideas about learning] go back to those experiences of making meaning with language when I was growing up. . . . [It] came from being alone as a 16-year-old. Alone in a world where I didn't understand the culture, I didn't know a word in the language, [except] maybe how to say, "Hello. Pleased to meet you." And becoming part of that culture, . . . [part of] a family, and stumbling through the language because I just kept trying. I had no real academic learning [of French]. . . . [Just] that sense of taking a risk to try to make some meaning that would connect with another human being. . . . You'd get the laughter of the incredible bungling thing that you had said, but also the affirmation [that you tried]. . . . That was a very conscious moment.

Mrs. Sampson's memory of learning to speak French while living in France provides a vivid image of the human drive to make meaning in order to connect to other human beings, and the risks that the learner will take in order to make that connection. Mrs. Sampson says that, at that time, she "didn't have labels" for the learning that she was doing, but later in her graduate-level studies of early literacy she encountered constructivist ideas about language learning in more formal garb. Mrs. Sampson was taking courses in literacy and the development of reading at a time when cognitive theories of learning were making their way into that field. She read the work of Frank Smith, a psycholinguist who argues that children develop language by actively constructing rules about how words work, testing hypotheses and thereby making childlike "errors," and then developing more accurate rules (Smith, 1971). She also studied the ideas of Don Holdaway who, following Smith in his insistence that meaning was central to language and literature, argues that the learning of reading and writing are developmental processes, which begin with immersion in an environment in which reading and writing are being used in purposeful and meaningful ways. Children independently and spontaneously experiment with reading and writing and engage in self-regulation, correcting their errors to get closer and closer to accurate behavior. In his view, adults should reinforce even rough approximations of the target behavior, the pace of learning should be determined by the learner, and the environment should be secure and supportive (Holdaway, 1979). While early language learning and second language learning are different from each other in important ways, Mrs. Sampson interpreted such theories of language learning as providing conceptual structure, or "labels," for the experiences she had had while living in France, and viewed that experience itself as providing her with a sense of the inner "feel" of a constructivist view of language learning.

From very early in her career as an educator, then, Mrs. Sampson was aware of the theory that children are inherently the active constructors of their own knowledge, that they see the world through the knowledge structures that they have at any given point in time, and that they continually work with new experiences, trying to fit them into current knowledge structures or change those structures to accommodate them. A corollary to this active view of learning, which Mrs. Sampson said she also adopted, is that such learning requires safe environments, without negative reinforcement.

Episodes from Administrative Practice

Mrs. Sampson told us that she chose to take the principalship of the Port Arthur School as a way to get close to students again. Her focus on children and a family-like community is noticeable immediately on arriving at the Port Arthur School. The first room one passes on entering is called the "Community Room"—a large room with old couches around the walls and rugs on the floor. It looks welcoming. The principal's office is directly across the hall from the Community Room and is unusual because, again, there is an open floor area with a rug. Several students might be playing on the floor there. Her office and the Community Room are part of Mrs. Sampson's explicit efforts to make the school feel safe for learners and are very different from the more typical office, which has no open floor space or rug for playing. Students who are in a principal's office are often those who have been sent there for discipline, and they may sit in a chair silently and alone with sullen or angry looks on their faces. The principal's office at the Port Arthur School, in contrast, is welcoming.

Mrs. Sampson says she has conceptualized the Port Arthur School as a community of people (children, staff, parents, and other community supporters) who think carefully about students, teaching, and learning. She thinks that building a professional community among the adults in the school is critical:

> Professional community . . . teachers working closely together,
> thinking about ideas, asking themselves big questions about all of the

factors that enter into how children learn, and how they teach . . . is really the foundational element of a good school. Without it, I think you might have some wonderful teachers, but . . .

Mrs. Sampson cites Newmann's (1996) book *Authentic Achievement: Restructuring Schools for Intellectual Quality* as a good source for her of ideas about professional community. In that book professional community among teachers is said to include five elements that tend to occur together: clear values and norms, a focus on student learning, reflective dialogue, deprivatization of practice, and collaboration (p. 202). All of these occur at the Port Arthur School.

Mrs. Sampson characterizes the Port Arthur School as having "multiple layers of reflection—you've got kids thinking about what they're doing and you've got us [Mrs. Sampson and the teachers] thinking about how does this make sense in the context of this one person's learning or this class learning, and then there's the whole level of the school as a learning community and that's where the forum [for parents] comes in." We can see Mrs. Sampson's sense of the Port Arthur School as a nested set of reflective communities by looking at her views and actions with regard to learning and teaching in classrooms, the school's governance structures, and the way that parents are involved in school life.

Learning and Teaching. Mrs. Sampson told us that she believes that the essence of teaching is learning—learning about children's thinking and how it develops and observing what works and doesn't work in the classroom. Mrs. Sampson first began to think these ideas through in the context of the whole language movement where, as she understood it, teachers were to be learners about children's work who exercised their judgment about the next instructional move.

> With the whole language movement . . . we really began to take back the profession in little ways. . . . When you start to feel a little power over your day as a teacher, over what you teach, over your relationships with other people, you start to be a learner in a new way. . . . When everything is dished out to you and your expectations are external, you're not a thinker, . . . you're just doing what you were hired to do, which is to dish out somebody else's curriculum. . . .
>
> [As principal] you . . . create a culture, and a soil that's fertile for [teachers] to think, and pretty soon they say, "Those basal readers aren't nearly as good as trade books," and "Writing is such a powerful way for children to understand written words, to become spellers, to become thinkers," and all of a sudden . . . teachers understand

teaching and learning better. . . . Once you get those seeds planted in a school, it works because teachers see kids differently. They see each [mind] as different and they start seeing cultures as different.

In this statement Mrs. Sampson describes what she believes are the advantages of the whole language form of instruction in reading and writing. Of course, there are also critiques of the whole language method, evidence to support phonics-based methods, and evidence to support combinations of whole language and phonics methods that have been shown to contribute substantially to the development of children's reading (cf. Snow, Davis, & Griffon, 1998). Although her view of language learning may not be shared by everyone, Mrs. Sampson's view of the nature of learning and teaching is profoundly and passionately anchored in student thinking. For her, teaching begins by listening to children's ideas and trying to understand the sense that they are expressing. From there, teachers use professional judgment about the next instructional move to make. They ground their teaching on their understanding of their students' thinking, not on the external demands of a curriculum they may be asked to "dish out."

Staff and Governance. In Mrs. Sampson's view, the entire culture of the school needs to be characterized by an orientation toward reflection and inquiry.

A school probably needs to have many different ways in which people can reflect. There needs to be time when you can just be off by yourself, which means that teachers should not think that all the work they do is the contact time with children, [but] that there is time you can get away and write in a journal, take a walk for that matter—the things that we don't give ourselves permission to do. . . . That's reflection and that's very personal. Beyond that, some of the greatest reflection I think happens in company. So what are the structures that you can provide for teams to get together? . . . I really support that each of the grade-level teaching teams gets together.

In addition to encouraging individual reflection, at the Port Arthur School the entire staff—classroom teachers, the librarian, and the physical education teacher—meets together every Tuesday afternoon. This is one of several organizational structures at the school where teachers, individually and collectively, have the opportunity to reflect on how they are working with their students.

Mrs. Sampson also believes that in such a school her own role needs to be different; she is an asker of questions, along with the teachers, rather than a provider of answers. This affects many aspects of school life, among them the Tuesday staff meeting:

> I think part of it is developing a culture within the school [such] that the staff meeting is a place where you can ponder as well as pass out information or solve problems. . . . I think it's the whole culture of the school that needs to somehow be a culture of inquiry. . . . I'm trying to ask questions rather than say, "I've got some answers." . . . I think you have to nurture the process of inquiry every step along the way, too. Just like for kids, you have to model what you believe. And the way the principal can help that process along is to ask inquiring questions, real questions that you want to hear real puzzlings about, and not have a set agenda.

Parental Involvement. Mrs. Sampson told us that she believes it is important to create the Port Arthur School as a place where parents, too, can reflect on the nature of learning and can participate in the school as a learning enterprise. She has created a number of contexts for parent involvement, each designed to support parents' learning as well as their oversight of their child's progress. In addition to having individual conversations with parents about their children, Mrs. Sampson includes parents on the school's governing council and on a set of curriculum advisory committees, and holds regular forums for parents and teachers, as well as informal morning conversations, all focused on central issues of learning and teaching. For example, the school's first parents' forum was in the evening, with a free spaghetti dinner and child care. About a hundred parents and teachers attended, and the driving question was, "How does your child learn?" In her description of that forum, Mrs. Sampson reveals her attention to parents' ideas about learning and what it might take for them to consider a variety of ideas in their thinking about learning:

> We started out just thinking about what it meant to be a learner, and then what it meant to be a learner in the context of this particular school. . . . People asked very challenging questions. . . . They struggled with the whole issue of skill, drill, practice, what it means to be competent. . . . There were a lot of people there who have had a more traditional schooling themselves and wondered how skill emerges in this kind of context. The question, "How does your child learn?" asked us all to dig into what matters to us in our own learning.

Analysis

Louise Sampson's beliefs about learning and how it occurs appear to infuse all aspects of the Port Arthur School. She believes that, in order to learn, both children and adults must be actively thinking about the topic at hand, developing and testing ideas about it in an environment in which it is safe to make the inevitable errors that active learning requires. She has put a number of organizational structures and practices in place to make this kind of learning available for everyone—students, teachers, and parents. And she, herself, is deeply engaged in every level. In this case study we have presented only Mrs. Sampson's view of the Port Arthur School, but independent observations in her school and interviews with teachers confirm that the Port Arthur School is a community centered on thinking about learning and teaching.

AN INSTRUCTIONAL LEADER'S DILEMMA—ACTIVE INVOLVEMENT OR HANGING BACK: ROB BOUVIER

But not every school is like Mrs. Sampson's school, a community of practice centered on thinking. Rob Bouvier, principal of suburban Whitestone School, is beginning to understand constructivist theories about how children learn mathematics, but has not thought yet about the possibility that teachers may need encouragement and support to think through constructivist ideas about mathematics learning before they can think productively about how they might want to modify their instruction. In Chapter 2, we saw how his insight that students' procedural competence with mathematics problems did not necessarily imply conceptual understanding affected what he looked for in classrooms and his ideas about the assessment of student understanding. In brief, Mr. Bouvier had developed an appreciation for the nature of children's mathematical thinking and for the importance of children's having the opportunity in math class to articulate their mathematical ideas and listen to each other's thinking. However, his understanding of instruction that would support students' development of rigorous thinking focused primarily on the teaching *behaviors* he wanted to see in classrooms. He wanted to see classrooms that had been arranged to foster discussion—desks facing each other to promote eye contact among students, the display of student work on the walls to indicate its importance ("to give strength to it"), and the frequent use of the overhead projector so that ideas could be shared among all students. He wanted students to do the majority of the talking in the classroom, and teachers to ask open-ended questions of students and help students build on each other's ideas. These instructional behaviors and arrangements are characteristic of standards-based classrooms and Mr. Bouvier was quite emphatic and consistent in his insistence that classrooms in his school look and sound like this. Identifying these behaviors, however, is only part of understanding how instructional practice can strengthen students' conceptual knowledge. There is still the need to understand what teachers need to know and know how to do to engage in such instructional practice and what students learn through such practice. Mr. Bouvier, we believe, was poised to move—but had not yet moved—to this next level of understanding.

An Episode from Administrative Practice

During the year we spent with Mr. Bouvier, the Whitestone School was preparing to select a new elementary mathematics curriculum. For the previous 5 years, the school had been using a program published by Addison Wesley, which the teachers in the school now thought was out of date. In order to address this situation, Mr. Bouvier and faculty representatives from each grade met once a month after school to work on selecting a new mathematics program. This process included reviewing the state's mathematics frameworks, creating their own scope and sequence for elementary mathematics instruction, and pilot-testing several candidate curricula. Mr. Bouvier also planned to use these meetings as a context for working with teachers on the idea that students construct their own mathematics knowledge.

The committee's discussions were wide-ranging. Several influential teachers pushed for mathematics programs that covered all of the topics in the district's scope and sequence and contained components such as drill-and-practice activities and end-of-unit tests. While there were some teachers who argued for a mathematics program that could engender students' excitement and a high level of mathematical thinking, the school's more traditional teachers argued that this could be accomplished by adopting a traditional program with open-ended activities as a supplement. The teachers who advocated programs that supported the development of children's mathematical thinking expressed skepticism that curricula with such different underlying philosophies could simply be "married." One teacher asked,

> I don't know how well they marry them together. Like is it that you do this and you do that or do they really flow together where you're working out of both of them at the same time?

In the end, the traditional teachers prevailed. The committee decided to select the newest edition of the more traditional Addison Wesley curriculum as the school's principal program and to use units from the more constructivist curricula, *Investigations in Number, Data, and Space* (Russell & Tierney, 1998) and *Mathscape* (1998), as supplementary materials or replacement units. This combination of materials was seen as providing a single, coherent, comprehensive basic curriculum with constructivist options for those teachers who wanted to provide their students with opportunities for mathematical exploration.

This decision gave each side some of what it wanted and provided instructional materials for teachers of every persuasion, but this mix of materials did not represent a consistent and intellectually coherent mathematics program, nor was it likely to achieve the outcome that Mr. Bouvier most wanted: strengthening students' conceptual understanding of mathematics. The Addison Wesley curriculum materials, on one hand, and *Investigations* and *Mathscape* on the other, are based on quite different views of what it means to learn mathematics. The Addison Wesley materials by and large stress the absorption of mathematical facts and practice with procedures; *Investigations* and *Mathscape* are built on the idea that children should build their own mathematical ideas through the investigation of mathematical ideas and problem solving. Mr. Bouvier did not appear to understand that these curricula were built on different philosophical premises, and was quite satisfied that the choice of materials would provide a high-quality mathematics education for students at the Whitestone School. From his point of view, collectively these materials covered the requisite mathematical content and gave teachers with different teaching styles materials they would be comfortable with.

Mr. Bouvier evidently was not aware of an argument running through the mathematics education community that mathematics content can be thought of as both the ideas or topics studied and the ways of doing the mathematics—the way problem solving is done, the kind of reasoning that justifies an answer, and so on. From this perspective, the process of doing mathematics in philosophically different ways actually produces qualitatively different understandings of the mathematical ideas (see Wilson, 2003). From this perspective, the nature of mathematical understanding that would likely be achieved through work with the Addison Wesley materials would be quite different than that achieved through work with *Investigations* and *Mathscape*. It would not be a simple matter to move from one to the other and produce seamless, coherent instruction. As we argued in Chapter 1, it is possible, even desirable, to teach mathematical concepts, facts, and procedures for calculation in relation to each other; but doing this well is a subtle matter and likely not achieved by simply combining units from instructional materials that are designed according to very different premises about what it means to learn mathematics.

As it turned out, Mr. Bouvier did not use the curriculum meetings as a context to explore with his teachers the idea of students constructing their own mathematics knowledge, as he had intended. Instead, he viewed his role as facilitating the teachers' process of designing the new district scope and sequence and being responsive to what they said was needed in commercial curriculum materials. He said that he assumed this role in part because math was not his area of expertise, but also because in those cases where teachers' views diverged from his own or from each other's he felt that voicing his own opinions would have the effect of shutting down the discussion.

This stance of hanging back in teacher meetings was not unusual for Mr. Bouvier. He told us that he had adopted his low-profile stance in recognition of a reality of school culture, namely, that voicing his views could change the nature of the discussion among teachers and preclude teacher ownership of the outcome:

> When a principal sits in and actively participates in curriculum development, the principal needs to be very careful not to lead. Certainly to be very vocal in what the beliefs are, what the belief system is . . . but not to pull, but rather to encourage, to coach, invite debate, invite opposing opinions. Because you can very quickly close the door. And you'll have the [curriculum], but it will sit on a shelf, and it will not be used if this grade-level representative committee doesn't feel partnership and ownership in the process.

In general, Mr. Bouvier considered that his role was to make what he called "administrative support decisions." He viewed his role as helping teachers prioritize and finding resources to support what teachers wanted to do:

> My role as a principal is to help [the teachers] decide priorities, reaffirm some core values that we have regarding mathematics instruction, and then provide the means to attain the goal. . . . Those solutions might be monetary, but they might also be providing coverage in the classroom to allow cross-grade discussions. It might be providing a champion effort to the parents, teachers, and friends organization to support a speaker that would come in. I mean, there are all types of support that teachers can expect from an administrator.

Much as he preferred to not voice his views in teacher meetings, Mr. Bouvier was clear that he had a responsibility to ensure that his substantive views were among those that the teachers would consider.

> I have never been in a situation in which my perspective has been unvoiced. In that situation I would have to—after all, I am still the building administrator. My view is important. If it's not voiced, it needs to get out.

Sometimes, in order to get his views out, he felt that he needed to work behind the scenes:

That's an administrative strategy. . . . Plant seeds of "I want you to ask this question at the meeting because it's very important for me to get an answer. If so and so says this, and I anticipate that they will, I would like you to share your experience and your dialogue." I do that all the time . . . behind the scenes.

But in the end, Mr. Bouvier sometimes had to live with teacher-made decisions that he might disagree with:

Sometimes [holding back] means as a building administrator, you've got to accept decisions that push against your beliefs and sometimes that's tough. But in my experience what I found is it is better to . . . allow the faculty to have some ownership and empowerment in making those kinds of choices. Very rarely will I unilaterally decide; [will I say], "This is what you feel. All of you. But this is the way we're going to run the school." . . . I've seen people that work that way and that does develop a certain effective school culture because, after all, a monarchy is the most effective form of government. It all sounds messy as democracy. But sometimes I find in the long run messy is better.

Analysis

Rob Bouvier's situation is quite familiar. Many elementary principals are torn between wanting to provide a context for professional teacher decision making in their schools, their wish to provide substantive leadership, and their fear that if they voice their own ideas they will dampen teacher discussion. Mr. Bouvier saw his choices as either to hold back his own ideas and beliefs, working behind the scenes to be sure that his ideas were in the mix, or to be a "monarch" and make unilateral decisions on behalf of everyone. In posing his choice as between monarchy and democracy, Mr. Bouvier's dilemma reflects a change in the way the field has viewed the relationship between principals and teachers over the past few decades, moving from viewing the principal as a strong, substantive authority, as in the effective schools movement (Edmonds, 1979, 1981), to viewing the principal's role as one of supporting the decision making of a group of highly educated, professional teachers (Darling-Hammond & Sclan, 1992; Sergiovanni & Starratt, 1998).

There is a third possibility, however, that does not seem to have occurred to Mr. Bouvier—being an intellectual colleague and guide. Mr. Bouvier's decision to hang back all through the curriculum selection process was very like what he wanted his teachers to do in their classrooms. His view of instruction that would support students' conceptual understanding involved making some physical changes in their classrooms and standing back: "Keep his or her mouth shut for a while, and allow and promote kids to talk to each other." He had not yet thought through the possibility that instruction that supported students' conceptual understanding would likely involve teachers and students in the work of thinking about mathematical ideas together, or that students need a teacher who listens to their mathematical thinking, judges its validity, and poses another mathematical task through which further thinking can be done.

Similarly, it did not seem to occur to Mr. Bouvier that his own work with his faculty could be about working with ideas. He did not appear to consider that in order to think through the issues entailed in selecting a new mathematics curriculum, he and the teachers would need to do the work of thinking through these issues together. What was the relationship between conceptual learning and drill and practice? Could very different curricula be "married"? Mr. Bouvier hung back and let the teachers work out a solution that apparently accommodated everyone, keeping his mouth shut and letting the teachers talk to each other.

There might be a variety of good reasons for a knowledgeable principal to choose not to be engaged with his teachers in deliberations about the nature of mathematics teaching and learning in his school: inadequate time, important other priorities that year, not enough knowledge about mathematics, good resources in the form of lead teachers or district math coordinators, and so on. Mr. Bouvier had said that math was not his field and he did not want to "shut down" the teachers' deliberations by his own participation. However, there were consequences to this decision. The Whitestone School's curriculum decision was a compromise between two different teacher positions, producing something for everyone but not a conceptually coherent instructional program. The curriculum choice does not seem to have been made by examining the conditions under which students could develop conceptual understanding of mathematics integrated with knowledge of mathematics facts and procedures for calculation, and thus an opportunity for learning and reflection among the staff appears to have been missed. And, in the end, the curriculum selection process did not serve as a context for Mr. Bouvier to work with teachers on the idea that students construct their own mathematics knowledge, as he had hoped.

We believe that Mr. Bouvier is at a place that is typical of a great many principals, and that is one of the reasons we chose to describe his work here. He has discovered a new view of mathematics instruction, but his view is partial. With his beginning understanding of a constructivist orientation toward mathematics learning, he is focused largely on desirable instructional strategies. He does not seem to have yet begun to consider that those instructional strategies are desirable because they afford teachers and students the opportunity to think about mathematics together, nor what teachers in his school would need to learn in order to engage in such instruction. Neither does he yet seem to have considered the implications for his own administrative behavior. However, his interest in children's mathematical thinking puts him in a good position to move forward, perhaps by arranging for professional development for his teachers to learn to attend to their students' mathematical thinking and reflect on the instructional implications of what they learn, much as he is now inclined to do.

INSTRUCTIONAL LEADERSHIP INVOLVING MORE THAN A "FORMULA TO PLUG INTO": COSTANZA WILSON

Costanza Wilson offers a picture of a principal who came to see things differently. Partway through a multiyear journey toward improving mathematics instruction in her school, she realized, "It has to start with me." Mrs. Wilson had the opportunity to deepen her own thinking about the nature of mathematics and to experience a learning environment in which her own thinking about mathematical ideas was both challenged and supported. She began to appreciate the value of a culture for learning built on respect for, and interest in, everyone's ideas and wanted such a culture for her school. These insights took her on a new, more engaged, path toward improving mathematics instruction in her school.

Mrs. Wilson is principal of the Montgomery School, one of 76 elementary schools in a large northeastern city. The school has approximately 160 students, Grades K–5, and 11 full-time classroom teachers. Mrs. Wilson had been principal of the Montgomery School for 8 years when we interviewed her.

Mrs. Wilson had always thought she was good at math; in her view, there was a formula for everything and all she had to do was know the formula and she would get the answer:

> [As a student] all I had to do was pay relatively close attention, understand what I was being told to do, and if I followed the directions . . . I would come across the answers.

Shortly after she became principal of the Montgomery School, she became concerned about the fact that the students in her school were not learning math. As she looked at classrooms, she saw that math was being taught the way she had learned it as a student and taught it when she was a teacher, but the standardized test scores were low and the students didn't know what they needed for the next grade. She saw fifth-grade teachers still teaching second-grade material. Further investigation revealed that the teachers were not getting all the way through the math texts each year, and some of the topics on the standardized tests had not been taught by the time those tests were administered in the spring. This data galvanized Mrs. Wilson to find a way to help the teachers in her school be better math teachers. "That's where the pursuit began," she said. "That was the charge: OK, I'm going to go at it as a principal and figure out how to help them be better math teachers."

An Episode from Administrative Practice

About 2 years after she became principal of the Montgomery School, Mrs. Wilson set out on her quest. At first she was looking for an instructional package that her school could easily "plug into."

> At first I was looking for the formula. I wanted [a program] we could plug into. Because that is so easy, just to plug into it and do it.

An early step involved taking a summer workshop about the constructivist-oriented curriculum *Investigations in Number, Data, and Space* (Russell & Tierney, 1998) with one of the teachers in her school. She reported that she and the teacher were very excited about what they learned, and they wrote a small grant to buy all of the teachers in the school everything they would need to implement *Investigations*. Mrs. Wilson mandated that all teachers implement some of the mathematical thinking units in the *Investigations* curriculum for a month at their grade level. "That was my way of making change occur," she said. She then tells what happened:

> So they all agreed that they would do that, and that's just what they did. They did it for that one month, . . . so I could check off that they did it, . . . and [then the books] all went into the closet, and everybody went back to what they were doing. . . . And we went back to our Scott Foresman [textbooks]. We went back to the way it was.

The teachers' resistance to doing the mathematical thinking units at their grade levels pushed Mrs. Wilson to continue her search for a way to improve mathematics instruction at the Montgomery School. A colleague suggested she join several other principals from their district in taking an experimental class about supervision in elementary mathematics that was being given at a local university. Mrs. Wilson decided to take the course, expecting that it would help her figure out how to be a better supervisor for her classroom teachers and also help her explain to her teachers the then-new *Curriculum and Evaluation Standards* published by the National Council of Teachers of

Mathematics (1989). But the course wasn't at all what she expected. It seemed that it was not going to provide her with a formula for change:

> After the first hour, it was clear that this class was not going to give me those answers. The class was going to require me to do some math. And that threw me. [I wondered,] why am I here? . . . I don't want to sit and do math.

But she was persuaded by her colleagues to stay. Gradually she realized that the class was about more than just doing math, but also about mathematical thinking and how children's mathematical thinking develops. It also offered opportunities to think about the nature of instruction that supports the development of children's mathematical thinking. Mrs. Wilson described the class:

> We did a little mental math and then we related it . . . to what happens in a classroom when you ask a child to do math without pencil and paper in front of them. It began my whole process of . . . realizing that I did have other strategies other than the ones that the teachers taught me, and I actually was using those strategies every single day, and very rarely used the techniques that the teachers had taught me: to divide, to add, to subtract, to come up with percentages. And I became really excited about that, about my own learning.

For Mrs. Wilson, the power in the class she was taking was doing mathematics herself: using her own strategies for solving mathematics problems, having the opportunity to talk about her mathematical thinking with other administrators in the class, and being supported by the facilitators in the development of her own mathematical understanding. From her descriptions of her mathematical experiences in the class we think it likely that Mrs. Wilson was beginning to develop a more flexible sense of how to work with numbers and beginning to see that the particular problem-solving strategies she had been taught in school were only one way to work with those numbers.

Mrs. Wilson described her experience with new methods of doing mathematics problems:

> That was the first time it dawned on me that there is more than one way of borrowing and carrying, and I don't have to draw that line, and I don't have to put that 1 up there, that I was still getting to the answer without doing all that.

While Mrs. Wilson wasn't explicit in our interview with her about what she was doing instead of the traditional methods of "borrowing and carrying," the course encouraged administrators to solve mathematics problems (like the problem in Chapter 1, 25 + ? = 42) in ways that seemed most sensible to them, which often involved using strategies to make the numbers easier to work with without necessarily "borrowing" 10 from the 40. Doing so involved them in thinking flexibly about how numbers were composed and how they might be decomposed and reconfigured for purposes of the calculation at hand.

Mrs. Wilson also was intrigued by what the course facilitators were doing to make mathematical ideas and mathematical thinking so accessible and exciting for her. She wondered if something similar would work for teachers and children.

> And I said, "Well, they [the facilitators] are teachers; they just happen to be teaching adults. And how do I then get our teachers to sort of do that with children, and can this be transformed into [instruction] for children and teachers?" I was beginning to get excited that change could happen and that there was a different way to do math, that we could create not only better students mathematically, but we could create a better culture for all learning to occur. That began [my] thinking about the type of professional development for teachers that I would look for.

Mrs. Wilson had noticed what many administrators in such classes notice, namely, that their instructors appear to be modeling the kind of instruction that teachers might employ with students. While the general principles of such instruction may be similar in several different contexts, the process of transforming those methods into courses for teachers and then having teachers develop teaching methods for students is considerably more complex than Mrs. Wilson's comment implies. There are significant differences between teaching adults and teaching children, and it would probably not be adequate for teachers simply to replicate with their students the methods they experienced in professional development classes. Further, teachers likely would need more than simply the modeling of new instructional methods in order to modify their teaching; they would also need to develop their own understanding of the mathematical concepts they were teaching and learn to make judgments about how, why, and under what conditions such methods would be effective in their own classrooms.

Nonetheless, in the course she took Mrs. Wilson experienced mathematics learning in such a way that the mathematics made sense, and this was exciting to her. She was beginning to believe mathematics learning could be exciting for teachers and students as well, and that mathematics learning needed to be done with a community of people who understand what it is like to explore mathematical ideas—"a better culture for all learning to occur," as she put it. What she now wanted for her school was most certainly not a "formula" that she and the teachers could "just plug into."

Mrs. Wilson then began to build a sense of shared enterprise among the teachers in her school, inviting them to investigate with her some new possibilities for mathematics instruction. She arranged for a group of her teachers to make a series of visits to another school in the city, where math was taught in the way she was coming to believe would be most effective. While she had seen classrooms like this on videotapes in the course she had taken, her teachers had not, and they were amazed.

> So, we all got in our cars and we went over to see [math at] the Tower School. We were all awed with what we saw. The culture of the school, of the classrooms that we visited, for me were the same classrooms that we had seen on the video. But the teachers—they hadn't seen the videos at this point—were just awed by the fact that students were sitting and listening to each other. And this was in all grades—second grade, third grade, fourth grade—that there was this culture of learning that was important, and that everybody had a right to say how they got to a particular answer, and that teachers were not saying whether it was right or wrong but were questioning, to help children [figure out] if this made sense. . . . And watching children correct themselves if they needed to, or say, "No, that doesn't get me what I wanted to get, let me go back." And also watching teachers move children to the next level. "Well, is counting being more efficient, is doing it that way—or is there another way that you can do it?" "Yeah, I can group it by twos or group it by fives and count a little faster, be a little more efficient."

Mrs. Wilson and the teachers talked together, and made lists of the things they saw that excited them. She reported about what they saw later:

> What we saw was not only about kids doing math, [but also] . . . this culture of children listening to each other; children feeling safe to share a strategy that no one else in the world may have thought of, but feeling comfortable and safe to do that. Teachers really probing and not judging.

Some of the teachers from the Montgomery School wanted to make changes in their classrooms right away. So Mrs. Wilson arranged for the professional development program in elementary mathematics that had helped the teachers at the Tower School, *Developing Mathematical Ideas*

(Schifter et al., 1999a, 1999b) to be offered to her entire faculty. She herself attended every session (48 hours) and did all the work, as a full participant.

> It was important for me that all of us do it together. Sitting in the classes with my colleagues, I learned something about them, I learned something about myself. But it also established a network that was important, and to this day we call each other up, about math and about other things. We wanted that networking and that culture that we saw [at the Tower School] to be created here at the [Montgomery] School as well.

Analysis

Thinking back on it later, Mrs. Wilson mused about how change had happened in the Montgomery School.

> Thinking about that journey, I said to myself, "Now, how did we get here?" A couple of years ago I couldn't get anyone to even think about math, and now they're thinking about it. . . . So what happened was . . . I was clearly looking at myself as a learner and things were being challenged in my own thought. And I was getting excited about that. I was reading things and I was realizing that I did like math and I did understand math and that I knew a lot more and had a lot more that I needed to know about math, and wanted to bring that excitement back to the teachers. . . . It became very clear that that began with me thinking about how I learned math. . . . [And] I realized that as a learner I needed to think about what was happening with the teachers as well.

Mrs. Wilson now believed that both teachers and children could experience the excitement and challenge of mathematics learning that she had experienced, but that this would not happen by finding a program to "plug into." Rather, the entire school community—children, teachers, and herself—would need to immerse themselves in this culture of math learning.

Mrs. Wilson's story is one of transition. Over time she had come to believe that centering the work of mathematics instruction on ideas and thinking is a different kind of enterprise than she had initially thought, requiring a change in the values that undergird the mathematics program—respect for students' mathematical thinking, probing rather than judging on the part of teachers, and so forth—as well as different instructional strategies in classrooms. She also had come to believe that if she herself became involved with thinking and ideas along with the teachers and students, a community of practice—a network and culture, as she called it—built around learning and teaching mathematics could grow in her school. However, these insights were relatively new for her and we do not know how they played out in subsequent years: whether the math program continued to develop along the lines that she had set out, whether ideas about teaching and learning conceived of as being about thinking and ideas took root in any other areas of instruction, or whether the embryonic community of practice that was developing at the Montgomery School around the need to understand how to improve mathematics instruction would continue to grow.

CONCLUSION

Not only do principals' ideas about the nature of mathematics, learning, and teaching affect what they see when they observe mathematics classes (discussed in Part I) and affect how they deal with the administrative processes of mentoring teachers, being accountable for student and teacher learning, and communicating with stakeholders outside of the school (discussed in Part II), but these ideas also affect how principals interpret the task of improving mathematics instruction in their schools (discussed in Part III). Principals who take a stance of inquiry in their instructional leadership may create a community of practice centered around learning about teaching and learning for themselves and their teachers. Principals who believe that mathematics instruction is fundamentally about fostering ongoing student and teacher thinking may also believe that achieving and sustaining mathematics instruction centered on student thinking may entail not only a set of technical changes in teaching technique that teachers can enact individually in their classrooms, but also the development of a schoolwide culture of learning that supports ongoing reflection and intellectual risk taking for all—students, teachers, and administrators.

In this chapter we explored the work of three principals who had quite different understandings of mathematics learning and teaching, looking to see how their understanding affected the way they engaged with mathematics instruction in their schools. Louise Sampson's beliefs about how children build their knowledge and the supports that help them do this led her to build her school around the ideas of reflection, inquiry, and support for intellectual work. Rob Bouvier came to believe that mathematics is a subject that is about ideas and concepts as well as about facts and procedures, but believed that the task of instructional improvement in mathematics was largely one of teachers developing new teaching techniques. He stood to the side as mathematics curriculum issues were being debated in his school. Costanza Wilson came to believe that the kind of mathematics instruction she wanted for students in the Montgomery School could not be achieved by finding a program to "plug into." Rather, she concluded that there is a culture of thinking in effective mathematics classes, and that one way that she and the teachers in her school could learn about this culture was to participate in such classes and be part of such a culture themselves.

We note that two of these principals—Mrs. Sampson and Mrs. Wilson—had had experiences in which the process of constructing their own knowledge had been heightened and made conscious. They remembered those experiences vividly and analyzed them to develop ideas about what students and teachers would need if they were to have similar experiences. While experiencing learning as the construction of knowledge and analyzing that experience is not the only thing that principals need to guide them in developing a culture of inquiry in their schools, and other principals might have learned other things from such experiences, for Mrs. Sampson and Mrs. Wilson their learning experiences supported the conviction that learning entailed grappling with ideas under conditions of uncertainty and risk and, therefore, required support on the part of teachers and the school's culture. Mrs. Sampson and Mrs. Wilson were able to use this insight as a guide in thinking about what it would mean to create such a community in their schools.

CONCLUSION

W E BEGAN this book with a scenario in which a fifth-grade class was developing strategies for multiplying whole and mixed numbers—generating creative ways to solve the problems posed, exploring the strategy of "doubling" and "halving," decomposing the numbers in ways that made sense to them, and utilizing the distributive property of multiplication. We then posed the question that underlies the main premise of this book: What can elementary principals do to increase the likelihood that such classrooms could thrive in their schools?

Our argument has been that principals' subject matter knowledge and beliefs about how elementary school subjects such as mathematics are learned and taught inform their professional judgment as instructional leaders. Such knowledge is a critical determinant of their ability to both support and constructively criticize such classrooms. It guides their identification of the salient features of a classroom, interchanges with teachers, or an administrative process like sending out report cards or choosing a math curriculum. Further, such knowledge affects how they act on those salient features. As we saw in Chapter 6 with Dr. Garfield facilitating his district's review of mathematics programs, when school and district administrators' knowledge and beliefs change, what they perceive as important to attend to also changes.

Through the stories of their practice, we have shown how several administrators' knowledge of mathematics, their understanding of how children develop mathematical knowledge, and their beliefs about how mathematics is best taught shaped their sense of what they could do to support high-quality mathematics instruction in their schools and districts. We also have examined how such understanding affected what they actually did in their day-to-day work. From these stories we have drawn out what we consider to be essential elements of effective instructional leadership as well as principles for launching administrators on trajectories of their own learning.

ELEMENTS OF EFFECTIVE INSTRUCTIONAL LEADERSHIP

Based on our decade of work with principals and other district administrators, we believe that administrators are greatly aided by having a conceptual grasp of subject matter content. For example, we saw that Ms. O'Brien, with her more procedural, and less conceptual, knowledge of mathematics, was limited in understanding what was happening in the mathematics classes she observed. Consequently, she was not positioned to help the teacher, Mr. Jones, figure out how to listen to students' mathematical thinking.

We also believe that it helps if principals' mathematics knowledge is flexible, so that they can follow the unexpected ways that students, like Josie in the fraction fringe episode in Chapter 1, make sense of the mathematics they are assigned. Principals who can use their own knowledge of mathematics to examine the constituent ideas in mathematics problems, are more likely able to identify ideas that students might have trouble with. Mr. Nash, as we also saw in Chapter 1, did this when he developed the problem about rafts and Popsicle sticks for his faculty to work on. Mrs. Cowan, however, stopped short of doing this when she and the teacher puzzled about what Josie understood about equivalent fractions.

Our work has also led us to believe that principals more readily shift what they see as the salient features of instruction when they understand how children's mathematical knowledge develops through working on complex mathematical problems (cf. Carpenter, Fennema, Peterson, Chiang, & Loef, 1989; Fennema, Franke, Carpenter, & Carey, 1993; Stein & Lane, 1996). Ms. Diggins, Ms. Goldstein, Mrs. Cowan, and Mrs. Wilson believed that mathematics learning involves making conjectures, discussing ideas, and inventing solutions, as well as mastering mathematical facts and procedures. When these administrators were faced with engaging teachers or other stakeholders in learning, they used this knowledge to productive ends. Ms. Goldstein, for instance, effectively trusted her belief that school committee members would understand the elementary program better by actually doing mathematics together.

We also hold that principals are aided greatly when they understand that teaching entails more than didactic skills. Ms. Diggins, for example, expected teachers in her school to be able to listen for the validity of students' mathematical ideas and ask responsive questions or pose mathematical tasks that make students reach just a little further than their current understanding. Further, administrators wanting to help teachers improve their instructional practice benefit when they themselves attend to the particulars of the teachers' moves in connection with the subject matter content and students' thinking about that content. Mr. Nash was able to do this when he used Margaret Riddle's article in a faculty meeting with his teachers.

Finally, we have observed that principals who understand how to build classroom and school cultures that provide safe environments for the intellectual risk-taking that is inherent in constructing new knowledge offer essential support in forwarding educational reform. We saw in Chapter 7 how Mrs. Sampson was able to bring her knowledge of supportive school culture to her highly effective and respected principalship.

As we examined the work of these principals and others, we looked at a large range of administrative practices that make up administrators' work as instructional leaders. Many of these administrative functions are usually thought of as independent of the subject matter at issue. However, we have seen in the vignettes of principals' work the difference it makes when ideas about subject matter, learning, and teaching serve as anchors for these functions. Having subject matter knowledge, principals can talk directly with teachers about what their students understand. They can work with curriculum selection committees on the ideas that will strengthen instruction in their districts. They can explain to parents how their children will be learning specific subjects. They no longer are limited to managing the processes and structures *around* instruction; they can work with teachers and others to improve instruction itself (Elmore, 2000).

ADMINISTRATORS AS LEARNERS

While we have posited here the central elements that we believe contribute to effective instructional leadership, we also emphasize that there is no "end state" of effective instructional leadership. Effective leaders are effective, generative learners.

We have presented here the varied and complex portraits of a particular set of individuals. As we can see, especially through the stories of those administrators whose practice we visited several times throughout the book, administrators are not unidimensional individuals, fixed in time. Each of the administrators we profiled was working on particular aspects of his or her own practice and had different strengths and challenges to contend with. Mr. Nash, for example, was able to bring an intellectually rich, mathematically informed stance to his work with his teachers yet puzzled about how to bring parents into this dialogue. Dr. Garfield was eagerly working on his ability to facilitate an exploration of ideas as he was facilitating the elementary mathematics curriculum review process but could not quite entertain how that same stance of learning was relevant—or safe—when working with the school committee. Some principals, like Ms. O'Brien, were only coming to see that mathematics instruction could be based on a different set of assumptions about how students learn mathematics. Others, like Mr. Bouvier, were beginning to see what listening to students' mathematical ideas meant and what one could learn from that.

While each of the administrators in this book was on his or her own learning trajectory, one feature that united them all was that they opened themselves up to be learners as well as leaders. They eagerly explored new ideas about mathematics, learning, and teaching. They wrestled with their own beliefs and knowledge. They asked questions and put aside their professional inclination to have ready answers. We believe that it was their orientation of curiosity and their willingness to critically examine their own ideas that positioned them to use outside resources (seminars and consultancies) and situations in their practice (issuing report cards, adopting new curricula, observing in classrooms) to learn more about how mathematics instruction worked and to explore what instructional practices would be best for their schools.

In our work with administrators we have observed that their deep and ongoing engagement with new ideas about mathematics teaching and learning often begins, much as Mr. Bouvier's did, with the realization and accompanying emotional jolt, that what had seemed to be adequate mathematics instruction was actually lacking a critical component—the opportunity for students to conceptually understand the mathematics with which they are working. This insight can set administrators off on a multiyear search to understand what mathematics instruction could be and, like all of the administrators whose work is depicted here, to experiment with how to get it to happen in their schools and districts.

IMPLICATIONS FOR MATHEMATICS EDUCATION, EDUCATIONAL POLICY, AND SCHOOL REFORM

In this book we have discussed the function of principals' knowledge by examining concrete events taken from their practice; this method has allowed us to embed ideas that might otherwise be quite abstract in easily recognizable administrative situations. We also have given voice to these administrators, so that their passions, struggles, and realities would be recognized as part of the fabric of instructional leadership. Now, we lay out the implication of these cases more broadly for mathematics education, educational policy, and school improvement.

Mathematics Education

In the last 15 years the mathematics education community has worked to develop standards for mathematics instruction (NCTM, 1989, 2000), curricula to support high-quality mathematics instruction, and professional development programs for teachers. However, scholars and reformers have long recognized the importance of the principal in the development and maintenance of academically excellent schools (Elmore, 1996; Hightower, Knapp, Marsh, & McLaughlin, 2002; Little & McLaughlin, 1993; Togneri & Anderson, 2003). Recent research has shown that administrators' understanding of high-quality mathematics instruction and their ideas about how they can support it are significantly influenced by their own ideas about the nature of mathematics, teaching, and learning (Nelson, 1998; Spillane, 2002; Spillane & Halverson, 1998; Spillane & Thompson, 1997; Stein & Nelson, 2003). The principals whose work we have examined in this book illustrate this point in considerable detail. As efforts to improve elementary mathematics instruction continue, educators will be well-advised to include plans for helping school and district administrators improve their own knowledge of mathematics, how it is learned, and how it is taught, as part of systemic plans for instructional improvement.

Educational Policy

We take the position advocated by Michael Lipsky 25 years ago, that principals are "street-level bureaucrats" who, in enacting policy, define it. Lipsky (1980) showed that public service workers make important decisions about the provision of services, and exercise wide discretion in their work:

> Policemen decide who to arrest and whose behavior to overlook. Judges decide who shall receive a suspended sentence and who shall receive maximum punishment. Teachers decide who will be suspended and who will remain in school, and they make subtle determinations of who is teachable. (p. 13)

Lipsky did not focus, as we do, on the ideas that street-level bureaucrats have about the nature of the services they provide. However, we align ourselves with Lipsky's notion that the daily decisions and actions of street-level administrators constitute the implementation of policy.

In recent years scholars in a variety of fields have begun to examine the role of administrators' and policymakers' subject-specific knowledge in their decision making. For example, scholars have argued that the content of the ideas that implementers come to understand or interpret from policy are an integral part of the policy implementation process. Spillane, Reiser, and Reimer (2002) argue that district-level implementers of new policies in mathematics and science education tend to assimilate those policies' qualitatively different ideas about mathematics and science instruction into their existing schemas and fail to recognize that new ideas about the nature of mathematics instruction underlie them. As we noted in Chapter 5, Cohen and Barnes (1993) argue that, since the enactors of new policies need to engage in learning in order to change their behavior, the education of enactors needs to be taken much more seriously. In fact, they argue, the pedagogy that has informed the education provided for policy enactors has itself been traditionally didactic. They question the circumstances under which such a traditional pedagogy is appropriate.

The principals whose work we examined in this book were engaged in policy implementation in a variety of ways. These included ensuring that teachers taught the adopted curriculum competently, helping teachers participate thoughtfully in debates about policies affecting mathematics instruction, and evaluating teachers and students using district-approved assessment forms. Our examination of their work can be viewed as an extended argument for the importance of cognitively oriented studies of policy implementation.

School Improvement

Early efforts to clarify the relationship between school leadership and student learning initially occurred in studies of effective schools in the 1970s and 1980s. These studies found that, in schools where academic achievement was independent of students' social class or race, principals set high expectations for all children, maintained an orderly environment, instituted regular testing programs, and focused on academic learning (Edmonds, 1979, 1981). Subsequent research showed that effective principal leadership is aimed at influencing internal school processes that are directly linked to student learning. These internal processes range from school policies and norms to the practices of teachers (Hallinger & Heck, 1998).

As Stein has reviewed (Stein & Nelson, 2003), for many years such research on instructional leadership focused primarily on identifying administrators' behaviors, disregarding the knowledge, understanding, and qualities of professional judgment that underlie their actions. In the late 1980s and early 1990s, researchers began to explore the cognitive underpinnings of effective leadership (Hallinger, Leithwood, & Murphy, 1993). Most of this work draws on earlier cognitive science research on problem solving and decision making and focuses on how school leaders identify and frame problems in their schools. Stein and Nelson (2003) have argued for the importance of what they call "leadership content knowledge"—the knowledge of subjects of instruction, how they are learned, and how they are taught—in instructional leadership at school and district levels. The cases in this book push this work further by exploring in detail how administrators' leadership content knowledge affects the practical judgment that they exercise in their administrative work.

THREE PRINCIPLES OF FACILITATING INSTRUCTIONAL
LEADERSHIP LEARNING

Finally, this book tacitly raises two critical questions: How much should (and can) administrators know? and How can they learn it?

There are as yet no clear answers to the question of how much administrators need to know about a subject such as mathematics, how it is learned, and how it is taught, and exactly what it is about mathematics learning and teaching they need to know, in order to engage in the kind of instructional leadership that we have seen in the administrators in this book. Stein and Nelson (2003) examined several case studies of administrators' work and suggested that different administrative tasks may require different amounts and kinds of knowledge, and that administrative functions closer to the classroom require more detailed knowledge than district-level functions that are further from the classroom, though the latter still need to be grounded in subject matter knowledge. Research into these questions and others like them is currently underway by a number of scholars, and we look forward to more precise answers than are now available.

Nor are there yet answers to the question of how it would be possible for administrators to know a sufficient amount about all of the subjects of instruction that they are responsible for supervising. Again, Stein and Nelson (2003) have proposed that administrators have depth of knowledge in one subject of instruction, so that they know how learning and teaching in that subject work. Then administrators could undertake short-term, highly focused explorations of teaching and learning in additional subjects. In-depth understanding of how the intellectual work of one subject takes place would prepare them to see how similar intellectual processes are worked out in other subjects. In addition, viewing leadership as a practice that is distributed among members of a team in a school or district allows the possibility that administrators could work with others whose knowledge may complement theirs. Making this strategy work, however, would require that team members collectively would need to have the requisite knowledge and be able to share it within the team.

We met all of the principals whose work we discussed in this book in the course of teaching them about mathematics, learning, and teaching, and many of the vignettes presented described contexts in which they continued to learn. In our decade of work with administrators we have developed three principles that we feel are fundamental in helping administrators think deeply about learning, teaching, and subject matter knowledge and in launching them on trajectories of learning so that they may continue to learn in and from their own practice. Together these principles offer a powerful opportunity for administrators to think through the relationship between educational and administrative ideas.

Our first design principle has been to operate seminars according to the pedagogical principles that inform mathematics classrooms based on a constructivist view of mathematics learning. This gives administrators the opportunity to directly experience for themselves "thinking in order to learn" and to analyze what has happened in the seminar to make such learning possible. A central component of these seminars is to have the administrators themselves do mathematics. The mathematics activities, while based on ideas of the elementary curriculum, are designed specifically for adults and are intended to help administrators deepen their own mathematical fluency.

Our second design principle, called *layering*, involves pointing out the direct links between children's mathematical thinking, teachers' mathematical and pedagogical thinking, and administrators' thought and practice. Such layering enables administrators to consider the possibility that standards-based mathematics classrooms have norms, values, and practices that might be valuable for the school as a whole and therefore for their own administrative practice.

Our third design principle is to situate the conceptual work of thinking about mathematics, learning, and teaching in areas of administrators' own work. That is, new ideas about mathematics, learning, and teaching affect not only the nature of instruction but also administrative functions that are related to instruction. Thinking about new ideas in the context of administrative tasks motivates administrators to do the hard work of reconceptualizing fundamental ideas. (See Nelson, 1999, for a fuller explication of these principles.)

Using the voices of school administrators and stories from their practice, our goal in this book has been to bring to light the qualities of high-quality instructional leadership that is anchored in a grounding in subject matter, how it is learned, and how it should be taught. These stories point to the intimate connection between administration and instruction, between managing a school and guiding instructional practice. School administrators clearly have to bring managerial skills to their work. But, as we have highlighted throughout this book, such skills alone will not serve administrators well in today's educational climate. They must be linked with an understanding of contemporary pedagogy, an appreciation of the complexity of subject matter knowledge, and a willingness to be a learner.

The principals and other administrators with whom we have worked over the years have come to recognize these imperatives. We have been most impressed by the energy and effort they have put into rethinking specifically what it means to understand mathematics, how mathematics instruction could work well, and how they can support high-quality mathematics instruction in their schools and districts. We are heartened by these administrators to believe that many more could take the same journey.

RESEARCH METHODOLOGY

T HE DATA in this book came from three sources: a qualitative study of how elementary principals link ideas about mathematics, learning, and teaching to their administrative practice; a teaching experiment in which we systematically collected data while teaching administrators about contemporary elementary mathematics instruction; and a consultancy, the qualitative study of an assistant superintendent directing the process of mathematics curriculum selection for his district. The research methods for each are described below.

LINKING IDEAS TO PRACTICE

This study, supported by the Spencer Foundation, examined five elementary school principals' instructional leadership in mathematics. The data in this book about Rob Bouvier, Sheila Diggins, Peter Nash, Libby O'Brien, and Marianne Cowan were collected and analyzed in this study.

The Sample

Participant Selection. A purposive sampling strategy was used to select the participants (Becker, 1998; Patton, 1990). We sought principals for whom ideas about mathematics, learning, and teaching were under lively reconsideration and who were likely thinking about how these ideas might affect specific aspects of their instructional leadership. Four of the five principals in this study had participated in a pilot course for administrators in elementary mathematics education. The fifth principal had been a participant in a prepilot version of the course as well as a long-term participant in, and then facilitator of, the *Developing Mathematical Ideas* course for elementary teachers (Schifter et al., 1999a, 1999b). All administrators were interested in understanding the ideas that underlie elementary mathematics education reform and, through their participation in these courses, had begun to examine their own ideas about mathematics, learning, and teaching.

Sampling Administrators' Work. We developed the construct of a *unit of practice* in order to generate a sample of administrative practice in which we could observe administrators' exercise of practical judgment. The notion of unit of practice emerged from our earlier work with school administrators. We found that in order for them to connect new ideas to their own practice, administrators needed opportunities to experience how the ideas played out in actual work settings. But, as we also discovered, they needed to carve out focused activities in which to start trying to use these ideas.

We worked with each participant to design a unit of practice. Four design criteria ensured that it would be possible to observe the connection between ideas about mathematics, learning, and teaching and the exercise of practical judgment:

1. Ideas about mathematics, teaching, and learning had to be relevant.
2. The practice to be studied would need to take place over a period of weeks or months and have specific occasions on which practical judgment was exercised.
3. The unit of practice work had to include making consequential decisions.
4. The exercise of practical judgment in the unit of practice had to be observable by the researchers.

Studying units of practice, so defined, excluded from the study deliberations and actions that occurred as part of an administrator's daily routine (e.g., telephone calls, hallway conversations, conversations on the margins of meetings called for another purpose). While our data are drawn from only select venues such as classroom observations or faculty meetings, the data generated by the unit of practice construct retains the characteristics of authenticity and consequence, while reducing the data to be analyzed to a manageable scope.

Data Collection

In this study we used the following data collection strategies: (1) interviews, (2) field observations of 3–5 scheduled events in each unit of practice, and (3) artifacts produced by the administrative activity. We administered the same preproject and postproject interviews to all administrators. We took field notes and/or audiotaped each unit of practice event we observed and then interviewed the administrator about the actions taken or not taken during the course of the event. We also interviewed two people who participated in the principal's unit of practice. By triangulating across various data sources using different methods, we reduce the limitations of any one method (Fielding & Fielding, 1986).

Data Analysis

Working with interview, field observation, and artifact data, we did both contextual and categorical analyses (Maxwell, 1996). Data analysis began during the first year, interwoven with data collection, and proceeded through a second year. Emergent interpretations both influenced the shape of subsequent interviews and observations and were tested by them (Miles & Huberman, 1994). Disconfirming evidence for emergent interpretations was sought.

Each unit of practice was regarded as a case, and both within-case and cross-case analyses were conducted (Stake, 1995). For each unit of practice we examined the data for evidence about: (1) the ideas about mathematics, learning, and teaching that were salient to the principal; (2) the principal's exercise of practical judgment; and (3) whether or not new administrative practice occurred and, if so, what it looked like. Data from each case were coded independently by two researchers. Discrepancies were adjudicated by the research group as a whole. Analytic memos about each case were written by one researcher.

TEACHING EXPERIMENT

This study was a naturalistic inquiry, supported by a grant from the National Science Foundation, in which we studied two consecutive yearlong professional development courses for administrators. The courses, which met monthly during the school year, focused on the ideas about mathematics, learning, and teaching that underlay the *Curriculum and Evaluation Standards* of the National Council of Teachers of Mathematics (1989). The data in Chapter 5 on Dana Goldstein, Charlotte Jenkins, and Joseph Garfield and the data in Chapter 7 on Louise Sampson were collected and analyzed in this study.

For this work we were both teachers and researchers (Ball, 1993; Hammer, 1995; Lampert, 1990). In this kind of work, data about the teaching process is collected in several ways: videotaping or audiotaping, retaining written student work, and keeping detailed teaching journals. Data is analyzed on a class-by-class basis to inform teaching decisions and after the course is finished to find general patterns and relationships. Combined with participant observation, the method's strengths are its sensitivity to context and the capacity to review data many times in order to understand events whose structure is too complex to be comprehended all at once (Corsaro, 1982; Erickson, 1992). The video or audio data also function as a triangulation with the more personalized data that emerges from the participant observation method (Patton, 1990). Our use of this method constituted *extreme case* sampling (Patton, 1990), in which the case (the seminar for administrators) was selected because it was rich in information about an unusual phenomenon (administrators' ideas about learning and teaching in elementary mathematics).

We and our colleagues designed and taught the seminar studied here. We assigned readings, developed activities, and facilitated group discussions to give administrators the opportunity to examine more deeply their fundamental ideas about mathematics, learning, and teaching, and the intellectual culture of schools. Project staff intended these discussions to encourage administrators to articulate and examine their own understanding of learning, teaching, mathematics, and school culture. The project's goal was to promote administrators' reflection about how those ideas were helpful guides for practice in the current reform climate.

Sample

This teaching experiment was linked with a professional development project for teachers of elementary mathematics that was also supported by a grant from the National Science Foundation. In conjunction with our work with teachers, we offered the seminar for principals of the teachers' schools and each district's elementary mathematics coordinator and assistant superintendent of curriculum and instruction. About 40 administrators from participating districts were invited to participate. Some administrators participated in the first year of the seminar, some in the second year, and some in both. Participation was voluntary and carried no requirements on which participants were evaluated. The data used here came from the first year of the seminar, which 26 administrators attended regularly.

Data Collection

Ethnographic field notes were taken at all seminar meetings. These meetings were also audiotaped, and the tapes were transcribed. Administrators' writing also was collected. In-depth interviews were conducted with all administrative participants at the beginning and end of the program.

Data Analysis

The episodes from the administrative practice of Dana Goldstein, Charlotte Jenkins, and Joseph Garfield described in Chapter 5 are based on analysis of the transcripts and ethnographic field notes of the last session of the seminar. The episode from the administrative practice of Louise Sampson described in Chapter 7 is based on analysis of the transcripts and ethnographic field notes of several sessions of the seminar, subsequent follow-up interviews in which Ms. Sampson described her school, several visits to her school in which ethnographic field notes were taken, and interviews with several teachers from her school.

Two researchers independently read and coded this data. We check-coded to establish interobserver reliability (Miles & Huberman, 1994). In analyzing the transcripts of seminar sessions, categories emerged from the data, as in grounded theory research (Glaser & Strauss, 1967). Preliminary categories were identified and the data was reread to refine or disconfirm those categories. Our goal was to describe what administrators valued and noticed in their analyses of mathematics instruction as a way of beginning to sketch out the principles and understanding that might be guiding their practical judgment.

THE CONSULTANCY

All administrators who participated in the mathematics education seminar were invited to participate in a *consultancy*, in which project staff would regularly visit with the administrator at his or her place of work to consult on an administrative task of the administrator's choice related to mathematics education. This work was done under a grant from the National Science Foundation. Two administrators volunteered for consultancies, and the data on Joseph Garfield's work with his district's elementary mathematics curriculum selection committee, described in Chapter 6, were collected in the context of this consultancy. The purpose of the consultancy was to provide the opportunity for individual administrators and project staff to examine the conceptual underpinnings of some aspect of the administrator's current practice.

Data Collection

Ethnographic field notes were taken of all meetings of the district's mathematics curriculum selection committee, which met eight times over the school year. Interviews were held with Dr. Garfield at the beginning and end of the project, and immediately after each meeting of the curriculum selection committee. All interviews were audiotaped and transcribed.

Data Analysis

A researcher who had not collected the data coded it, identifying themes that emerged. The data were check-coded by another researcher to establish interobserver reliability (Miles & Huberman, 1994).

REFERENCES

Abelmann, C., & Elmore, R. (with Even, J., Kenyon, S., & Marshall, J.). (1999). *When accountability knocks, will anyone answer?* Philadelphia: Consortium for Policy Research in Education, University of Pennsylvania.

Acheson, K. A., & Gall, M. D. (1980). *Techniques in the clinical supervision of teachers.* White Plains, NY: Longman.

Ball, D. L. (1993). With an eye on the mathematical horizon: Dilemmas of teaching elementary school mathematics. *The Elementary School Journal, 93*(4), 373–397.

Ball, D. L. (2000). Bridging practices: Intertwining content and pedagogy in teaching and learning to teach. *Journal of Teacher Education, 51*(3), 241–247.

Ball, D. L., & Cohen, D. K. (1999). Developing practice, developing practitioners: Toward a practice-based theory of professional education. In L. Darling-Hammond & G. Sykes (Eds.), *Teaching as the learning profession: Handbook of policy and practice* (pp. 3–32). San Francisco: Jossey-Bass.

Becker, H. (1998). *Tricks of the trade: How to think about your research while you're doing it.* Chicago: University of Chicago Press.

Bransford, J. D., Brown, A. L., & Cocking, R. R. (Eds.). (1999). *How people learn: Brain, mind, experience, and school.* (Committee on Developments in the Science of Learning, Commission on Behavioral and Social Science and Education, National Research Council.) Washington, DC: National Academy Press.

Brophy, J., & Good, T. L. (1986). Teacher behavior and student achievement. In M. C. Wittrock (Ed.), *Handbook of research in teaching* (3rd ed., pp. 328–375). New York: Macmillan.

Brown, A. L., & Campione, J. C. (1994). Guided discovery in a community of learners. In K. McGilly (Ed.), *Classroom lessons: Integrating cognitive theory and classroom practice* (pp. 229–270). Cambridge, MA: MIT Press/Bradford Books.

Brown, A. L., & Campione, J. C. (1996). Psychological theory and the design of innovative learning environments: On procedures, principles and systems. In L. Schauble & R. Glaser (Eds.), *Innovations in learning: New environments for education* (pp. 289–325). Mahwah, NJ: Erlbaum.

Brown, J. S., Collins, A., & Duguid, P. (1989). Situated cognition and the culture of learning. *Educational Researcher, 18*(1), 32–42.

Brown, J. S., & Duguid, P. (1991). Organizational learning and communities of practice: Toward a unified view of working, learning, and innovation. *Organizational Science, 2*(1), 40–57.

Carpenter, T. P., Ansell, E., & Levi, L. (2001). An alternative conception of teaching for understanding: Case studies of two first-grade mathematics classes. In T. Wood, B. S. Nelson, & J. Warfield (Eds.), *Beyond classical pedgogy: Teaching elementary school mathematics.* Mahwah, NJ: Lawrence Erlbaum.

Carpenter, T. P., Fennema, E., Peterson, P. L., Chiang, C., & Loef, M. (1989). Using knowledge of children's mathematical thinking in classroom teaching: An experimental study. *American Educational Research Journal, 26*(4), 499–532.

Cobb, P., Wood, T., Yackel, E., Nicholls, J., Wheatley, G., Trigatti, B., et al. (1991). Assessment of a problem-centered second-grade mathematics project. *Journal for Research in Mathematics Education, 22*(1), 3–29.

Cohen, D. K. (1988). Teaching practice: Plus ça change. In P. Jackson (Ed.), *Contributions to educational change: Perspectives on research and practice* (pp. 27–84). Berkeley, CA: McCutcheon.

Cohen, D. K., & Barnes, C. A. (1993). Pedagogy and policy. In D. K. Cohen, M. W. McLaughlin, & J. E. Talbert (Eds.), *Teaching for Understanding: Challenges for policy and practice* (pp. 207–239). San Francisco: Jossey-Bass.

Corsaro, W. (1982). Something old and something new: The importance of prior ethnography in the collection and analysis of audiovisual data. *Sociological methods and research, 11*(2), 145–166.

Darling-Hammond, L., & Sclan, E. (1992). Policy and supervision. In C. Glickman (Ed.), *Supervision in transition. 1992 Yearbook of the Association for Supervision and Curriculum Development* (pp. 7–29). Reston, VA: Association for Supervision and Curriculum Development.

Edmonds, R. R. (1979, March/April). Some schools work and more can. *Social Policy, 9*(5), 28–32.

Edmonds, R. R. (1981, September/October). Making public schools effective. *Social Policy, 12*(2), 56–60.

Elbow, Peter. (1986). *Embracing contraries.* New York: Oxford University Press.

Eliasoph, Nina. (1996). Making a fragile public: A talk-centered study of citizenship and power. *Sociological Theory, 14*(3), 262–289.

Elmore, R. F. (1996). Getting to scale with good educational practice. *Harvard Educational Review, 66*(1), 1–26.

Elmore, R. F. (2000, Winter). *Building a new structure for school leadership.* Washington, DC: Albert Shanker Institute.

Erickson, F. (1992). Ethnographic microanalysis of interaction. In M. D. LeCompte, W. L. Millroy, & J. Preissle, (Eds.), *The handbook of qualitative research in education* (pp. 201–226). Boston: Academic Press.

Feinman-Nemser, S., & Remillard, J. (1995). Perspectives on learning to teach. In F. Murray (Ed.), *The teacher educator's handbook* (pp. 63–91). San Francisco: Jossey-Bass.

Fennema, E., Franke, M. L., Carpenter, T. P., & Carey, D. (1993). Using children's mathematical knowledge in instruction. *American Educational Research Journal, 30*(3), 555–583.

Fielding, N., & Fielding, J. (1986). *Linking data*. Beverly Hills, CA: Sage.

Fink, E., & Resnick, L. B. (2001, April). Developing principals as instructional leaders. *Phi Delta Kappan, 82*(8), 598–606.

Forester, J. (1999). *The deliberative practitioner: Encouraging participatory planning processes*. Cambridge, MA: MIT Press.

Fosnot, C. T., & Dolk, M. (2002). *Young mathematicians at work: Constructing fractions, decimals, and percents*. Portsmouth NH: Heinemann.

Franke, M. L., Carpenter, T. P., Fennema, E., Ansell, E., & Behrend, J. (1998). Understanding teachers' self-sustaining, generative change in the context of professional development. *Teaching and Teacher Education, 14*(1), 67–80.

Franke, M. L., Carpenter, T. P., Levi, L., & Fennema, E. (2001). Capturing teachers' generative change: A follow-up study of professional development in mathematics. *American Educational Research Journal, 38*(3), 653–689.

Fuson, K. C. (1992). Research on whole number addition and subtraction. In D. A. Grouws (Ed.), *Handbook of research on mathematics teaching and learning* (pp. 243–275). (A project of the National Council of Teachers of Mathematics.) New York: Macmillan.

Gardner, H. (1985). *The mind's new science: A history of the cognitive revolution*. New York: Basic Books.

Glaser, B., & Strauss, A. (1967). *The discovery of grounded theory*. Hawthorne, NY: Aldine.

Grant, C. M., Nelson, B. S, Davidson, E., Sassi, A., Weinberg, A., & Bleiman, J. (2003a). *Lenses on learning, module 1: Instructional leadership in mathematics*. Parsippany, NJ: Dale Seymour Publications.

Grant, C. M., Nelson, B. S., Davidson, E., Sassi, A., Weinberg, A., & Bleiman, J. (2003b). *Lenses on learning, module 2: Teacher learning for mathematics instruction*. Parsippany, NJ: Dale Seymour Publications.

Grant, C. M., Nelson, B. S., Davidson, E., Sassi, A., Weinberg, A., & Bleiman, J. (2003c). *Lenses on learning, module 3: Observing today's mathematics classroom*. Parsippany, NJ: Dale Seymour Publications.

Greeno, J. G. (1998). The situativity of knowing, learning, and research. *American Psychologist, 53*(1), 5–26.

Greeno, J. G., Collins, A. M., & Resnick, L. B. (1996). Cognition and learning. In D. C. Berliner & R. C. Chalfee (Eds.), *Handbook of educational psychology* (pp. 15–46). New York: Macmillan.

Hallinger, P., & Heck, R. (1998). Exploring the principal's contributions to school effectiveness. *School Effectiveness and School Improvement, 9*(2), 157–191.

Hallinger, P., Leithwood, K., & Murphy, J. (Eds.). (1993). *Cognitive perspectives on educational leadership*. New York: Teachers College Press.

Halverson, R. (2003). Systems of practice: How leaders use artifacts to create professional community in schools. *Educational Policy and Analysis Archives, 11*(37), 1–33.

Halverson, R., & Zoltners, J. (2001, April). *Distribution across artifacts: How designed artifacts illustrate school leadership*. Paper presented at the annual meeting of the American Educational Research Association, Seattle, WA.

Hammer, D. (1995). *Epistemological considerations in teaching introductory physics.* Newton, MA: Center for the Development of Teaching, Education Development Center, Inc.

Hightower, A. M., Knapp, M. S., Marsh, J. A., & McLaughlin, M. W. (Eds.). (2002). *School districts and instructional renewal.* New York: Teachers College Press.

Holdaway, D. (1979). *The foundations of literacy.* New York: Ashton Scholastic.

Hummel, R. P. (1991). Stories managers tell: Why they are as valid as science. *Public Administration Review, 51*(1), 33–41.

Hunter, M. (1984). Knowing, teaching and supervising. In P. L. Hosford (Ed.), *Using what we know about teaching* (pp. 169–192). Alexandria, VA: Association for Supervision and Curriculum Development.

Joyce, B., & Showers, B. (1988). *Student achievement through staff development.* New York: Longman.

Kilpatrick, J., Swafford, J., & Findell, B. (Eds.). (2001). *Adding it up: Helping children learn mathematics.* (Mathematics Learning Study Committee, Center for Education, Division of Behavioral and Social Sciences and Education, National Research Council.) Washington, DC: National Academy Press.

Kliman, M., & Russell, S. J. (1998). Building number sense: The number system (Grade 1). In S. J. Russell & C. Tierney, *Investigations in number, data, and space.* White Plains, NY: Dale Seymour Publications.

Knapp, M., et al. (May, 2002). *Leadership for teaching and learning: A framework for understanding and action.* Field test draft, Center for the Study of Teaching and Policy, University of Washington, Seattle.

Kohn, A. (1998, April). Only for *my* kid: How privileged parents undermine school reform. *Phi Delta Kappan, 79*(8), 569–577.

Lampert, M. (1990). When the problem is not the question and the solution is not the answer: Mathematical knowing and teaching. *American Educational Research Journal, 27*(1), 29–63.

Lampert, M. (2001). *Teaching problems and the problems of teaching.* New Haven, CT: Yale University Press.

Lave, J., & Wenger, E. (1991). *Situated learning: Legitimate peripheral participation.* New York: Cambridge University Press.

Leithwood, K., Jantzi, D., Coffin, G., & Wilson, P. (1996). Preparing school leaders: What works? *Journal of School Leadership 6*(3), 316–342.

Lipsky, M. (1980). *Street-level bureaucracy: Dilemmas of the individual in public services.* New York: Russell Sage Foundation.

Little, J. W., & McLaughlin, M. W. (Eds.). (1993). *Teachers' work: Individuals, colleagues, and contexts.* New York: Teachers College Press.

Luhm, T., Foley, E., & Corcoran, T. (1998). *The accountability system: Defining responsibility for student achievement* [Research report]. Philadelphia, PA: Consortium for Policy Research in Education, University of Pennsylvania.

Marris, P. (1975). *Loss and change.* New York: Anchor Press/Doubleday.

Mathscape: Seeing and thinking mathematically. (1998). Mountain View, CA: Creative Publications.

Maxwell, J. (1996). *Qualitative research design.* Thousand Oaks, CA: Sage.

Miles, M., & Huberman, M. A. (1994). *Qualitative data analysis* (2nd ed.). Thousand Oaks, CA: Sage.

Milstein, M. M. (1990). Rethinking the clinical aspects in administrative preparation: From theory to practice. In S. L. Jacobson & J. Conway (Eds.), *Educational leadership in an age of reform* (pp. 119–130). New York: Longman.

Milstein, M. M., Bobroff, B. M., & Restine, L. N. (1991). *Internship programs in educational administration: A guide to preparing educational leaders.* New York: Teachers College Press.

Murphy, J. (1999, April). *Reconnecting teaching and school administration: A call for a unified profession.* Paper presented at the annual meeting of the American Educational Research Association, Montreal, Canada.

National Council of Teachers of Mathematics (NCTM). (1989). *Curriculum and evaluation standards for school mathematics.* Reston, VA: Author.

National Council of Teachers of Mathematics (NCTM). (2000). *Principles and standards of school mathematics.* Reston, VA: Author.

Nelson, B. S. (1998). Lenses on learning: Administrators' views on reform and the professional development of teachers. *Journal of Mathematics Teacher Education, 1*(2), 191–215.

Nelson, B. S. (1999). *Building new knowledge by thinking: How administrators can learn what they need to know about mathematics education reform.* Newton, MA: Center for the Development of Teaching, Education Development Center, Inc.

Nelson, B. S., Benson, S., & Reed, K. M. (2004, April). Leadership content knowledge: A construct for illuminating new forms of instructional leadership. Paper presented at the annual meeting of the National Council of Teachers of Mathematics, Philadelphia, PA.

Nelson, B. S., & Sassi, A. (2000). Shifting approaches to supervision: The case of mathematics supervision. *Educational Administration Quarterly, 36*(4), 553–583.

Newmann, F., and associates. (1996). *Authentic achievement: Restructuring schools for intellectual quality.* San Francisco: Jossey-Bass.

No Child Left Behind Act (NCLB) of 2002, 20 U.S.C. Sec. 6301 et seq.

Nussbaum, M. (1990). Perceptive equilibrium: Literary theory and ethical theory. In *Love's knowledge: Essays on philosophy and literature* (pp. 168–193). New York: Oxford University Press.

Patton, M. (1990). *Qualitative evaluation and research methods* (2nd ed.). Newbury Park, CA: Sage.

Pendlebury, S. (1990). Practical arguments and situational appreciation in teaching. *Educational Theory, 40*(2), 171–179.

Pendlebury, S. (1995). Reason and story in wise practice. In H. McEwan & K. Egan (Eds.), *Narrative in teaching, learning, and research* (pp. 50–65). New York: Teachers College Press.

Phillips, D. (1987). The good, the bad, and the ugly: The many faces of constructivism. *Educational Researcher, 24*(7), 5–12.

Piaget, J. (1977). *The essential Piaget* (H. E. Gruber & J. J. Vonèche, Trans.). London: Routledge & Kegan Paul.

Prestine, N. A., & Nelson, B. S. (2003, April). *How can educational leaders support and promote teaching and learning?: New conceptions of learning and leading in schools.* Paper presented at the annual meeting of the American Educational Research Association, Chicago, IL.

Reitzug, U. C. (1997). Images of principal instructional leadership: From supervision to collaborative inquiry. *Journal of Curriculum and Supervision, 12*(4), 356–366.

Resnick, L. B. (1981). Instructional psychology. *Annual Review of Psychology, 32,* 659–704.

Resnick, L. B. (1987). *Education and learning to think.* (Committee on Mathematics, Science, and Technology Education, Commission on Behavioral and Social Sciences and Education, National Research Council.) Washington, DC: National Academy Press.

Resnick, L. B., & Hall, M. W. (1998). Learning organizations for sustainable education reform. *Daedalus, 127*(4), 89–118.

Richardson, V. (1994). Conducting research on practice. *Educational Researcher, 23*(5), 5–10.

Riddle, M. (1996). Beyond stardom: Challenging competent math students in a mixed-ability classroom. In D. Schifter (Ed.), *What's happening in math class?: Vol. 1. Envisioning new practices through teacher narratives* (pp. 136–149). New York: Teachers College Press.

Romberg, T. A., & Carpenter, T. P. (1986). Research on teaching and learning mathematics: Two disciplines of scientific inquiry. In M. C. Wittrock (Ed.), *Handbook of research on teaching* (3rd ed., pp. 850–873). New York: Macmillan.

Rosenshine, B., & Stevens, R. (1986). Teaching functions. In M. C. Wittrock (Ed.), *Handbook of research on teaching* (3rd ed., pp. 376–391). New York: Macmillan.

Rowan, B. (1995). Learning, teaching, and educational administration: Toward a research agenda. *Educational Administration Quarterly, 31*(3), 344–354.

Rowe, M. B. (1986). Wait times: Slowing down may be a way of speeding up. *Journal of Teacher Education, 37*(1), 43–50.

Russell, S. J. (1999). Developing fluency. In *Relearning to teach arithmetic: Addition and subtraction: A teacher's study guide.* Parsippany, NJ: Dale Seymour Publications.

Russell, S. J., & Tierney, C. (1998). *Investigations in number, data, and space* [Curriculum]. White Plains, New York: Dale Seymour Publications.

Russell, S. J., Schifter, D., Bastable, V., Yaffee, L., Lester, J. B., & Cohen, S. (1995). Learning mathematics while teaching. In B. S. Nelson (Ed.), *Inquiry and the development of teaching: Issues in the transformation of mathematics teaching* (pp. 9–25). Newton, MA: Center for the Development of Teaching, Education Development Center, Inc.

Saphier, J., & Gower, R. (1987). *The skillful teacher.* Carlisle, MA: Research for Better Teaching, Inc.

Sassi, A. (2002). *Cultivating perception: Helping teachers to attend to the salient features of their mathematics classrooms.* Newton, MA: Center for the Development of Teaching, Education Development Center, Inc.

Schifter, D., Bastable, V., & Russell, S. J. (1999a). *Developing mathematical ideas: Making meaning for operations.* Parsippany, NJ: Dale Seymour Publications.

Schifter, D., Bastable, V., & Russell, S. J. (1999b). *Developing mathematical ideas: Building a system of tens.* Parsippany, NJ: Dale Seymour Publications.

Schifter, D., & Fosnot, C. T. (1993). What's so special about math? Lisa Yaffee. In *Reconstructing mathematics education: Stories of teachers meeting the challenge of reform* (pp. 119–144). New York: Teachers College Press.

Schön, D. A. (1983). *The reflective practitioner: How professionals think in action.* New York: Basic Books.

Schön, D. A. (1984). Leadership as reflection in action. In T. Sergiovanni & J. Corbally (Eds.), *Leadership and organizational culture.* Chicago: University of Illinois Press.

Schön, D. A. (1988). Coaching as reflective teaching. In P. Grimmett & G. Erickson (Eds.), *Reflection in teacher education.* New York: Teachers College Press.

Sergiovanni, T. J., & Starratt, R. J. (1998). *Supervision: A redefinition* (6th ed.). New York: McGraw Hill.

Shepard, L., & Bliem, C. (1995). Parents' thinking about standardized tests and performance assessments. *Educational Researcher, 24*(8), 25–32.

Shulman, L. S. (1986). Paradigms and research programs in the study of teaching: A contemporary perspective. In M. C. Wittrock (Ed.), *Handbook of research on teaching* (3rd ed., pp. 3–36). New York: Macmillan.

Shulman, L. S. (1992). Toward a pedagogy of cases. In J. H. Shulman (Ed.), *Case methods in teacher education* (pp. 1–30). New York: Teachers College Press.

Simon, M. A. (1997). Developing new models of mathematics teaching: An imperative for research on mathematics teacher development. In E. Fennema & B. S. Nelson (Eds.), *Mathematics teachers in transition.* Mahwah, NJ: Erlbaum.

Smith, F. (1971). *Understanding reading: A psycholinguistic analysis of reading and learning to read.* New York: Holt, Rinehart & Winston.

Snow, C. E., Davis, M. S., & Griffon, P. (Eds.). (1998). *Preventing reading difficulties in young children.* (Committee on the Prevention of Reading Difficulties in Young Children, Commission on Behavioral and Social Sciences and Education, National Research Council.) Washington, DC: National Academy Press.

Spillane, J. P. (2002). Local theories of teacher change: The pedagogy of district policies and programs. *Teachers College Record, 104*(3), 377–420.

Spillane, J. P. (2004). *Standards deviation: How schools misunderstand education policy.* Cambridge, MA: Harvard University Press.

Spillane, J. P., & Halverson, R. (1998, April). *Local policy-makers' understandings of the mathematics reforms: Alignment and the progress of the mathematics reforms.* Paper presented at the annual meeting of the American Educational Research Association, San Diego, CA.

Spillane, J. P., Halverson, R., & Diamond, J. B. (2001). Investigating school leadership practice: A distributed perspective. *Educational Researcher, 30*(3), 23–28.

Spillane, J. P., Reiser, B., & Reimer, T. (2002). Policy implementation and cognition: Reframing and refocusing implementation research. *Review of Educational Research, 72*(3), 387–431.

Spillane, J. P., & Thompson, C. L. (1997). Reconstructing conceptions of local capacity: The local education agency's capacity for ambitious instructional reform. *Educational Evaluation and Policy Analysis 19*(2), 185–203.

Stake, R. E. (1995). *The art of case study research*. Thousand Oaks, CA: Sage.

Steffe, L. P., & Thompson, P. W. (2000). Teaching experiment methodology: Underlying principles and essential elements. In A. E. Kelly & R. Lesh (Eds.), *Handbook of research design in mathematics and science education* (pp. 267–306). Mahwah, NJ: Erlbaum.

Stein, M. K., & D'Amico, L. (2000, April). *How subjects matter in school leadership*. Paper presented at the annual meeting of the American Educational Research Association, New Orleans.

Stein, M. K., & Lane, S. (1996). Instructional tasks and the development of student capacity to think and reason: An analysis of the relationship between teaching and learning in a reform mathematics project. *Educational Research and Evaluation, 2*(1), 50–80.

Stein, M. K., & Nelson, B. S. (2003). Leadership content knowledge. *Educational Evaluation and Policy Analysis, 25*(4), 423–448.

Tharp, R. (1993). Institutional and social context of educational practice and reform. In E. A. Forman, N. Minick, & C. A. Stone (Eds.), *Contexts for learning: Sociocultural dynamics in children's development* (pp. 269–282). New York: Oxford University Press.

Togneri, W., & Anderson, S. E. (2003). *Beyond islands of excellence: What districts can do to improve instruction and achievement in all schools—A leadership brief*. Washington, DC: Learning First Alliance.

Vygotsky, L. S. (1978). *Mind in society: The development of higher psychological processes*. Cambridge, MA: Harvard University Press.

Wenger, E. (1998). *Communities of practice: Learning, meaning, and identity*. Cambridge, U. K.: Cambridge University Press.

Wenger, E., McDermott, R., & Snyder, W. M. (2002). *Cultivating communities of practice: A guide to managing knowledge*. Boston, MA: Harvard Business School Press.

Wiggins, D. (1978). Deliberation and practical reason. In J. Raz (Ed.), *Practical reasoning*. New York: Oxford University Press.

Wilson, S. M. (2003). *California dreaming: Reforming mathematics education*. New Haven, CT: Yale University Press.

Wood, T., Nelson, B. S., & Warfield, J. (Eds.). (2001). *Beyond classical pedagogy: New forms of instruction in elementary school mathematics*. Mahway, NJ: Erlbaum.

INDEX

Abelmann, C., 70, 78
Accountability, 3, 35, 54, 77, 78, 169. *See also* Assessment
Acheson, K. A., 73
Administrative practice
  and articulating ideas, 40–44
  and assessment, 80–82, 84–86, 88–95
  conceptual learning in, 128–32
  and culture for pondering, 153–56
  and dilemma of instructional leaders, 158–61
  and doing mathematics with school committee, 102–4
  and elements of effective instructional leadership, 173
  and engaged instructional leader, 150, 151, 153–56, 158–61, 164–68
  implications of principals' ideas for, 55–56
  and instructional leadership as more than a formula, 164–68
  and learning theories, 33
  and learning through instructional leadership, 126, 127–32, 141–46, 147–48, 149
  and narratives as supplements, 88–95
  and parents' forum, 108–11
  and questioning skills, 66–70
  and reflection, 61–63
  and report cards, 80–82
  and rules versus conceptual understanding, 49–51
  and schools as communities of practice, 126, 128–32, 141–46, 147–48, 149, 150, 151, 153–56, 158–61, 164–68
  and scripting a lesson, 84–86
  and sense making, 36–39

and situating ideas in practice, 61–63, 66–70
and stakeholders as learners, 102–4, 108–11, 116
and studies as way to learn from practice, 133–37, 141–46
and transforming administrative process into context for conceptual learning, 141–46
See also specific person
Administrators
  behavior of, 176
  challenges facing, 113
  as instructional leaders, 2–4
  as intermediaries between parents and teachers, 98
  knowledge of mathematics and mathematics learning of, 7–8, 9–31, 32–54
  as learners, 127, 171, 173–74
  as mentors, 56, 58–76, 169
  roles/functions of, 54, 58, 125, 158–63
  use of knowledge in work of, 55–120
  See also specific person or topic
Anderson, S. E., 175
Ansell, E., 58, 80, 127
Aristotle, 55
Articulation of ideas, 39–47, 51–52, 53, 54, 157
Assessment
  and administrative practice, 80–82, 84–86, 88–95
  and content, 77, 94, 96–97
  and doing mathematics with school committee, 102–3, 105
  and engaged instructional leader, 157
  externally imposed, 78, 97

Assessment (*continued*)
  functions of, 77, 90
  and implications of principals'
    knowledge, 56, 176
  inadequate forms for, 88–96, 97
  of instruction, 3, 56, 77
  and knowledge, 78, 79, 81, 88
  and learning, 78, 79, 81, 82, 83, 89, 96,
    148
  and motivation, 78
  and narratives as supplements, 88–96,
    97
  and nature of learning, 53
  and parents' forum, 109
  and report cards, 79–83, 95–96, 97
  and rewards/incentives, 78
  and roles/functions of instructional
    leaders, 3, 98
  and rules versus conceptual
    understanding, 50–51, 52, 54
  and schools as communities of practice,
    148, 157
  and scripting a lesson, 79, 83–88, 96–97
  and situating ideas in formal
    accountability structures, 77–97
  specificity in, 96, 97
  and stakeholders as learners, 102–3, 105,
    110
  and standards, 77, 78, 89, 90–91, 93, 97
  of teachers, 56, 58, 77, 78, 79, 83–95,
    110, 176
  and teaching, 82, 88–95, 96
  and thinking, 82, 87, 88, 93, 94
  tools for, 77, 78–79, 88–95, 96, 148
  and values, 78
  and written records, 77

Ball, D. L., 21, 34, 58, 127, 181
Barnes, C. A., 99, 106, 176
Bastable, V., 58, 66, 80, 89, 167–68, 179
Becker, H., 179
Behaviorism, 32, 33–34, 35–36, 39, 53, 54
Behrend, J., 58, 127
Beliefs
  and administrators as learners, 174
  and assessment, 78, 83, 95
  as changing, 171
  and conceptual learning, 130
  and culture for pondering, 156–57

  and doing mathematics with school
    committee, 105
  and elements of effective instructional
    leadership, 172
  and engaged instructional leader, 150,
    151, 156–57, 169
  importance of, 98, 171
  and learning through instructional
    leadership, 130, 138, 148, 149
  and narratives as supplements, 95
  and parents' forum, 113
  and presentations as political
    performances, 116–17
  and report cards, 83
  and schools as communities of practice,
    122, 123, 130, 138, 148, 149, 150,
    151, 156–57, 169
  and stakeholders as learners, 100, 105,
    116–17, 119
  and studies as way to learn from
    practice, 138
Benson, S., 22
Bleiman, J., 24, 28, 29
Bliem, C., 80, 82
Bobroff, B. M., 126
Bouvier, Rob, 35, 47–53, 54, 151, 157–63,
  169, 174, 179
Bransford, J. D., 11, 32, 34
Brophy, J., 46, 73
Brown, A. L., 3, 11, 32, 34
Brown, J. S., 3, 32, 39
Building Number Sense (Kliman and
  Russell), 37, 67
Burns, Marilyn, 51

Campione, J. C., 3
Carey, D., 172
Carpenter, T. P., 10, 32, 34, 58, 74, 80,
  127, 172
Checklists, 46, 73
Chiang, C., 172
Cobb, P., 39
Cocking, R. R., 11, 32, 34
Coffin, G., 126
Cognition, 10, 12, 52–53, 64, 94, 96, 152,
  176
Cohen, D. K., 10, 21, 32, 58, 99, 106, 127,
  176
Cohen, S., 58

Collaborative learning
and culture for pondering, 154
and doing mathematics with school
committee, 103–6, 118
and engaged instructional leader, 151,
154
and learning through instructional
leadership, 139, 149
and parents' forum, 106–13, 118, 119
and presentations as political
performances, 113–18, 119
and schools as communities of practice,
139, 149, 151, 154
and stakeholders as learners, 98–119
and studies as way to learn from
practice, 139
Collins, A., 32, 34, 39, 94
Communities, classrooms as, 39, 58, 68
Communities, learning, 139, 148
Communities of practice, schools as
building trust and confidence within, 112
characteristics of, 151, 154
current interest in developing, 3
and engaged instructional leader, 150–70
implications of principals' knowledge for
building, 31, 121–23
and learning through instructional
leadership, 125–49
and stakeholders, 98, 112
and transforming administrative process
into context for conceptual learning,
140
Computational strategies, 1–2, 171
Conceptual knowledge
and administrators as learners, 174
and engaged instructional leader, 157–
58, 159, 161–62
and facilitating instructional leadership
learning, 178
and knowing elementary mathematics, 9,
10–13, 30
and questioning skills, 65–66
and rules versus conceptual
understanding, 47–53, 54
and schools as communities of practice,
157–58, 159, 161–62
and situating ideas in practice, 65–66
and understanding students'
mathematical thinking, 18–23

See also Conceptual learning; *specific
principal*
Conceptual learning, 14, 128–32, 139–47,
148, 149. *See also* Conceptual
knowledge
Constructivism
and articulating ideas, 40, 44, 46, 47
and assessment, 79, 82, 94
basic tenets of, 32
and culture for pondering, 152, 153
and curriculum, 34–35
definition of, 35–36
and doing mathematics with teachers, 14
and engaged instructional leader, 150,
152, 153, 157, 158, 162, 164
and facilitating instructional leadership
learning, 178
and instructional leadership as more than
a formula, 164
as learning theory, 32, 33, 53, 54
and learning through instructional
leadership, 140
and limits of rules for practice, 73–74
and principals' use of knowledge, 56
and professional development, 34–35
and questioning skills, 71
and report cards, 82
and rules versus conceptual
understanding, 51, 52
and schools as communities of practice,
140, 150, 152, 153, 157, 158, 162,
164
as sense making, 35–36, 39
and situating ideas in practice, 71, 73–74
and teaching, 34–35
and transforming administrative process
into context for conceptual learning,
140
Consultancy, 141–46, 183–84
Content
and articulating ideas, 47
and assessment, 77, 94, 96–97
and elements of effective instructional
leadership, 172–73
and engaged instructional leader, 159
and implications of principals'
knowledge, 175
and learning through instructional
leadership, 125, 126

Content (*continued*)
  and limits of rules for practice, 74
  and listening, 28–29, 30
  and narratives as supplements, 94, 97
  and parents' forum, 109
  and "pedagogical content" knowledge,
    57
  and presentations as political
    performances, 113–18
  and questioning skills, 75
  and reflection, 74–75
  and rules versus conceptual
    understanding, 47
  and schools as communities of practice,
    125, 126, 159
  and scripting a lesson, 96–97
  and situating ideas in practice, 57, 74–
    75
  and stakeholders as learners, 109, 113–18
Context
  and culture for pondering, 156
  and engaged instructional leader, 156,
    158, 159, 162, 166
  and facilitating instructional leadership
    learning, 178
  and instructional leadership as more than
    a formula, 166
  and learning theories, 32–33
  and learning through instructional
    leadership, 139–47, 149
  and schools as communities of practice,
    139–47, 149, 156, 158, 159, 162,
    166
  and transforming administrative process
    into context for conceptual learning,
    139–47
Corcoran, T., 78
Corsaro, W., 182
Counting, 37–38, 39, 45, 53
Cowan, Marianne, 13, 18–23, 31, 79, 83–
    88, 96–97, 127–128, 132–39, 148,
    149, 172, 179
Culture
  and elements of effective instructional
    leadership, 173
  and engaged instructional leader, 151–
    57, 160, 161, 163, 166, 167, 168,
    169, 170
  and instructional leadership as more than
    a formula, 163, 166, 167, 168, 169

  and learning through instructional
    leadership, 125
  and parents' forum, 109
  for pondering, 151–57
  and reflection, 60
  and schools as communities of practice,
    123, 125, 151–57, 160, 161, 163,
    166, 167, 168, 169, 170
  and situating ideas in practice, 60
  and stakeholders as learners, 110
Curriculum
  Addison Wesley, 158, 159
  and administrators as instructional
    leaders, 3
  and constructivism, 34–35
  and culture for pondering, 155
  and doing mathematics with school
    committee, 102, 103
  and doing mathematics with teachers,
    14–15
  and engaged instructional leader, 155,
    158–63, 169
  and implications of principals'
    knowledge, 176
  and learning through instructional
    leadership, 139–47, 148–49
  and parents' forum, 107, 108
  and presentations as political
    performances, 113–18
  and principals' knowledge of
    mathematics and mathematics
    learning, 7
  and schools as communities of practice,
    139–47, 148–49, 155, 158–63, 169,
    173
  selection of new, 14–15, 100, 139–47,
    148–49, 158–63, 169, 173
  and stakeholders as learners, 102, 103,
    107, 108, 113–18
  and transforming administrative process
    into context for conceptual learning,
    139–47
*Curriculum and Evaluation Standards for
  School Mathematics* (NCTM), 75,
    101, 103, 108, 115, 141, 164–66,
    174–75, 181

D'Amico, L., 3
Darling-Hammond, L., 46, 161
Davidson, E., 24, 28, 29

Davis, M. S., 155
Davis, Ted, 37–39, 88–95
Developing Mathematical Ideas (DMI)
    course (Schifter et al.), 66, 69, 89–90,
    94, 167–68
Diamond, J. B., 3, 76, 83
Diggins, Sheila, 35–39, 45, 53, 58–59, 65–
    72, 75, 79–83, 88–97, 172, 174
Discourse, 148, 149
Disequilibrium, role of, 110
Doing mathematics
    and engaged instructional leader, 159,
        165–66
    and facilitating instructional leadership
        learning, 178
    and instructional leader's dilemma, 159
    and instructional leadership as more than
        formula to plug into, 165–67
    with school committee, 100–106, 118,
        172
    with teachers, 13–18, 22, 31
Dolk, Maarten, 1–2
Duguid, P., 3, 32, 39

Edmonds, R. R., 161, 176
Educational reform, 173
Elbow, Peter, 111
Eliasoph, Nina, 100
Elmore, R., 10, 78, 97, 121, 173, 175
Environment, 153, 157, 163, 167, 170,
    173, 176
Equity, 60, 133–37
Equivalent fractions, 19–23, 83, 86, 172
Erickson, F., 182
Exploration, mathematical, 133–39, 148,
    158, 167

Facts, mathematical, 14, 18, 34, 48, 53,
    56, 65, 172
Feedback, 33, 67, 69, 111–13. *See also*
    Postobservation conferences
Feinman-Nemser, S., 127
Fennema, E., 58, 74, 127, 172
Fielding, J., 181
Fielding, N., 181
Findell, B., 7, 10, 11, 30, 34
Fink, E., 121
Foley, E., 78
Forester, J., 106, 116, 117, 126
Fosnot, Catherine Twomey, 1–2, 14

Fraction fringe, 19–23, 83, 84, 88, 136,
    172
Franke, M. L., 58, 74, 172
Fuson, K. C., 37

Gall, M. D., 73
Gardner, H., 32, 34
Garfield, Joseph, 100, 113–18, 119, 128,
    139–49, 171, 173, 181, 183–84
Gattegno, Caleb, 14
Glaser, B., 183
Goldstein, Dana, 99–106, 118, 172, 181,
    183
Good, T. L., 46, 73
Governance, 155–56
Gower, R., 85
Grant, C. M., 24, 28, 29
Greeno, J. G., 32, 34, 94
Griffon, P., 155
Groupings, heterogenous and
    homogeneous, 14–18, 31, 59–64, 75,
    106–7, 108, 109, 127, 128–29, 131–
    32, 147, 148

Hall, M. W., 121
Hallinger, P., 176
Halverson, R., 3, 76, 83, 175
Hammer, D., 181
Heck, R., 176
Hightower, A. M., 175
Holdaway, Don, 152, 153
Holloway, Theresa, 66–71, 75
Huberman, M. A., 181, 183, 184
Hummel, R. P., 126 Hunter, M., 46, 73

Ideas
    and administrators as learners, 173, 174
    articulation of, 39–47, 51–52, 53, 54,
        157
    and assessment, 81, 86, 87, 90, 94, 96–
        97
    and culture for pondering, 153, 156,
        157
    and elements of effective instructional
        leadership, 172
    and engaged instructional leader, 150,
        151, 153, 156, 157, 162, 163, 166,
        167, 168, 169, 170
    and facilitating instructional leadership
        learning, 178

Ideas (*continued*)
  and implications of principals'
    knowledge, 55–56, 175–76
  and instructional leader's dilemma, 157
  and instructional leadership as more than
    a formula, 163, 166, 167, 168, 169
  and learning theories, 33
  and learning through instructional
    leadership, 142, 145, 146, 147, 148
  and limits of rules for practice, 72–74,
    75
  and narratives as supplements, 90, 94,
    97
  and questioning skills, 71–72, 75
  and report cards, 81
  and rules versus conceptual
    understanding, 51–52
  and schools as communities of practice,
    123, 142, 145, 146, 147, 148, 150,
    151, 153, 156, 157, 162, 163, 166,
    167, 168, 169, 170
  and scripting a lesson, 86, 87, 96–97
  sharing of, 51, 53, 54
  and situating ideas in practice, 57–76
  study about linking practice and, 179–
    81
  and transforming administrative process
    into context for conceptual learning,
    142, 145, 146, 147
"Images of Good Teaching" (parents'
    forum), 100, 106–13, 128
Instruction
  and administrators as learners, 174
  assessment of, 3, 56, 77
  direct, 33–34
  and engaged instructional leader, 157–
    58, 162, 163, 165, 167, 168, 169
  and facilitating instructional leadership
    learning, 178
  goal of, 94
  and implications of principals'
    knowledge, 175, 176
  and instructional leader's dilemma, 163
  and instructional leadership as more than
    a formula, 165, 167, 168
  and learning through instructional
    leadership, 125, 133–37, 148
  and schools as communities of practice,
    125, 133–37, 148, 157–58, 162,
    163, 165, 167, 168, 169

  and studies as way to learn from
    practice, 133–37
  See also Instructional leadership;
    Teaching; *specific teacher or
    administrator*
Instructional leadership
  characteristics of, 125
  definitions of, 126
  and dilemma of instructional leaders,
    157–63
  elements of effective, 172–73
  engaged, 150–70, 174
  and facilitating instructional leadership
    learning, 177–78
  and functions of leaders, 98
  and implications of principals'
    knowledge, 4, 176
  and importance of subject matter
    knowledge and beliefs, 7–8, 171
  learning through, 125–49
  as more than a "formula to plug into,"
    163–69
  risks of, 99
  and schools as communities of practice,
    122–23, 125–49, 150–77
  and split between instruction and
    administration, 121–22
  studies of, 176, 179–84
  See also specific person or topic
Instructional materials, 4, 51, 54
Investigations in Number, Data, and Space
    curriculum (Russell and Tierney), 35,
    37, 66, 67, 137, 158, 159, 164

Jantzi, D., 126
Jenkins, Charlotte, 99–106, 118, 181, 183
Jones, Jeremy, 25–28, 40–47, 72–74, 75, 172
Joyce, B., 73

Kilpatrick, J., 7, 10, 11, 30, 34
Kliman, M., 37, 67
Knapp, M. S., 3, 175
Knowing elementary mathematics, 10–13,
    21, 30
Knowledge
  and elements of effective instructional
    leadership, 172, 173
  and facilitating instructional leadership
    learning, 177–78
  flexibility of, 139, 171, 172

function of principals', 174
and how it is learned, 75
and how much principals need to know,
     75–76
implications of principals', 3, 7–8, 9, 13,
     22–23, 31, 55–120, 121–23, 175,
     176
importance of, 98, 171
and knowing elementary mathematics,
     10–13
and knowing where you're going, 9–31
"leadership content," 3
and learning theories, 32
limited, 7, 22–30, 31, 65, 72, 172
overview of principals', 7–8
"pedagogical content," 57
procedural, 9, 13, 29, 30–31, 50–51, 52,
     53, 75
students' construction of own
     mathematics, 158–63, 169
and studies as way to learn from
     practice, 132, 138, 139
See also Conceptual knowledge; *specific*
     person or topic
Kohn, Alfie, 106

Lampert, M., 34, 39, 181
Lane, S., 172
Languages, learning, 152–53, 154–55
Lave, J., 122, 126
Layering, 178
Leadership
   distributed, 76, 83
   traditional, 3
   See also Instructional leadership
"Leadership content knowledge," 3
Learning
   active view of, 152–53
   and administrators as learners, 127, 171,
        173–74
   assumptions about, 113–18, 141, 173
   as continuous, 57, 58–59, 74, 75–76,
        127, 173–74
   disjunct between complexities of learning
        and need for order and control, 99
   and elements of effective instructional
        leadership, 172, 173
   and facilitating instructional leadership
        learning, 177–78
   goals for, 7

and implications of principals'
     knowledge, 7–8, 31, 121–23, 175,
     176
importance of administrator's knowledge
     about, 7–8, 31, 98, 171
through instructional leadership, 125–
     49
languages, 152–53, 154–55
nature of, 53
prior, 33
project-based, 34
romantic view of, 35–36, 39
theories of, 32–34, 53–54, 152
transmission view of, 56
See also Collaborative learning;
     Conceptual learning; *specific theory*
     or topic
Leithwood, K., 126, 176
Lenses on Learning course (Grant et al),
     24, 28, 29, 46, 50, 51
Lester, J. B., 58
Levi, L., 74, 80
Lipsky, Michael, 175
Listening
   and administrators as learners, 174
   and culture for pondering, 155
   and elements of effective instructional
        leadership, 172
   and engaged instructional leader, 155,
        157, 162, 167
   and instructional leadership as more than
        a formula, 167
   and learning through instructional
        leadership, 126, 146, 148, 149
   and limits of rules for practice, 72–74
   and principals' conceptual knowledge of
        mathematics and mathematics
        learning, 23–30, 31
   and questioning skills, 65, 67, 71–72
   and reflection, 75
   and rules versus conceptual
        understanding, 51–52, 54
   and schools as communities of practice,
        126, 146, 148, 149, 155, 157, 162,
        167
   and situating ideas in practice, 57, 65,
        67, 71–74, 75
   and teachers as "listening more and
        talking less," 40–44, 51–52, 53–54,
        72–74, 110

Listening (*continued*)
  and transforming administrative process
    into context for conceptual learning,
    146
Little, J. W., 175
Loef, M., 172
Luhm, T., 78

Management, classroom, 28, 29, 68, 85,
  88, 89
Manipulatives, 83, 106–13, 135–37
Marris, P., 32
Marsh, J. A., 175
"Math stars," 128–32, 148
Mathematics, defining of, 30
Mathematics education
  and discipline-based reform movement,
    10
  goals of, 12–13
  implications of principals' knowledge
    for, 174–75
  and math movement of 1950s and
    1960s, 10
  in Progressive Era, 10
Mathscape curriculum, 158, 159
Maxwell, J., 181
McDermott, R., 122, 151
McLaughlin, M. W., 175
Memorization, 14, 18, 34, 48, 53, 65
Mentors, administrators as, 56, 58–76, 169
Miles, M., 181, 183, 184
Milstein, M. M., 126
Motivation, 78, 110, 125, 132
Murphy, J., 3, 121, 176

Narratives, as supplements to inadequate
  forms, 88–95
Nash, Peter, 13–18, 22, 31, 58, 59–64, 72,
  73–75, 100, 106–13, 118, 119, 127,
  128–32, 146, 147, 148, 149, 172, 173,
  179
National Council of Teachers of
  Mathematics (NCTM), 10, 11, 12, 30,
  68, 75, 101, 103, 108, 115, 141, 164–
  65, 174–75, 181
National Research Council, 10, 12
National Science Foundation, 181, 182, 183
Nelson, B. S., 3, 22, 24, 28, 29, 32, 35, 56,
  58, 116, 121–22, 175, 176, 177, 178
Newman, F. N, 154

Nicholls, J., 39
No Child Left Behind (NCLB) legislation,
  3, 13, 23, 35, 54, 77, 78
Nussbaum, M., 55

O'Brien, Libby, 13, 23–30, 31, 39–46, 51,
  52, 53–54, 58–59, 72–74, 75, 172,
  173, 179

Parents
  and assessment, 78, 96
  building political capital with, 106–13,
    118, 119
  and culture for pondering, 154, 156
  and elements of effective instructional
    leadership, 173
  and engaged instructional leader, 154,
    156
  forums for, 100, 106–13, 118, 119, 128,
    154, 156, 173
  principals as intermediaries between
    teachers and, 98
  and principals' use of knowledge in their
    work, 56
  and schools as communities of practice,
    154, 156
  as stakeholders, 98
  See also Report cards; School committee
Patterns, mathematical, 26–28, 29, 44,
  72
Patton, M., 179, 182
"Pedagogical content" knowledge, 57
Pendlebury, S., 55
Peterson, P. L., 172
Phillips, D., 32
Piaget, J., 10, 32, 109
Policy, educational, 98, 175–76
Politics
  and communicating with outside
    stakeholders, 56
  and doing mathematics with school
    committee, 100–106, 118
  and parents' forum, 106–13, 118, 119
  and presentations as political
    performances, 113–18, 119
  and school committees, 100–106, 113–
    18, 119
  and stakeholders as learners, 98–119
  and values, 56
Pondering, culture for, 151–57

Portfolios, math, 51, 52
Postobservation conferences
  and assessment, 84, 85
  and learning as process of articulating
    ideas, 43–44, 45
  and learning through instructional
    leadership, 133, 138, 149
  and limits of rules for practice, 72
  and listening, 28–29
  and questioning skills, 69
  and schools as communities of practice,
    133, 138, 149
  and scripting a lesson, 84, 85
  and situating ideas in practice, 69, 72
  and studies as way to learn from
    practice, 133–37, 138
Practical/professional judgment, 55–56,
    171, 176
Practice
  and administrators as learners, 174
  and culture for pondering, 154, 157
  distributed, 177
  and elements of effective instructional
    leadership, 172
  and engaged instructional leader, 154,
    157–58
  and facilitating instructional leadership
    learning, 177, 178
  and implications of principals'
    knowledge, 176
  knowledge as situated in, 59, 127
  learning through, 100, 139
  and learning through instructional
    leadership, 126, 127, 132–39, 145,
    147, 148
  limits of rules for, 72–74, 75
  linking ideas and, 179–81
  and reflection, 59–64
  and schools as communities of practice,
    126, 127, 132–39, 145, 147, 148,
    154, 157–58
  situating ideas in, 57–76
  and stakeholders as learners, 100
  studies as way to learn from, 132–39
  and transforming administrative process
    into context for conceptual learning,
    145, 147
  as unique venue for learning, 147
  See also Administrative practice;
    Communities of practice, schools as

Preobservation conferences, 27, 28, 66–67,
    70, 72, 133–37, 138
Prestine, N. A., 3, 121–22
Problem solving
  and articulating ideas, 40–47, 54
  and conceptual learning in
    administrative practice, 128–32
  and doing mathematics with school
    committee, 103–5
  and elements of effective instructional
    leadership, 172
  and engaged instructional leader, 165–
    66
  and implications of principals'
    knowledge, 7, 176
  and instructional leadership as more than
    a formula, 165–66
  and limits of rules for practice, 72
  and listening, 23–30
  and questioning skills, 66
  and reflection, 61–63, 74–75
  and rules versus conceptual
    understanding, 47–48, 49–51, 52
  and schools as communities of practice,
    165–66
  and situating ideas in practice, 61–63,
    66, 72, 74–75
  and stakeholders as learners, 103–5
Problems, real-world, 47, 48, 104
Procedural knowledge, 9, 13, 29, 30–31,
    50–51, 52
Process-product program of research on
    teaching, 34, 46, 73
Professional development
  and articulating ideas, 46
  and assessment, 89, 95, 96
  and constructivism, 34–35
  and engaged instructional leader, 163,
    164–66, 167–68
  functions of, 95
  and implications of principals'
    knowledge, 56, 175
  and instructional leader's dilemma, 163
  and instructional leadership as more than
    a formula, 164–66, 167–68
  and learning through instructional
    leadership, 128, 137, 142, 147
  and listening, 30
  and narratives as supplements, 95
  and questioning skills, 65–66

Professional development (*continued*)
  and roles/functions of instructional
    leaders, 3, 98
  and schools as communities of practice,
    128, 137, 142, 147, 163, 164–66,
    167–68
  selection of programs for, 4
  and situating ideas in practice, 57, 65–
    66, 75–76
  and studies as way to learn from
    practice, 137
  and teaching experiment study, 181–
    83
  and transforming administrative process
    into context for conceptual learning,
    142, 147
Project-based learning, 34

Questions
  and administrators as learners, 174
  anticipating, 117
  and articulating ideas, 41–44, 46–47
  and conceptual learning in administrative
    practice, 130, 131, 132
  and culture for pondering, 153–54, 155–
    56
  and elements of effective instructional
    leadership, 172
  and engaged instructional leader, 153–54,
    155–56, 157, 167, 169, 170
  and facilitating instructional leadership
    learning, 177
  and instructional leadership as more than
    a formula, 167
  and learning through instructional
    leadership, 127, 130, 131, 132, 133–
    39, 141–42, 143–44, 145, 146, 148,
    149
  and limits of rules for practice, 72–73
  and parents' forum, 108, 111
  and presentations as political
    performances, 117–18
  and questioning skills, 65–72, 75
  and rules versus conceptual
    understanding, 49, 50, 52
  and schools as communities of practice,
    127, 130, 131, 132, 133–39, 141–42,
    143–44, 145, 146, 148, 149, 153–54,
    155–56, 157, 167, 169, 170
  and sense making, 36

  and situating ideas in practice, 57, 65–73,
    75
  and stakeholders as learners, 108, 111,
    117–18
  and studies as way to learn from practice,
    133–39
  and transforming administrative process
    into context for conceptual learning,
    141–42, 143–44, 145, 146

Reed, K. M., 22
Reflection
  and assessment, 85, 86, 96
  and conceptual learning in
    administrative practice, 130
  and culture for pondering, 154, 155, 156
  and engaged instructional leader, 150,
    151, 154, 155, 156, 162, 163, 169
  and instructional leader's dilemma, 163
  and learning through instructional
    leadership, 126, 130, 133, 137–38,
    139, 141, 142, 145, 148
  and parents' forum, 113, 119
  and practice, 58, 59–64
  and schools as communities of practice,
    126, 130, 133, 137–38, 139, 141,
    142, 145, 148, 150, 151, 154, 155,
    156, 162, 163, 169
  and scripting a lesson, 85, 86
  and stakeholders as learners, 99, 113, 119
  and studies as way to learn from
    practice, 133, 137–38, 139
  and transforming administrative process
    into context for conceptual learning,
    141, 142, 145
Reimer, T., 33, 34, 175–76
Reiser, B., 33, 34, 175–76
Reitzug, U. C., 46
Remillard, J., 127
Report cards, 56, 77, 78–83, 96
Resnick, L. B., 11, 32, 34, 94, 121
Respect, 150, 163, 168
Restine, L. N., 126
Richardson, V., 127
Riddle, Margaret, 59, 61–64, 74–75, 128–
  32, 148, 172
Risk-taking, 152, 169, 170, 173
Romantic view, 35–36, 39
Romberg, T. A., 10, 32, 34
Rosenshine, B., 33

Rowan, B., 3
Rowe, Mary Budd, 110
Rules, 47–53, 72–74
Russell, S. J., 11, 35, 37, 58, 66, 67, 80, 89, 137, 158, 164, 167–68, 179

Sampson, Louise, 122, 151–57, 169, 170, 173, 181, 183
Saphier, J., 85
Sassi, A., 24, 28, 29, 56, 58, 64, 67, 73, 87
Scaffolding, 110, 141
Schifter, D., 14, 58, 66, 80, 89, 167–68, 179
Schön, D. A., 126, 137
School committee
    and administrators as learners, 173
    and disjunct between complexities of learning and need for order and control, 99
    doing mathematics with, 100–106, 118, 172
    and elements of effective instructional leadership, 172, 173
    Garfield's presentation to, 100, 113–18, 119
    image control in, 101
    Jenkins's and Goldstein's presentation to, 100–106, 118, 172
    and pilot high school mathematics program, 100, 113–18
    and presentations as political performances, 113–18, 119
    rules, norms, and procedures for interacting with, 99–100, 105
    structure of, 102, 103
    timing and focus of presentation to, 101–2
School reform, implications of principals' knowledge for, 176
Sclan, E., 46, 161
Scripting a lesson, 79, 83–88, 96–97, 132
Selnes, Dawn, 1–2
Sense making, 35–39, 53, 54, 59, 65, 70, 83, 154, 172
Sergiovanni, T. J., 161
Shepard, L., 80, 82
Showers, B., 73
Shulman, L. S., 34, 57, 63
Simon, M. A., 127
Smith, Frank, 152

Snow, C. E., 155
Snyder, W. M., 122, 151
Social studies, mathematics classroom as resembling, 47–48
Socioconstructivism, 32–33, 34, 35, 39
Spencer Foundation, 179
Spillane, J. P., 3, 33, 34, 76, 83, 100, 140, 175–76
Staff, 155–56
Stake, R. E., 181
Stakeholders
    definition of, 98
    and doing mathematics with school committee, 100–106
    and engaged instructional leader, 169
    as learners, 98–119, 128
    and parents' forum, 106–13
    and presentations as political performances, 113–18
    rules, norms, and procedures for interacting with, 99–100
    and schools as communities of practice, 169
    values and communicating with outside, 56
    See also specific stakeholder
Standardized tests, 46, 73, 77, 78, 80, 82, 163, 164
Standards
    and assessment, 77, 78, 89, 90–91, 93, 97
    and doing mathematics with school committee, 102, 103
    and engaged instructional leader, 157
    and facilitating instructional leadership learning, 178
    and limits of rules for practice, 74
    and narratives as supplements, 89, 90–91, 93, 97
    and presentations as political performances, 115
    and questioning skills, 68
    and schools as communities of practice, 157
    and situating ideas in practice, 68, 74
    and stakeholders as learners, 102, 103, 115
Starratt, R. J., 161
Stein, M. K., 3, 58, 116, 172, 175, 176, 177

Stevens, R., 33
Story problems, writing, 27–29
Strauss, A., 183
Studies
    and consultancy, 183–84
    of effective schools, 176
    and facilitating instructional leadership
        learning, 177
    and implications of principals'
        knowledge, 176
    of instructional leadership, 176
    and learning through instructional
        leadership, 148
    of linking ideas to practice, 179–81
    and schools as communities of practice,
        148
    and teaching experiment, 181–83
    as way to learn from practice, 132–39
Supervision, teacher
    checklists for, 73
    and learning through instructional
        leadership, 133–39, 148
    and principals' use of knowledge in their
        work, 56, 57–76
    and schools as communities of practice,
        133–39, 148
    and situating ideas in practice, 57–76
    and studies as way to learn from
        practice, 133–39
    See also specific teacher or principal
Swafford, J., 7, 10, 11, 30, 34

Teachers
    and administrators as mentors, 56, 58–
        76, 169
    behavior of, 45–46, 47, 54, 73–74, 75,
        157
    checklist for use in supervision of, 46
    "de-skilling" of, 61
    doing mathematics with, 13–18, 22, 31
    evaluation of, 56, 58, 77, 78, 79, 83–95,
        110, 176
    as learners, 57–76
    and learning through instructional
        leadership, 127
    as "listening more and talking less," 40–
        44, 51–52, 53–54, 72–74, 110,
        157
    and parents' forum, 109

permanent records of, 88–95
principals as intermediaries between
    parents and, 98
recruitment of, 4
roles of, 127
and schools as communities of practice,
    127
and situating ideas in practice, 57–76
See also Professional development;
    Supervision, teacher; Teaching;
    specific person
Teaching
    and administrators as learners, 174
    assumptions about, 141
    and constructivism, 34–35
    "efficient," 109
    and elements of effective instructional
        leadership, 172, 173
    and engaged instructional leader, 150,
        151, 154–55, 156, 157, 166, 169,
        174
    and facilitating instructional leadership
        learning, 177–78
    "good," 46, 73, 108–9, 129, 130, 131
    and implications of principal's
        knowledge, 13, 121–23, 175, 176
    and importance of subject matter
        knowledge and beliefs, 171
    and learning theories, 32, 33–34, 53–
        54
    and learning through instructional
        leadership, 126, 128, 130, 131, 141,
        142, 147, 149
    process-product program of research on,
        34, 46, 73
    and schools as communities of practice,
        121–23, 126, 128, 130, 131, 141,
        142, 147, 149, 150, 151, 154–55,
        156, 157, 166, 169
    and socioconstructivism, 34, 35
    and stakeholders as learners, 108–18,
        119
    transmission view of, 56
    See also Instruction; Instructional
        leadership; *specific person or topic*
Teaching experiment, 181–83
Testing, 3, 7, 23, 30–31, 50–51, 52, 78,
    125, 176. *See also* Standardized tests
Textbooks, 7, 46, 142, 164

Tharp, R., 127
Thinking
  and elements of effective instructional
    leadership, 172
  and engaged instructional leader, 150,
    151, 154, 155, 157, 162–66, 168,
    169, 170
  and facilitating instructional leadership
    learning, 178
  and importance of principals' knowledge
    of mathematics and mathematics
    learning, 18–23, 31
  and learning through instructional
    leadership, 127, 131, 132, 133–37,
    139, 140, 142, 145, 146, 147, 148
  and principals' use of knowledge in their
    work, 56
  and schools as communities of practice,
    127, 131, 132, 133–37, 139, 140,
    142, 145–48, 150, 151, 154, 155,
    157, 162–66, 168, 169, 170
  sharing, 47, 48–49
  understanding, 18–23, 31
  See also specific topic

Thompson, C. L., 175
Tierney, C., 35, 66, 137, 158, 164
Togneri, W., 175
Trigatti, B., 39

Validity, 46–47, 51, 57, 162, 172
Values, 56, 78, 108, 150, 151, 154, 168,
  178
Vygotsky, L., 39

Warfield, J., 32
Weinberg, A., 24, 28, 29
Wenger, E., 122, 126, 151
Wheatley, G., 39
Wiggins, D., 55
Wilson, Costanza, 151, 163–70, 172
Wilson, P., 126
Wilson, S. M., 10, 159
Wood, T., 32, 39

Yackel, E., 39
Yaffee, L., 58

Zoltners, J., 83

ABOUT THE AUTHORS

BARBARA SCOTT NELSON is a senior scientist and director of the Center for the Development of Teaching at Education Development Center (EDC), Inc., Newton, MA. She holds an Ed.D. in educational policy studies from the Harvard Graduate School of Education. Dr. Nelson's current research focuses on school and district administrators' practical judgment; in particular, how administrators' ideas about the nature of mathematics, learning, and teaching affect their administrative practice. She is one of the authors of the *Lenses on Learning* instructional materials for school and district administrators. Dr. Nelson has published numerous articles on administrator and teacher learning and edited two volumes on teacher learning: *Mathematics Teachers in Transition*, with Elizabeth Fennema, and *Beyond Classical Pedagogy*, with Terry Wood and Janet Warfield.

ANNETTE SASSI is an educational researcher and evaluator who was a senior research associate at EDC when the work on this book was done. She is currently a research associate at Education Matters, Inc., in Cambridge, MA. She received a Ph.D. in city and regional planning from Cornell University and was a National Academy of Education postdoctoral fellow. She also holds degrees in sociology and anthropology. Her work has focused on understanding the nature of teachers' and school administrators' professional judgment and how they develop it. She has continually addressed the need for teachers or school administrators to cultivate an ability to listen to students and understand the ideas that they are grappling with. She is one of the authors of the *Lenses on Learning* courses, which are aimed at helping school administrators connect the work of learning and teaching with the work of school administration.